THE IRAQ WAR

This volume covers the Iraq War from a wide range of perspectives, providing several academic, as well as military-oriented analyses. It provides an historical background to current events and analyses the behaviour of several of the most important actors of the Iraq War. Although its emphasis is on the links between US foreign policy, US strategy and the US conduct of war, the volume also covers Iraqi grand strategies, the consequences of the war for transatlantic relations and the role of international law in the conflict. In analysing the war and the behaviour of its main parties, the chapters draw upon literature in international relations, political science, strategic thought and military theory, international law and media studies. Several experts on military strategy and operations focus on the land war, the air war, and on the US use of coercive strategies. In a concluding chapter, the Iraq War is put into a broader perspective, and the lessons learned are suggested, while remaining questions are highlighted.

Jan Hallenberg is a specialist on US foreign and security policy and has published *The Demise of the Soviet Union: Analysing the Collapse of a State* (Ashgate, 2002). **Dr. Håkan Karlsson** is a specialist on US strategy and nuclear weapons. His publications include *Bureaucratic Politics and Weapons Acquisition: The Case of the MX ICBM program* (two volumes, 2002).

Both editors work in the Department of Security and Strategic Studies at the Swedish National Defence College.

THE IRAQ WAR

European perspectives on politics, strategy and operations

Edited by Jan Hallenberg and Håkan Karlsson

Routledge
Taylor & Francis Group

LONDON AND NEW YORK

CONTENTS

CONTENTS

NOTES ON CONTRIBUTORS

Jan Angstrom, researcher at the Department of War Studies, Swedish National Defence College (SNDC) since 2002 and research student at the Department of War Studies, King's College, London. Angstrom has published several articles in scholarly journals such as *Security Studies*, *Studies in Conflict and Terrorism*, *Civil Wars* and *European Political Science*.

Magnus Bengtsson, major. Teacher in tactics in the Air Operations Branch, Department of War Studies, SNDC since 2003.

Claes Bergström, lieutenant-colonel. Teacher in air operations at the Department of War Studies, SNDC since 2002.

Nils-Göran Bernebring, lieutenant-colonel. Course Director and teacher at the Department of War Studies, SNDC since 2002. Bernebring has held several different positions during his 30 years in the Swedish Armed Forces.

Ove Bring, LLD. Professor of International Law at Stockholm University and the Swedish National Defence College. Head of the International Law Centre at SNDC. Member of the Swedish Ministry of Foreign Affairs delegation on international law. Chairman of the Swedish branch of the International Law Association. Board member of the San Remo Institute of International Humanitarian Law and the Swedish Helsinki Committee.

Per Broström, LLM. University lecturer. Assistant Head of the International Law Centre at SNDC. Reserve officer and legal adviser to the Chief of the Joint Forces Command. Member of the Swedish Total Defence Council on International Law. Served in Lebanon 1981, Honduras 1990–1992, El Salvador 1992 and Israel 1997–1998.

Anders Cedergren, lieutenant-colonel. Head of the Land Operations Branch at the Department of War Studies, SNDC since 2000. During the last few years Cedergren has edited or participated in several edited volumes, of which the latest is Cedergren and Mattsson (eds) *Uppdragstaktik: En ledningsfilosofi i förändring* (*Mission Command and Control in Transition*) (Stockholm: SNDC). Cedergren has also written articles in Military Theory and Military Pedagogics.

Lars Ericson, Associate Professor of History at Åbo Akademi University. Senior Lecturer in Military History at the Department of War Studies, SNDC since 2000. Previously at the Military Archives of Sweden from 1983–2000. Ericson has, apart from many papers, published more than a dozen books, among the latest of which is *Svensk militärmakt: Strategi och operationer i svensk militärhistoria under 1.500 år* (*Swedish Military Power: Strategy and Operations in Swedish Military History during 1,500 years*) (Stockholm: SNDC, 2003).

Jan Hallenberg, Professor of Political Science. Hallenberg is Director of Studies at the Department of Security and Strategy, SNDC since 2000. He has been Research Fellow at Princeton University, Harvard University and the University of California, Berkeley. He is the author of three academic monographs, the latest of which is *The Demise of the Soviet Union: Analysing the collapse of a state* (Aldershot: Ashgate, 2002).

Bo Huldt, Professor of Security and Strategy, SNDC. Professor Huldt has previously been Director of the Swedish Institute of International Affairs, the International Institute of Strategic Studies in London, and the Department of Strategy at the SNDC.

Anders Johansson, lieutenant-commander, R(Sw)NR, MA. Johansson is a Ph.D. candidate at Örebro University and Head teacher at the Media and Communication Studies Section, Department of Security and Strategic Studies, SNDC. He served as the Chief Public Information officer at the Nordic-Polish Brigade in SFOR, Doboj, Bosnia, 1998–1999.

Roland Jostrup, lieutenant-colonel. Teacher at the Air Operations Branch, Department of War Studies, SNDC. Jostrup has a military background in ground-based air defence, in particular the Hawk.

Håkan Karlsson, Ph.D. in political science. Karlsson is a research associate at the Department of Security and Strategic Studies, SNDC. He is the author of *Bureaucratic Politics and Weapons Acquisition: The Case of the ICBM Program* (2 volumes, Stockholm: Stockholm University, 2002).

Roger Karlsson, major, BA. Teacher in political science at the Department of Security and Strategic Studies. Karlsson has several years of service in international operations, most recently as Liaison Officer at UNIKOM's office in Baghdad. He has also served as Liaison Officer in SFOR in Sarajevo and has also had positions at the UN missions UNIFIL and UNPROFOR.

Richard Lindborg, major. Teacher in tactics at the Air Operations Branch at the Department of War Studies, SNDC. Lindborg has previously been an instructor at the Swedish Air Force Air Battle Simulation Centre.

Lars-Johan Nordlund, major. Teacher in tactics and air operations at the Air Operations Branch, Department of War Studies, SNDC. Nordlund has previously served as staff officer in the Swedish Armed Forces Head-quarters.

Jan Reuterdahl, lieutenant-colonel. MA with honours in Military Studies Air Warfare at the American Military University. Head of the SNDC Air Operations Branch. Reuterdahl has an operational background in the Swedish Air Defence Control system as a fighter controller and tactical director. He has commanded various air defence units and has served in various staff positions at joint commands and on national level. In 1994–5 he headed the Air Operations Branch of the United Nations mission in former Yugoslavia.

Kristina Riegert, Ph.D. in Political Science. Lecturer in Media Studies and Research Fellow at the Media and Communication Studies Section, Department of Security and Strategic Studies, SNDC. Riegert is the author of several books and reports on the role of media in international conflicts and in information warfare, and of the relationship between media and identity in the Nordic countries' coverage of its Baltic Sea neighbours. Her most recent publications are found in K. Riegert (ed.) *News of the Other: Tracing Identity in Scandinavian Constructions of the Eastern Baltic Region* (Gothenburg: Nordicom, 2004).

Stefan Ring, lieutenant-colonel. Head teacher in Strategy at the Department of Security and Strategic Studies. He is a member of the Royal Swedish Academy of War Sciences.

Charlotte Wagnsson, Ph.D. in political science. Assistant Professor at the Department of Security and Strategic Studies, SNDC since 1999. Wagnsson's present project compares Russia and the EU concerning differences in the norms of security policy from the Kosovo bombings in 1999 to the Iraq War in 2003. She has published a number of texts, nationally and internationally, on Russian foreign and security policy.

Johan Wiktorin, major. Teacher in joint operations at the Department of War Studies, SNDC since 2003. Assistant to the Director JFS (2000–01). He commanded the 3rd Ranger Battalion until 2000.

PREFACE

This book is the result of a collaboration between academics and officers at the Swedish National Defence College (SNDC). As one of the editors it is a pleasure to note that what was originally intended to be an in-house publication largely for the teaching of Swedish officers has now become a book for the Anglo-Saxon market. Our ambition with this book was to have a broader approach than the usual analysis of a war, not only a military or a political scientist/historical book, but a volume that covers both these aspects and more. We wanted to avoid the trap of analysing a complex process from a single perspective. I want to thank all the authors for their efforts in making the publication of this book possible.

There are two people, in particular, that deserve to be singled out for their contributions to the birth and completion of this book. First, I owe thanks to my colleague Jan Angstrom who first came up with the idea of making an in-house volume in Swedish into an internationally published book and then asked me to be the editor of the English version. In addition to these crucial steps, he also contributed a first chapter to this book that helped set the frames for the succeeding analyses. Second, I owe thanks to my colleague and long-term friend Håkan Karlsson, the second editor of this book. I know of no-one who can read an academic text, whether in English or Swedish, and come up with as strict and constructive editorial critique, leading to suggestions for improvement, as Håkan. There is no doubt in my mind that Håkan Karlsson has greatly contributed to whatever analytical qualities that this book may possess.

Finally, there have been other people who have contributed to the production of this volume. I wish to single out Ms Petra Nilsson and Ms Elsa Johannesson, especially, for their valuable help at various stages of our work. Our editor at Routledge, Andrew Humphrys, has also consistently supported this project, for which I am grateful. As for myself, I also wish to thank my wife Ulrika Mörth for her consistent support and encouragement.

Stockholm, September 2004
Jan Hallenberg

LIST OF ABBREVIATIONS

AAA	Anti-aircraft artillery
ABM	Anti-ballistic missile
AMC	Air Mobility Command
ASFAO	Anti-surface force air operations
AWACS	Airborne Warning and Control System
BBC	British Broadcasting Corporation
BCT	Brigade combat team
BDA	Battle damage assessment
CAO	Counter air operations
CAOC	Combined air operations centre
CAS	Close air support
CBO	Congressional Budget Office
CBS	Columbia Broadcasting System
CENTCOM	Central Command
CNN	Cable News Network
CoG	Centre of gravity
CPA	Coalition Provisional Authority
CSCE	Conference on Security and Co-operation in Europe
C-SPAN	Cable-Satellite Public Affairs Network
DCA	Defensive counter air
EBO	Effects-based operations
ESDP	European Security and Defence Policy
EU	European Union
EW	Electronic warfare
FCO	Foreign and Commonwealth Office
FCSL	Fire control support line
GBAD	Ground-based air defence
GBU	Guided bomb unit
GEM	Guidance enhanced missile
GPRC	Global personnel recovery system
GPS	Global positioning system
HARM	High-speed anti-radiation missile

IAEA	International Atomic Energy Agency
ICC	International Criminal Court
ID	Infantry division
IFOR	Implementation Force (in Bosnia)
IHL	International humanitarian law
IISS	International Institute for Strategic Studies
INA	Iraqi News Agency
INS	Inertial navigation system
IPI	International Press Institute
ISAF	International Security Assistance Force (in Afghanistan)
ITV	Independent Television
JDAM	Joint direct attack munition
JFACC	Joint force air component commander
JRC	Joint rescue centre
JSTARS	Joint Surveillance Target Attack Radar System
KFOR	Kosovo Force
KLA	Kosovo Liberation Army
MEF	Marine Expeditionary Force
MSNBC	Microsoft/National Broadcasting Company
NATO	North Atlantic Treaty Organization
NBC	National Broadcasting Company
NBC	Nuclear, biological, and chemical (weapons)
NCO	Non-commissioned officer
NCW	Network-centric warfare
NSD	National Security Directive
OCA	Offensive counter air
OMG	Operational Manoeuvre Group
OODA	Observation, orientation, decision and action
OSCE	Organization for Security and Co-operation in Europe
POW	Prisoner of war
QDR	Quadrennial Defense Review
RAF	Royal Air Force
RFID	Radio frequency identification
ROE	Rules of engagement
SA	Strategic attack
SEAD	Suppression of enemy air defences
SFOR	Stabilization Force (in Bosnia)
SUPAO	Supporting air operations
TAV	Total asset visibility
TBM	Tactical ballistic missile
TRADOC	Training and Doctrine Command
TST	Time sensitive target
UAV	Unmanned aerial vehicle

UBO	Intelligence and battle area (underrättelse-och bekämpningsområde)
UCAV	Unmanned combat air vehicle
UN	United Nations
UNMOVIC	United Nations Monitoring, Verification, and Inspection Commission
UNOCHI	United Nations Office of the Humanitarian Co-ordinator for Iraq
UNSC	United Nations Security Council
UNSCOM	United Nations Special Committee
UNTAC	United Nations Transitional Authority in Cambodia
USAF	United States Air Force
USCENTAF	United States Central Command Air Forces
USMC	United States Marine Corps
VTsIOM	Russian Centre for Public Opinion and Market Research
WEU	Western European Union
WMD	Weapons of mass destruction
WTO	World Trade Organization
WW I	World War I
WW II	World War II

1

PUZZLES AND PROPOSITIONS OF THE IRAQ WAR

Jan Angstrom

Introduction

The war in Iraq in 2003 – and the political process which led up to it – challenged the conventional wisdom of international politics, strategy, war and warfare in several ways. For example, the traditional understanding of war and peace rests uneasily with the notion of an 'inter-war' period of peace between the Gulf War in 1991 and the Iraq War in 2003, considering that coalition forces carried out air strikes on average every third day during the period, including launching over 500 Tomahawk missiles against targets in Iraq.[1] Moreover, considering that the Iraqi forces were most likely aware that they faced a technologically superior and heavily mechanized enemy, it would have made sense to prepare and destroy bridges early so as to hamper the advancement of the coalition forces. But they did not. Why? The Iraq War did, however, also conform to other expectations more commonly found in analyses of international discord and collaboration. For example, the US attempt to build an international coalition before the war followed an established post-cold war pattern of US policy-makers searching for burden-sharing in military operations. Hence, there are also important continuities that need to be taken into consideration when analysing the Iraq War. How should the Iraq War be approached? What are its central puzzles and propositions?

This chapter aims to address three central puzzles in the study of modern war and their connection to the war in Iraq. Although the three puzzles are partly interrelated, this broad categorization will help to introduce the chapters in this volume as well as set studies of the Iraq War within a broader scholarly framework. The notion of a 'puzzle' is intimately, although not exclusively, linked to inconsistencies with what Stephen Toulmin has termed 'ideals about the natural order'.[2] The puzzle is therefore often framed as an anomaly – a departure from the norm. Arguably, the puzzle's great worth in scientific study is that it drives scholars to search for explanations.

This chapter poses some research questions for the study of the Iraq War. Specifically, the central puzzles here are to explain when the war actually took place, why it took place, and how it was fought. Even though the discussion in this chapter is mainly conceptual, it will not impose a conceptual hierarchy for the rest of the chapters. It will, however, provide an analytical framework within which the different contributions to the book can be usefully examined. The concluding chapter, therefore, returns to the when, why and how of the Iraq War and on the basis of the contributions suggests possible answers to the overall puzzles.

It should be pointed out that a final assessment of the Iraq War is still premature. In itself this is hardly surprising, and studies of the Iraq War suffer no more in this respect than studies of other contemporary wars. It is still important, though, to realize that sources and data on the Iraq War are provisional at best, and part of the parties' attempt to manipulate information for operational or political purposes at worst. In turn, this raises questions regarding the quality of conclusions that can be drawn from early studies of the Iraq War. This is no easy matter to decide without the benefit of hindsight. Hence, caution is in place.

The discussion is also related to a more general question of how far-reaching conclusions about warfare can be drawn from the Iraq War. At least two positions need to be considered. On the one hand, one can argue that hardly any conclusions for future warfare can be drawn, as the coalition forces were overwhelmingly superior to the degraded Iraqi forces, which had gradually been starved of resources, training and equipment throughout the 1990s. Karl Mueller recently made a similar point when arguing that caution is necessary since there are hardly any replicas of Warsaw Pact-organized armed forces around anymore. The Iraq War, therefore, may be the last of its kind.[3]

On the other hand, one can argue that the Iraq War is perhaps the way of the future. At the moment, it is difficult to envision any potential challengers with capabilities equal to those of the US forces (or any US-led coalition). Hence, as has been suggested, the post-cold war era may be one of 'hegemonic wars' and 'expeditionary warfare', characterized not by campaigns and battles between equally organized and equipped armed forces but between highly trained and well-equipped professionals on one hand, and poorly equipped low-tech irregulars (or regulars), on the other. In this interpretation, the Iraq War, together with the war in Afghanistan, may be the rule rather than the exception. This is not to say that warfare is turning one-sided, however. Despite their great strength, even US forces can still encounter resistance which is difficult to overcome – as developments in Iraq subsequent to the end of major conventional warfare have demonstrated.

This chapter proceeds as follows. First, I discuss the puzzle of *when* wars take place. This has immediate importance for the Iraq War, as assumptions of when the war took place partly determine what we can consider caused it. This puzzle is also inextricably linked to questions about the nature of war. Second, I discuss the causes of war and how this question relates to the Iraq War. Considering that wars are costly and risky, *why* did the second war between the US and Iraq break out? What theoretical questions and propositions can be formulated when approaching the possible causes of the Iraq War? Third, I discuss the conduct of the war and introduce analytical approaches for understanding *how* the war in Iraq was fought. This puzzle naturally focuses on identifying the balance between practising force economy (as even superpowers have limited resources) and achieving the goals of military operations. And how should the conduct of the war be understood and explained?

When did the war in Iraq take place?

The first issue to be considered when attempting to analyse any aspect of the Iraq War is to determine, or at least make an assumption about, *when* the war took place. This, of course, is just another way of framing the question of *what* war is, but it also serves to pinpoint a potential weakness in studies of war in general, which more often than not treat this issue only tacitly.[4] Its importance is obvious in that the understanding of the term 'cause' implies that it occurs before its effect. Consequently, it is necessary to delineate the dependent variable, not only spatially but also temporally in studies of the causes of war. In this way, assumptions on *when* the war in Iraq occurred influence our notion of what caused it. Moreover, the notion of *jus in bello* assumes that there is a distinction between war and peace, which the actors in the war can identify. These notions are rendered meaningless if war and peace cannot be separated. Accordingly, it is appropriate to begin an analysis of puzzles in the Iraq War with a discussion of when the war took place.

Dating wars – as with other historical events – requires that it is possible to determine both when they break out and when they stop.[5] In European wars, the parties have traditionally used declarations of war and peace treaties as means to clear any lingering confusion as to whether or not they are at war. This custom, in turn, provided analysts with a means to date wars. However, Kalevi Holsti has noted that the practice of formally declaring war has gradually decreased. Instead, armed conflicts since the Second World War have largely been characterized by the absence of immediate crises preceding the outbreak of hostilities, the absence of declarations of war, and the absence of formal peace treaties (in favour of more or less adhered-to ceasefires) to end hostilities.[6] In itself, this fact does not suggest that we live in an era of perpetual war – or peace – but it does suggest that the conventions on how both analysts and parties separate these phenomena have changed.

3

As Christopher Coker has pointed out, even when these conventions were used by the parties in their interaction, it was far from problem-free for analysts to use them as indicators to determine when wars took place.[7] While Coker uses difficulties to date the Second World War to illustrate his point, his argument is easily transferred to current world politics. The US-proclaimed 'war on terrorism' highlights additional problems. Lawrence Freedman has suggested that: 'wars are fought between opposing political entities and not against tactics'.[8] The inherent problem with this concept is that war as a term entails the possibility of a beginning and an end, but does a war against a tactic – or, for that matter, against drugs – have a conceivable end? When wars occur, therefore, depends on how we understand war (and peace).

The first issue on the agenda in the search for new indicators for dating war is, quite naturally, to understand what is meant by war and peace. Perhaps the most commonly found notion depicts war and peace as opposites on a scale of possible ways that states (or other social actors) can relate to each other. In this view peace is a state in which individuals, groups, or states pursue their goals through dialogue, the rule of law and, normally, non-armed competition. During war, meanwhile, using force and violence is the rule, rather than the exception.[9] This understanding, however, may not be helpful in describing the relationship between the US and Iraq in the past 15 years considering that Western forces carried out air strikes, including Tomahawk missile strikes on a number of occasions, during the interim period between the two major outbreaks of large-scale military operations. Should Clausewitz's dictum be reversed insofar as peace being the continuation of war with similar means to accommodate US–Iraqi relations?

Traditionally, war has been conceptualized as 'organized large-scale armed conflict' or simply 'organized large-scale violence'.[10] Although war is usually understood to be a phenomenon intimately connected to the state, there is no apparent contradiction in incorporating other actors as well.[11] The traditional understanding follows Carl von Clausewitz's influential ideas of war as a rational and political phenomenon. Following his famous dictum that war is a continuation of politics by other means,[12] the term 'organized' signifies that war is a controlled rational and collective phenomenon with more or less developed (and adhered to) norms which govern the parties' behaviour, rather than chaotic, irrational and random acts of violence.[13] In this interpretation, it makes sense to talk of war as a *tool* to achieve an end. What Clausewitz had in mind was a political end, but David Keen among others has suggested that war could be understood as a means to an economic end.[14] Nevertheless, both these interpretations emphasize the fact that war is essentially a tool, which in turn suggests that making the Iraq War intelligible comes down to identifying ends which the war may serve. A central query is, therefore, investigating the rationale of the Iraq War, either through analysis of its conduct to identify operational patterns, which may indicate what the war is about, or through analysis of the political pretext for the war.

There are, however, other ways of understanding the meaning of war. Closely related to the understanding of war as a tool is the notion that war occurs between actors. It is a social phenomenon. This means that war presupposes reciprocity. At 'the heart of the matter', Clausewitz argued, 'war is a violent "duel"; two forces of will, standing opposed to each other, each trying to overpower the other'.[15] In this context, some aspects of the Iraq War seem puzzling. Why, for example, did Iraqi forces not prepare and destroy bridges to hamper the advance of coalition forces? To what extent did Iraqi commanders consider contingencies for post-Saddam Iraq? Although a fully evolved Clausewitzian 'duel' may not have materialized during major operations in Iraq, it does not mean that there was no fighting. Indeed, the protracted low-level fighting, in which the US forces have suffered more casualties than during the major combat operations ending in May 2003, also suggests that the notion of reciprocity in war is still valid. The fact that there have been more coalition casualties after May 2003 rests uneasily with the notion that the war ended at that time.

The notion of war as a duel invokes yet another separate understanding of war. It suggests that war is an *institution* – a social ritual with its own set of rules and norms – to manage conflicts when other instruments fail.[16] A closely related interpretation frames war as a decision-making mechanism. If two parties fail to reach an agreement, they can let war decide the issue.[17] In this respect, war has similarities with tossing a coin. This understanding of war, however, presupposes that the parties involved in the conflict view war in a similar fashion and share a similar perception of what constitutes defeat and victory. If war involves asymmetric interest, Paul Pillar argues, at least one of the parties will be less inclined to leave the matter to a decision-making mechanism, in which justice is uncared for. In such situations, war is transformed and becomes part of a bargaining game.[18] War, in this interpretation, is a form of communication.[19] Hence war does not replace politics, but constitutes a different form of politics. Understanding war in these terms still points to some puzzling behaviour in the Iraq War. What signals did the US try to send during the 1990s and why did the Saddam regime fail to understand them – or did it understand them, but chose to ignore them? To what extent, if any, did the way in which the coalition fought during the operations contribute to the problems which have occurred since major operations ended? The much-heralded 'rapid decisive operations' and 'strategic dislocation' may not signal clearly enough to the opponent that 'You have lost: Surrender!'. Should that be the case, attrition warfare may still have its advantages, although it is frequently derided in current doctrinal and theoretical debate. This final argument touches upon a different understanding of war. What makes war special as a form of communication, as a decision-making mechanism, or as a tool to solve conflicts is that wars are carried out with violent means. As Martin Shaw has pointed out, the German word *Schlacht*, which Clausewitz used, means both 'battle' and 'slaughter'.[20] Thus violence is not only inherent in war, but the degree of violence may also carry explanatory value.

In stark contrast to viewing war as a controlled and rational act, some – most notably Martin van Creveld – have argued that war is an end in itself.[21] Following the Dutch philosopher Johan Huizunga's notion of *Homo Ludens*, i.e. the 'playing man', van Creveld suggests that war is not instrumental but rather an end in itself, as it allows mankind to participate in a game with the highest stakes.[22] It thus opens the possibility to understand war as a non-rational phenomenon. The argument suggests that war is not necessarily linked to politics or any higher end. What van Creveld had in mind was so-called 'low-intensity conflict'. Surprising some, but not others, as soon as major combat operations in Iraq ended the situation turned into a quagmire of repeated minor skirmishes, bombings, and rioting. There are even reports that al-Qaeda operatives have been active in recruiting and participating in attacks against the international presence in Iraq. To what extent is the resistance against coalition forces organized and hierarchical? This is an empirical question, but answering it would make a substantial contribution to the debate on the nature of war.

From these different conceptions of war, it is possible to extract operational criteria, which can be used to measure when the war in Iraq took place. An analysis of these, however, provides an ambivalent answer. If one considers military operations as an indicator, the number of air sorties over Iraq suggests that there are hardly grounds for postulating an 'inter-war' period and, similarly, it would suggest that the war is still ongoing. If one considers strike sorties, the result is not all that different. If one considers the casualty rate, it becomes even more puzzling because data collection is notoriously difficult to verify, which has meant that some conflict databases, e.g. the Uppsala Conflict Database, have not included the Iraq War in their databanks. Solving this riddle is not only important for analytical purposes. If war and peace are becoming more difficult to separate – and admittedly, they may always have been difficult to separate – it becomes more difficult to sustain aspects of international law.

Why did the war in Iraq happen?

Traditionally, causes of war as a research object has been a major concern for international relations; it has even been argued that it forms an integral part of the discipline's identity.[23] The puzzle involved in the causes of war is usually framed in terms of asking why wars happen even though they are risky, costly and destructive.[24] Understanding the puzzle in this way automatically leads analysts to consider rational explanations of war that focus on identifying the political goals and motivations of governments. Although the assumption of rationality is reasonable, it does not necessarily explain all facets of the Iraq War. How, then, should this puzzle be approached according to a theory of international relations, assuming rational behaviour, and to what extent can it provide propositions for the Iraq War? Below, I outline some preliminary propositions on the causes of war in Iraq that follow the levels of analysis.[25]

Explanations at the individual level of analysis are usually framed as being either derived from the psychological set-up of man, his biological nature, or – in some cases – the more elusive 'nature' of man. The standard criticism of such explanations is that they have difficulty explaining variance. For example, if one assumes that human nature is power-seeking, as for example Hans Morgenthau did, it becomes difficult to explain altruistic behaviour.[26] In connection with the war in Iraq, some have argued that the motives and rationales behind US and Iraqi behaviour can be found at the individual level of analysis. For example, it has been suggested – mostly by commentators in the media critical of the Bush administration – that US action was triggered by a personal vendetta between the Bush family and Saddam Hussein. Evidence to support this thesis, however, has not appeared en masse. Arguments stressing misperceptions have, so far, been even less frequent in analyses of the causes of the Iraq War.

Explanations and propositions derived from the state level are more common and seem more promising. An obvious puzzle in relation to the causes of war in Iraq concerns the actions of Saddam Hussein and the Iraqi regime. Saddam, if one tries to analyse his behaviour from the standpoint of a rational actor, behaved quite enigmatically. Why did the war happen at all, given the fact that he ought to have understood that Iraq did not have a chance and that the coalition meant business? When the UN Security Council declared Iraq to be in material breach of resolution 1441, the negotiation 'win-set' – to use Robert Putnam's term – was still sufficiently broad to avoid war.[27] Why, then, did the Iraqi regime not come clean? Why did Saddam manipulate information to appear to have weapons of mass destruction when he could easily have averted international pressure, and thus been in a better position to avoid war altogether? Surely, by allowing weapons inspectors to return to Iraq at an early stage in the process, he might have succeeded in the same game in which he was successful during the 1990s. The mystery can perhaps be solved by studying Saddam's precarious situation as a balancing act between internal and external pressures. The reasoning so far assumes that the Iraqi leader had the information needed to make an informed decision. It may still be some time before we can estimate the impact of 'groupthink' or other cognitive bias in the regime's policies.[28]

Equally obvious puzzles surround the behaviour of the US. If the US had been attacked by Iraq or by terrorists undoubtedly supported by the Iraqi

7

regime, the US war policy would, arguably, have represented no puzzle at all. However, as Hallenberg points out (in this volume), the Iraq War was a 'war of choice' for the Bush administration. The fact that Washington did not have to go to war when it did begets a puzzle in view of the great dangers always associated with military warfare. A fundamental insight that Hallenberg puts forward is that there are many explanations for the US invasion of Iraq: the difficulty is to identify the most important explanations. In trying to solve the puzzle of why the US went to war despite wars being risky undertakings, Hallenberg evaluates the explanatory power of a number of conceivable policy ends. He distinguishes between the declared goals of the Bush administration, those that were presented publicly to ensure political support for the decision to invade Iraq and the 'real' goals that actually led to the decision. The public justifications, dominated by the stated objective of disarming Iraq, were largely discredited when the war was over. In retrospect, they have raised puzzling questions about the knowledge, judgement and sincerity of the decision-makers in Washington. To put it bluntly, did the President and his aides try to hoodwink the American people and the international community?

This question is also related to a wider issue of trends and transformation in US foreign policy behaviour and US grand strategy since the end of the cold war and since the September 11 attacks.[29] One trend that seems to be gaining popularity in the field is how to relate the concept of empire to the current US hegemony in world politics.[30] The notion of 'imperial over-stretch' could perhaps be fruitful in explaining US military misfortunes, considering that the US currently has its armed forces stationed worldwide. There are also those exploring the agenda-setting effects of the war on terror upon US unilateralism or multilateralism.[31] Moreover, while seeking burden-sharing in its military operations has become a pattern, albeit in a slightly more ad-hoc Rumsfeldian 'the mission determines the coalition'-way, the US attempt to build a broad coalition in the UN Security Council before the war in Iraq failed. Why did this fail when the US had succeeded in building a similar coalition less than two years earlier regarding operations in Afghanistan? Why did the permanent members of the Security Council allow the issue to become an open conflict, when all of them would be worse off should the US and the UK still go through with their plans? France and Russia would suffer, as a non-UN sanctioned attack against Iraq would undermine the legitimacy of the UN (which is arguably their major opportunity to show their status as world powers), while the US would suffer in so far as it pursued an operation without the legitimacy of the international community behind it. Yet neither party backed down. Why? The puzzle is further confounded in the case of Russia, considering that the challenge jeopardized Russia's improved but still uneasy relationship with Washington.

Although public opinion or other state level factors may have swayed some Western leaders to oppose the war in Iraq, there are also explanations derived from the system level of analysis which may prove valuable for understanding the political pretext for the war. An as yet unexplored avenue may be to explain the crisis within the UN Security Council as a so-called 'chicken game'. In game theory, chicken games are used to explain breakdown in cooperation leading to suboptimal outcomes for the parties involved.[32] At first glance this seems promising, as the parties in the diplomatic crisis all failed in their tasks and the resulting situation arguably left them worse off than before. Nevertheless, it is likely that the partial breakdown of cooperation in transatlantic relations regarding Iraq will be highlighted in future debate both as a case of the problem in alliance politics as well as in connection with the question of whether or not states balance or bandwagon with power.[33]

Another system level explanation of the war draws heavily upon the alleged US fear that the Iraqi regime would supply terrorist networks with weapons of mass destruction. This argument could easily be linked with the notion of a 'security dilemma'.[34] The security dilemma is central to realism as a theory of international relations, as it provides realism with a causal mechanism to explain why wars break out despite the fact that no party intends to go to war. It does so by arguing that anarchy among states forces them to act upon worst case scenarios and that these actions have a tendency to lead to unintended suboptimal consequences, i.e. war. There is, however, a substantial debate within realism as to whether or not power-seeking or status-quo ambitions drive states in their international behaviour.[35] To what extent does the evidence on US Iraq policy lend itself to these competing interpretations? Did the US go to war out of fear or out of ambition, for its security or for oil, for Middle Eastern democratization or to extend its power? The US Administration has made it clear, not least in its national security strategy, that in the post-9/11 world there are no margins for error in dealing with terrorists with weapons of mass destruction. In view of the US analysis that deterrence against terrorism does not work, pre-emptive attacks made sense. The Bush administration may thus have felt it had a valid reason for invading Iraq.

Whether the war has made the US more secure or not remains unclear. International terrorism has not abated. Is there even evidence of the US-led attack leaving al-Qaeda better off than before insofar as the war further provoked already alienated young men, pushing them into the hands of the network?

Even among those who reject international law as an explanatory factor in international politics, most would acknowledge that it is still important as one source of legitimacy for military operations. To what extent was the war sanctioned by, and conducted according to, international law? This discussion raises several puzzles and relates to a much wider scholarly debate. Is the Iraq War an example of international law being created or was it the swan song of international law? To what extent did US foreign policy-makers take international law into consideration in the process that led to the war?

How was the war in Iraq fought?

Another central puzzle in the study of war focuses on the way war is conducted. Arguably, for as long as war has been a part of human experience, this issue has been closely related to the question of how to win wars.[36] It has traditionally been the focus of so-called military theory (or strategic thought, as it sometimes is referred to) and military history.[37] From this perspective, what is puzzling about warfare in Iraq? How, for example, should the onset of major combat operations be understood? The attempted surgical strike against Saddam and the near instantaneous start of the ground and air operations did not comply with analyses before the war stressing that the initial phases – as in the Gulf War a decade ago – would consist of an extended air bombardment. However, it must be said that Operations Southern and Northern Watch may, at least with hindsight, have served as a prolonged effort to set the stage for immediately obtaining air superiority over the theatre of operations in case of war. This seems to be supported by evidence that from June 2002 coalition strike sorties increased, even though no one at the time could be certain whether or not this was a prelude to war.

The central dilemma of strategy, as James Gow frames it, is to achieve a balance between force economy to maintain freedom of action if the conflict escalates or transforms or if forces are needed elsewhere, and the achievement of policy goals.[38] The inherent difficulties and vested interests in this balancing act are aptly captured in the debate on US force allocation during the war and during the post-war stabilization operations. While coalition forces seemingly easily beat the Iraqi forces during March and April in 2003, they have struggled with major difficulties since. The post-war situation proved to be much harder to deal with than the war itself. Critics of the war effort maintain that one reason for this was 'too few boots on the ground'. In other words, the US and its allies did not deploy sufficient troops to secure the peace. An intriguing question is why the coalition forces, after conducting major combat operations seemingly flawlessly and thereby achieving a swift military victory, seemed so ill-prepared for the aftermath of the war and apparently fell short of what was needed to stabilize Iraq. Can partial answers to this puzzle be provided by analysing the development of US military strategy and operational concepts of US armed forces?

The war in Iraq also brings further evidence to the so-called 'great air power debate'.[39] This discussion, in short, deals with whether air power alone can decide the outcome of wars or if air power is most efficiently used in support of ground operations in 'joint warfare'. The rationale behind the latter is so-called 'combined arms theory', in which the aim is to put one's enemy in a position where he has no good alternatives for action. For example, at the operational level in the Iraq War, allied ground forces sought to mass their forces to coerce the Iraqis into concentrating their forces in response. Concentration, however, made the Iraqis sitting ducks against the superior coalition air component, and if the Iraqis stayed dispersed they would be easy targets of the concentrated effort of the allied ground forces.

Discussing the air operations leads to several other general puzzles. First, the use of US air power also has links to international law insofar as targeting processes currently involve not only military and political views but also juridical considerations. The efforts that the US and coalition air forces made to avoid collateral damage suggest that the idea of separating civilians and soldiers is alive and well. Second, Iraqi conduct of the air war also posed some major puzzles. Why, for example, did the Iraqis literally bury parts of their air force? Most importantly this indicates that someone was planning for contingencies. But who took these decisions? Third, air power, through the increased use of precision-guided munitions, is closely linked with the notion of an impending 'revolution in military affairs'. To what extent did the US conduct its operations according to the guiding principles of network-centric warfare?

There are nearly innumerable ways of classifying warfare, although the more recent literature dealing with the operational level of war seems to focus on the dichotomy between manoeuvre warfare and attrition warfare on the one hand and on the impact of the much-debated revolution in military affairs on the other.[40] How should the US-led coalition's operations in Iraq be understood? Did the Marine Corps conduct its operations differently from the US Army? How did the force to space ratio matter in coalition operations? And how should the current counter-insurgency campaign be understood in relation to manoeuvre and attrition warfare?

One of the possible contingencies that has been mentioned is that the Iraqi regime aimed to conduct a lengthy guerrilla warfare campaign. This part of the war would be carried out simultaneously as the Iraqi regular forces would force the coalition troops to fight their way through the city centres: the idea would be that the coalition advance would grind to a halt in urban warfare. The creation and endowment of Saddam's *Fedayyin* militia may be a case to the point. Yet the campaign in urban environments never took place. Why? Why did the Iraqi forces not put up a fight where the coalition's main advantage, air power, would not be able to make an easy impact? This seems even more puzzling considering the degree of success that Shia militias, those apparently still faithful to Saddam, and cells or individuals possibly linked to al-Qaeda have had since May 2003 in their operations against the coalition.

Another influential tradition in this field has been to analyse warfare according to who conducts the war. As Thomas Mahnken puts it: 'The notion that there is a connection between a society and its style of warfare has a long and distinguished pedigree.'[41] Accordingly, there are those who maintain that there is an 'American way of war'. Most notably, Russell Weighley's analysis of how the US has conducted its major wars still influences the discourse. Weighley claimed that the American way of war is one aiming for decisive battles and unconditional surrender while being pursued through grinding attrition, massive firepower and technological superiority.[42] To what extent does evidence from the war in Iraq lend itself to this interpretation? Was the Iraq War conducted in an 'American' way? Max Boot argues that it was,[43] but a general deficiency in this literature is the lack of comparative analysis. It is difficult to sustain the claim that there is a uniquely American way of war without comparisons examining whether other nations behave in a similar way, strategically, operationally and tactically, when faced with a similar opponent as US forces. Hence, there is a danger that 'national' categorizations are false. The superimposed 'national' may obscure analyses and prevent scholars from uncovering the real pattern. Comparative studies of the way British and US forces conducted their operations in the Iraq War may illuminate the issue.

Organization of this study

This chapter has outlined some central puzzles and propositions in the study of the Iraq War. By posing these questions, the chapter has provided the overall volume with a general structure and set the scene for the following chapters which contain analyses of various aspects of the Iraq War, US and Iraqi grand strategy, military strategy and operations.

The study comprises two major analytical sections. Part I deals mainly with strategy and politics before the war, while Part II deals mainly with strategy and operations during the war. In Chapter 2, by seeking to identify the Bush administration's goals, Jan Hallenberg tries to solve the puzzle of why the US went to war voluntarily despite wars being risky undertakings. In Chapter 3, Bo Huldt analyses how transatlantic relations influenced the political prelude to the Iraq War as well as how the war has influenced transatlantic relations during the 15 months or so since major combat operations ended. Chapter 4, by Charlotte Wagnsson, provides an analysis of Russian foreign policy behaviour during the Iraq War crisis. Wagnsson seeks an explanation of Russian behaviour mainly in the long-term goals of Russian foreign policy. Roger Karlsson, in Chapter 5, provides insights into the problems and constraints that faced the Iraqi regime as it developed its grand strategy. In Chapter 6 Lars Ericson provides an historical perspective on the current conflict by examining the war which *created* Iraq in 1914–1921.

In Chapter 7, which serves as a link between the political pretext and military operations, Ove Bring and Per Broström analyse the Iraq War from the perspective of international law. In Chapter 8, Stefan Ring investigates the extent to which brute force and coercion were used against Iraq to analyse US strategy. In Chapter 9, Anders Cedergren examines US ground operations during the war, focusing in no small part on the notion of combined arms theory as well as whether technology or force employment can explain the conduct of the war. Chapter 10, by Jan Reuterdahl *et al.* provides an analysis of the air operations and their impact during the war. In Chapter 11, Kristina Riegert and Anders Johansson explore the role of the media during the war. Finally, in the concluding chapter Jan Hallenberg and Håkan Karlsson summarize some of the contributions to the volume in the light of the puzzles presented here and identify further puzzles to be examined.

Notes

1 I will continuously refer to the Gulf War in 1991 and the Iraq War in 2003, not as analytical categories, but rather as a reflection of the common perception among scholars as well as policy-makers that during these periods there were wars between Iraq and various Western-led coalitions. Data on air strikes was compiled from the US Department of Defense, *Annual Report to the President and the Congress, 1992–2003*.
2 Quoted in J. Asplund, *Om undran inför samhället*, Lund, Sweden: Argos, 1970, pp. 111–115.
3 K. Mueller, 'Man in the Loop: Human Factors in Operation Iraq Freedom', paper presented at the biannual RAF Air Power conference in London, 11–12 May 2004.
4 This is arguably a lesser problem in quantitative studies of war, in which coding issues usually consist of a notion of when war happens. I am grateful to Birger Heldt for pointing this out, thus limiting the criticism.
5 J. L. Gaddis, *The Landscape of History: How Historians Map the Past*, Oxford: Oxford University Press, 2002, p. 19.
6 K. J. Holsti, *The State, War, and the State of War*, Cambridge: Cambridge University Press, 1996, pp. 19–40.
7 C. Coker, 'How Wars End', *Millennium*, 26, 3 (1997), 615–629.
8 L. Freedman, 'The Third World War?', *Survival*, 43, 4 (2002), 63.
9 M. Wight, 'Why is there no International Theory?', in H. Butterfield and M. Wight (eds) *Diplomatic Investigations: Essays in the Theory of International Politics*, London: Allen & Unwin, 1966, p. 33. For a criticism, see G. J. Ikenberry, *After Victory*, Princeton, NJ: Princeton University Press, 2001, pp. 6–7.
10 See, for example, Holsti op. cit., pp. 1–2.
11 M. Smith, 'Strategy in an age of low-intensity warfare: why Clausewitz is still more relevant than his critics', in I. Duyvesteyn and J. Angstrom (eds) *Rethinking the Nature of War*, London: Frank Cass, 2005, pp. 28–64. Wars are not only conducted by states, they are also closely related to the creation of states. See, for example, C. Tilly, *Coercion, Capital, and European States, AD 990–1990*, Oxford: Blackwell, 1992.
12 C. von Clausewitz, *On War*, trans. Michael Howard and Peter Paret, London: Everyman's Library, 1993, p. 99.

13 J. A. Vasquez, *The War Puzzle*, Cambridge: Cambridge University Press, 1993, pp. 24–25 and J. Gow, *The Serbian Project and Its Adversaries: A Strategy of War Crimes*, London: Hurst, 2003, pp. 16–17.

14 D. Keen, 'Incentives and Disincentives for Violence', in M. Berdal and D. Malone (eds) *Greed and Grievance: Economic Agendas in Civil Wars*, Boulder, CO: Lynne Rienner, 2000, p. 27.

15 Clausewitz, op. cit., p. 83.

16 Margaret Mead has argued that mankind invented or learned war to solve otherwise unsolvable conflicts. Quoted in Vasquez, op. cit., pp. 31–32, 39.

17 Vasquez, op. cit., p. 48.

18 P. Pillar, *Negotiating Peace: War Termination as a Bargaining Process*, Princeton, NJ: Princeton University Press, 1983, p. 28.

19 For a discussion of war as a form of communication and its inherent limitations as a form of sending unambiguous signals, see C. R. Mitchell, *The Structure of International Conflict*, London: Macmillan, 1981, pp. 143–162.

20 M. Shaw, *War and Genocide: Organized Killing in Modern Society*, Cambridge: Polity Press, 2003, p. 19.

21 For further discussion, see J. Angstrom, 'Introduction: Debating the Nature of Modern War', in Duyvesteyn and Angstrom (eds) op. cit., pp. 1–27.

22 M. van Creveld, *Transformation of War*, New York: Free Press, 1991, pp. 161–187.

23 W. Olson and N. Onuf, 'The Growth of a Discipline: Reviewed', in S. Smith (ed.) *International Relations: British and American Perspectives*, Oxford: Blackwell, 1985, pp. 2–6. The causes of war is a vast field of study and this discussion can only glance at some preliminary points of departure. For a comprehensive review, see J. S. Levy, 'The Causes of War: A Review of Theories and Evidence', in P. E. Tetlock *et al.* (eds) *Behavior, Society, and Nuclear War*, vol. 1, New York: Oxford University Press, 1989, pp. 209–333.

24 See for example J. D. Fearon, 'Rationalist Explanations for War', *International Organization*, 49, 3 (1995), 379–414.

25 M. Hollis and S. Smith, *Explaining and Understanding International Relations*, Oxford: Clarendon Press, 1990.

26 H. J. Morgenthau, *Politics Among Nations*, New York: Knopf, 1948.

27 R. D. Putnam, 'Diplomacy and Domestic Politics: The Logic of Two-Level Games', *International Organization*, 42, 3 (1988), 427–460.

28 For a study that outlines the effects of cognitive factors on foreign policy, see Y. Vertzberger, *The World in Their Minds*, Stanford, CA: Stanford University Press, 1990.

29 For a review of recent literature, see C. Dueck, 'New Perspectives on American Grand Strategy: A Review Essay,' *International Security* 28, 4 (2004), 197–216.

30 See, for example, A. J. Bacevich, *American Empire: The Realities and Consequences of US Diplomacy*, Cambridge, MA: Harvard University Press, 2002.

31 T. G. Weiss *et al.* (eds) *Wars on Terrorism and Iraq: Human Rights, Unilateralism, and US Foreign Policy*, London: Routledge, 2004.

32 For an overview of the literature on social dilemmas, see P. Kollock, 'Social Dilemmas: The Anatomy of Cooperation', *Annual Review of Sociology*, 24 (1998), 183–214.

33 For a study of the diplomatic entanglements during the present crisis over Iraq, see P. H. Gordon and J. Shapiro, *Allies at War: America, Europe, and the Crisis over Iraq*, New York: McGraw-Hill, 2004. See also R. L. Schweller, 'Bandwagoning for Profit: Bringing the Revisionist State Back In', *International Security*, 19, 1 (1994), 72–107.

34 For other influential analyses, see J. Herz, 'Idealist Internationalism and the Security Dilemma', *World Politics*, 2, 2 (1950), 157–180 and R. Jervis, 'Cooperation under the Security Dilemma', *World Politics*, 30, 2 (1978), 167–214.
35 For studies outlining the intra-realist debate, see for example S. G. Brooks, 'Dueling Realisms', *International Organization*, 51, 3 (1997), 445–477.
36 For the debate on when wars first took place, see for example R. C. Kelly, *Warless Societies and the Origin of War*, Ann Arbor, MI: University of Michigan Press, 2000.
37 Some narratives of the Iraq War have already emerged, notably A. H. Cordesman, *The Iraq War: Strategy, Tactics, and Military Lessons*, Westport, CN: Praeger, 2003 and W. Murray and R. H. Scales, *The Iraq War: A Military History*, Cambridge, MA: Belknap Press, 2003.
38 Gow op. cit., pp. 16–17.
39 R. A. Pape, 'The True Worth of Air Power', *Foreign Affairs*, 83, 2 (2004), 116–130. For an extended discussion on strategic bombing, see B. Frankel (ed.) *Precision and Purpose*, London: Frank Cass, 2001.
40 See, for example, E. N. Luttwak, *Strategy: The Logic of War and Peace*, Cambridge, MA: Belknap Press, 1987.
41 T. Mahnken, 'The American Way of War in the Twenty-First Century', in E. Inbar (ed.) *Democracies and Small Wars*, London: Frank Cass, 2003, p. 73.
42 R .F. Weighley, *The American Way of War: A History of United States Military Strategy and Policy*, Bloomington, IN: Indiana University Press, 1973.
43 M. Boot, 'The New American Way of War', *Foreign Affairs*, 82, 4 (2003), 41–58.

References

Angstrom, J. 'Introduction: Debating the Nature of Modern War', in I. Duyvesteyn and J. Angstrom (eds) *Rethinking the Nature of War*. London: Frank Cass, 2005, pp. 1–27.
Asplund, J. *Om undran inför samhället*. Lund, Sweden: Argos, 1970.
Bacevich, A. J. *American Empire: The Realities and Consequences of US Diplomacy*. Cambridge, MA: Harvard University Press, 2002.
Boot, M. 'The New American Way of War', *Foreign Affairs*, 82, 4 (2003), 41–58.
Brooks, S. G. 'Dueling Realisms', *International Organization*, 51, 3 (1997), 445–477.
Clausewitz, C. von *On War*, trans. M. Howard and P. Paret. London: Everyman's Library, 1993.
Coker, C. 'How Wars End', *Millennium*, 26, 3 (1997), 615–629.
Cordesman, A. H. *The Iraq War: Strategy, Tactics, and Military Lessons*. Westport, CN: Praeger, 2003.
Creveld, M. van *Transformation of War*. New York: Free Press, 1991.
Dueck, C. 'New Perspectives on American Grand Strategy: A Review Essay', *International Security*, 28, 4 (2004), 197–216.
Fearon, J. D. 'Rationalist Explanations for War', *International Organization*, 49, 3 (1995), 379–414.
Frankel, B. (ed.) *Precision and Purpose*. London: Frank Cass, 2001.
Freedman, L. 'The Third World War?', *Survival*, 43, 4 (2002), 61–88.
Gaddis, J. L. *The Landscape of History: How Historians Map the Past*. Oxford: Oxford University Press, 2002.
Gordon, P. H. and Shapiro, J. *Allies at War: America, Europe, and the Crisis over Iraq*. New York: McGraw-Hill, 2004.
Gow, J. *The Serbian Project and Its Adversaries: A Strategy of War Crimes*. London: Hurst, 2003.

Herz, J. 'Idealist Internationalism and the Security Dilemma', *World Politics*, 2, 2 (1950), 157–180.

Hollis, M. and Smith, S. *Explaining and Understanding International Relations*. Oxford: Clarendon Press, 1990.

Holsti, K. J. *The State, War, and the State of War*. Cambridge: Cambridge University Press, 1996.

Ikenberry, G. J. *After Victory*. Princeton, NJ: Princeton University Press, 2001.

Jervis, R. 'Cooperation Under the Security Dilemma', *World Politics*, 30, 2 (1978), 167–214.

Keen, D. 'Incentives and Disincentives for Violence', in M. Berdal and D. Malone (eds) *Greed and Grievance: Economic Agendas in Civil Wars*. Boulder, CO: Lynne Rienner, 2000, pp. 19–41.

Kelly, R. C. *Warless Societies and the Origin of War*. Ann Arbor, MI: University of Michigan Press, 2000.

Kollock, P. 'Social Dilemmas: The Anatomy of Cooperation', *Annual Review of Sociology*, 24 (1998), 183–214.

Levy, J. S. 'The Causes of War: A Review of Theories and Evidence', in P. E. Tetlock *et al.* (eds) *Behavior, Society, and Nuclear War*, vol. 1. New York: Oxford University Press, 1989, pp. 209–333.

Luttwak, E. N. *Strategy: The Logic of War and Peace*. Cambridge, MA: Belknap Press, 1987.

Mahnken, T. 'The American Way of War in the Twenty-First Century', in E. Inbar (ed.) *Democracies and Small Wars*. London: Frank Cass, 2003, pp. 73–84.

Mitchell, C. R. *The Structure of International Conflict*. London: Macmillan, 1981.

Morgenthau, H. J. *Politics Among Nations*. New York: Knopf, 1948.

Mueller, K. 'Man in the Loop: Human Factors in Operation Iraq Freedom', paper presented at the biannual RAF Air Power conference in London, 11–12 May 2004.

Murray, W. and Scales, R. H. *The Iraq War: A Military History*. Cambridge, MA: Belknap Press, 2003.

Olson, W. and Onuf, N. 'The Growth of a Discipline: Reviewed', in S. Smith (ed.) *International Relations: British and American Perspectives*. Oxford: Blackwell, 1985, pp. 1–28.

Pape, R. A. 'The True Worth of Air Power', *Foreign Affairs*, 83, 2 (2004), 116–130.

Pillar, P. *Negotiating Peace: War Termination as a Bargaining Process*. Princeton, NJ: Princeton University Press, 1983.

Putnam, R. D. 'Diplomacy and Domestic Politics: The Logic of Two-Level Games', *International Organization*, 42, 3 (1988), 427–460.

Schweller, R. L. 'Bandwagoning for Profit: Bringing the Revisionist State Back In', *International Security*, 19, 1 (1994), 72–107.

Shaw, M. *War and Genocide: Organized Killing in Modern Society*. Cambridge: Polity Press, 2003.

Smith, M. 'Strategy in an age of low-intensity warfare: why Clausewitz is still more relevant than his critics', in I. Duyvesteyn and J. Angstrom (eds) *Rethinking the Nature of War*. London: Frank Cass, 2005, pp. 28–64.

Tilly, C. *Coercion, Capital, and European States, AD 990–1990*. Oxford: Blackwell, 1992.

US Department of Defence. *Annual Report to the President and the Congress, 1992–2003*. Washington, DC: Government Printing Office.

Vasquez, J. A. *The War Puzzle*. Cambridge: Cambridge University Press, 1993.

Vertzberger, Y. *The World in Their Minds*. Stanford, CA: Stanford University Press, 1990.

Weighley, R. F. *The American Way of War: A History of United States Military Strategy and Policy*. Bloomington, IN: Indiana University Press, 1973.
Weiss, T. G. *et al.* (eds) *Wars on Terrorism and Iraq: Human Rights, Unilateralism, and US Foreign Policy*. London: Routledge, 2004.
Wight, M. 'Why is there no International Theory?', in H. Butterfield and M. Wight (eds) *Diplomatic Investigations: Essays in the Theory of International Politics*. London: Allen & Unwin, 1966, pp. 17–34.

Part I

POLITICS AND STRATEGY
BEFORE THE WAR

2

WHAT WERE THE BUSH ADMINISTRATION'S GOALS IN INVADING IRAQ?

Jan Hallenberg

Introduction: how to study a single decision

During the 16 months that have passed since the US-led invasion of Iraq there has been an immense amount of speculation about what goals the Bush administration was pursuing in that undertaking. The premise of these speculations, as well as of this chapter, is that it was Washington's actions that were decisive in the process that led to the invasion and that Great Britain under Tony Blair merely adapted to US leadership.

This chapter analyses in an academic fashion the goals that the Bush administration pursued with the Iraq invasion. Before proceeding to do so, some points need clarification. The first concerns the actor or actors that are analysed. In the policy debate there have been numerous expressions such as 'the Americans want,' 'the Neo-Conservatives seek . . .', 'it is the goal of Colin Powell' etc. The second point has to do with the method by which I determine what goals the actor in question was pursuing.

The starting point for any analysis of a decision by the United States to apply military force abroad is that it must always focus on the executive branch, that is on the President and his advisers, because it is here that the initiative, and thereby in practice the decision, lies. It is true that it is stated in the US Constitution that the decision to start a war rests with Congress. Throughout American history, however, the initiative on this issue has gradually passed to the President. One important reason is that during many crises and small wars, from the Civil War in the 1860s until the present time, the President has taken initiatives to defend the Union, decisions subsequently being ratified by Congress. Only on five occasions has Congress declared War, while the US has applied military force abroad on hundreds of occasions.[1] This process has been based on two provisions in the Constitution, one being that 'The executive Power shall be vested in a President of the United States of America' and the other that the President is the Commander-in-Chief of the Armed Forces of the United States.[2]

In this chapter, the actor is defined as the Bush administration. The analytical problem with this definition is that, apart from the President himself at the centre of power, there are several actors within his administration that may play a role in a decision of this kind. To name just a few officials, Vice President Dick Cheney, Secretary of State Colin Powell, Secretary of Defense Donald Rumsfeld, National Security Adviser Condoleezza Rice and Deputy Defence Secretary Paul Wolfowitz have all been mentioned as important actors in the process that led to the decision to invade Iraq. This is not to mention all the conspiracy theories that identify 'the Christian Right' or 'the oil industry' or other forces as more or less responsible for different parts of US foreign policy. The decision to invade Iraq was taken in a wider political context than that analysed here. This, however, is not the place for a deeper analysis of this wider process.

This analysis focuses on the formal decision apparatus. A study of this formal apparatus can not of course explain all aspects of the foreign policy actions of the superpower, but without studying how that entity functions we have hardly any chance of understanding the broader context that can influence foreign and security policy.

The first assumption on which this analysis is based is that the decision to topple the Saddam regime was taken early at the presidential level. My own surmise is that the decision was taken in principle in the autumn of 2001, and was then formalized in the spring of 2002. Let me specify that the essence of this decision in all likelihood was that the Saddam regime had to be toppled, while the precise means whereby this was to be accomplished were not settled at that early stage.[3]

A second assumption in this chapter is that without the personal involvement of the President there would have been no invasion of Iraq. At the same time, it is too limited to study only the President's personal motives. A vital decision of this kind is taken in a broader circle, which makes the Bush administration a more reasonable approximation of the actor to study, than the President alone. This is not to say that 'the Bush administration' is a definition of the actor that is completely unassailable to criticism, but simply that it is the most workable approximation for the case at hand. The President takes the overall decision and implements it, but there are other actors, of the type mentioned, who play a role in the decision-making process.

It should be emphasized that it is precisely the crucial strategic decision which in a matter of this magnitude can, in the final analysis, only be taken by the President himself, which is analysed here. It is important to clarify this, because a decision of this enormity is so large and has so many secondary ramifications that these ramifications take on a life of their own and are then apt to be mentioned as the very goals that the administration sought to accomplish. To illustrate this, it is my contention that the fact that so many of the contracts for the supplies of the troops and the rebuilding of Iraq have been given to US companies after the conclusion of the war is a striking fact, but this does not mean that the decision to invade was taken with the express goal of supporting US companies. This is not because the Bush administration does not want to support these companies – on the contrary it strives very strongly to do so – but because this intention to support US companies is always there and thus cannot be an additional factor that in any way explains the decision to invade Iraq. On the other hand, given the general view that the Bush administration has of supporting US companies, together with the fact that Washington broke with several other large countries in pursuing the invasion, it was a consequence of the strategic decision that these companies received favourable treatment. It is an analytical problem for the researcher to delineate clearly what is the precise object of analysis when he analyses a strategic issue of the kind under consideration here.

As to the methodological issue, it is necessary to try to elucidate how the researcher is to determine what goals the Bush administration was pursuing with the invasion of Iraq. How and where can we find these goals? One possible method is to let the actor define this. In other words, the analysis could be based on the most important speeches given by the President, the Vice President, the Secretary of State and the Secretary of Defense given before 19 March 2003. A systematic analysis of these speeches may provide a list of the goals that these decision-makers publicly stated that the US wanted to pursue with the invasion.

An alternative method, the one chosen here, is to let the researcher decide analytically what goals he finds are the most likely ones that Washington pursued in Iraq. An analysis of this latter type does of course include a perusal of the material mentioned above, but it is also a critical assessment of public material based on previous academic research on relevant issues. It is obvious that it is not possible to conduct a completely valid and reliable analysis of the goals pursued by the Bush administration in this fashion. Another problem is that choosing this second approach means that there is a risk that the researcher may identify conflicting goals. This is to some extent the result of the analysis presented here, but this is part and parcel of this method and its consequences must be assessed in each separate case.

On the other hand, the decision to invade Iraq is a case where a pure content analysis of public records hardly leads to completely satisfactory analytical results either. It should be possible to clarify exactly what goals were mentioned by a limited number of decision-makers during a specified period. This way of proceeding is, however, in its turn impaired by the fact that for the decision-makers speaking publicly on the subject it has presumably been more important to receive political support for the decision already taken to invade than to give a completely truthful account of what the real goals were that led to the decision in the first place. It is reasonable to assume that the striving to get support has influenced both what goals have been presented and how these goals have been characterized.

It is also important to clarify which step in the usually three-step chain in the study of a policy this chapter focuses on.[4] The first step is to analyse the process that has led to a decision by a decision-making unit, including the taking of the decision itself. The second step is to analyse how the decision-making unit, if necessary, attempts to get support for its chosen policy. The third step is to analyse how the decision is implemented. This chapter focuses only on the first step in this chain.

A starting point for this analysis is that the decision to attack Iraq was a real choice, a single decision. It cannot be said that the President, during the months after 11 September, or during the spring of 2002, was in a political situation where he had to attack Iraq and topple Saddam Hussein. In this respect there is a clear difference between the decision to attack Afghanistan and the decision to attack Iraq. In the former case, the President was faced with a situation where it was a strategic imperative, a nearly absolute necessity to attack Afghanistan after terrorists who, in the view of the Bush administration, had had bases in that country carried out what were regarded as military attacks against continental America. In the latter case, the President had a true choice: there was nothing approaching the direct challenge to Washington's status as a superpower that existed in the case of Afghanistan. What is analysed here is a truly strategic decision taken by the President of the United States on a central political issue.[5]

The background to the decision

The decision to attack Iraq was a major one, even for a superpower like the United States. It is sometimes stated that President Bush took the decision because he wanted to increase his chances of winning the Presidential election in 2004. My view is, however, different. It was a very difficult decision that, if anything turned out badly, could lead to very damaging consequences in terms of the President's chances of getting re-elected. The President took the decision despite this risk, not because he thought that it would increase his chances of re-election.

At least two background factors have to be mentioned to place the decision-making process in this case into the proper perspective. One of these factors is the terrorist attacks on 11 September 2001. The other is that the policy option of invading Iraq and thereby toppling Saddam Hussein existed as a viable option in leading policy circles in the United States ever since Saddam invaded Kuwait in August 1990.

The attacks against the twin towers of the World Trade Center in New York and on the Pentagon outside Washington DC are regarded in the US as the first attack of military significance on the US mainland since Great

Britain burnt down Washington DC in 1814 during the British–American War. The Japanese attack on Pearl Harbour on 7 December 1941 was an attack on a part of the US that was outside the mainland, and on a territory that was, furthermore, not a state of the Union at that time.[6] The immense and multifaceted military forces that were built after the Second World War, including a gradually ever more sophisticated and deadly strategic nuclear force, meant that the citizens of the US came to regard their country as more or less invulnerable militarily. The exception was of course the threat of all-out nuclear war, but after the collapse of the Soviet Union in 1991 this rather unlikely threat more or less ceased to exist. The shock was thus the greater when 19 men succeeded in hijacking four civilian airplanes and in using three of these to attack targets of immense symbolic value to the political class, as well as to the broader public in the US.[7]

The first step in responding to these attacks was that the Bush administration decided to attack Afghanistan and topple the Taliban regime, which was regarded as at least partly responsible for the 11 September attacks. The training camps that al-Qaeda had had in Afghanistan for some years were, according to the view prevailing in official Washington, a direct precondition for carrying out the 11 September attacks. As mentioned, this meant that it became a strategic imperative for the Bush administration to attack Afghanistan, topple the Taliban regime, and strive to weaken al-Qaeda as much as possible. In this view, Al Gore would also have attacked Afghanistan during roughly the same period if he had won the Presidential election in 2000. A superpower such as the US cannot absorb an attack that is defined as military, as the Bush administration did, without responding with a military counterattack. This is out of concern for the credibility of the superpower's will and ability to act in situations where vital national interests are at stake.

Besides directly causing the Afghanistan War, the 11 September attacks also created opportunities for the President to carry out policies that had been impossible to get through the US political system prior to these events. The attack against Iraq is the clearest example of this. Apparently, the idea of invading Iraq had existed and circulated in policy circles in Washington under three Presidents, but it was not a serious policy option.[8] The readers of this book are aware of at least some of the complexities of the federal decision-making apparatus in Washington DC. It is not least the division of powers between the three branches that makes it difficult to get large decisions accepted by Congress, as well as supported by a majority of the American people. The 11 September attacks created what political scientist John Kingdon has called a 'policy window', a situation in which political actions that are otherwise impossible to carry out can be taken.[9]

There are several indications that at least one influential member of the Bush administration, Deputy Defence Secretary Paul Wolfowitz, asserted immediately after 11 September that in his view Iraq ought to be attacked

at the same time as Afghanistan.[10] Before the terrorist attacks any suggestion that Iraq be invaded would have been regarded as unrealistic: afterwards it suddenly became politically possible to act upon it. In other words,
if 11 September had not occurred, Saddam Hussein would still be in power
as of this writing, in the summer of 2004.

Three interconnected goals

It is no exaggeration to state that the issue of what goals the Bush administration had when invading Iraq has been widely, as well as intensively, discussed, before, during and after the war.[11] One favourite explanation of
what the Administration was trying to accomplish has been that the main,
if not the only, reason for the US invasion was a wish to control Iraq's oil
reserves. Two main variants of this explanation exist. One is that by invading
Iraq the US wanted to control all of that country's oil. The other is that the
US wanted to control the oil trade.

The overriding counterargument to both of these beliefs is that global oil,
broadly seen, is a functioning global market. The global oil market is
immense and not easily controlled by a single state, even if that state is as
powerful as today's United States. And why should the US want to use
weapons and spend tens of billions of dollars to control a good that the
country could otherwise obtain on normal commercial terms? Conversely,
what would Saddam Hussein's regime do with its oil, except sell it on the
world market and thus get sorely needed hard currency income? Any Iraqi
regime, whether led by Saddam Hussein or anyone else, must sell its oil to
make its value serve the interests of the Iraqi regime and its people. The
US bought more oil from Iraq during Saddam's last years in power than
any other state.

This means that it is not reasonable to assume that the US had either control of Iraqi oil, or control of its oil exports, as the main reason for invading
Iraq. Instead, the Bush administration pursued three broad goals with its
invasion. The first main goal was *to demonstrate political and military power
by toppling the Iraq regime* in a situation where the decision-makers in
Washington regarded it as both politically and militarily fairly simple to do.
This goal of regime change for the sake of a power demonstration is linked
to the other two main goals, but it also has its own separate explanatory
power.

The second main goal was to *prevent the danger that the regime of Saddam
Hussein* – which, so the US decision-makers were convinced, had access to
weapons of mass destruction (WMD) – *might use WMD to threaten the
US or in the future might form an alliance with al-Qaeda* and supply this organization with WMD. There is no reason to believe that President Bush was
not truthful when he stated immediately after 11 September that he realized
that for the rest of his presidency he would be evaluated first and foremost on

his ability to prevent another attack similar to this one. This statement is a reminder of the fact that even scenarios that may be less than plausible in an objective sense can influence a decision-maker's actions in a situation where the decision-maker's political career appears to be at stake.

The third main goal, which is directly linked to several more detailed objectives, was that the US government wanted to start the process of *building a more democratic and thus more stable Middle East*. This third goal and its logical corollaries demand a more thorough analysis than the other two main goals. Among other things, this is probably the only one of the three goals identified here over which there were some differences of opinion among the small circle of decision-makers on which this chapter focuses.

The first main goal of the US in the Iraq War is connected to a broad sense within the Bush administration that the toppling of the Taliban regime in Afghanistan was not enough to demonstrate that the US government could forcefully repel the threats that it faced after the attacks of 11 September. There was a need to demonstrate that even if the superpower had been defenceless against the terrorist attacks, it had the ability to attack wherever al-Qaeda, and with it affiliated organizations, lived and worked. In discussion of why the Bush administration chose to invade Iraq, the expression 'pick the low-lying fruit' was used. It meant that the toppling of Saddam Hussein was something that had been discussed in the US for a long time but had been impossible to carry it through for various political reasons. An invasion of Iraq after 11 September would, according to this reasoning, mean that the US government got rid of a hated regime and at the same time demonstrated Washington's superior military strength. This factor is also linked to the long tradition within the US of using military force to reach political goals within its foreign and security policy.[12] The signal that the US government retained both its ability to make difficult decisions and to carry them out forcefully was directed at both a domestic and an international audience. The public in the US was intended to be assured that the Bush administration did not lack either the will or the power to strike at forces it regarded as threatening the nation's security. Potential enemies, as well as allies and neutral forces outside the country, would similarly be assured that the claims by Osama bin Laden that the US was an impotent superpower that had no ability to sustain military casualties over a period of time were wrong. The signal was to make it abundantly clear that the superpower retained the power to make difficult decisions, as well as the strength and the ability to carry decisions through into practical action.

Several actors within the Bush administration, particularly Vice President Richard Cheney, have several times reiterated that there is proof that Saddam Hussein had cooperated with al-Qaeda before 11 September.[13] The main point in this chapter is not whether or not this was indeed a connection that did exist before the terror attacks – there is really no substantial proof of this at the time of writing. This, however, does not necessarily mean that leading members of the Bush administration may not have believed that such a link did in fact exist at the time they made the decision to attack Iraq. Even if the chances of any alliance between the agnostic, or even atheistic Saddam Hussein and the extreme Islamist Osama bin Laden were exceedingly small, any such alliance would, given the assumption that the same actors believed that Saddam had WMD, have led to a risk of a catastrophic terrorist attack, an attack on a scale that would have made 11 September but a pale shadow. Even if such a turn of events in any objective sense was extremely unlikely to occur, the disaster that an attack of the form outlined here would have constituted for the Bush administration meant that it is very probable that one goal that they wanted to reach with the invasion was a definite end to any such risk.

It should be added that the second main goal, which implied both removing the Iraqi regime and eliminating Iraqi WMD, was the one most frequently mentioned by members of the Bush administration when they looked for support in their decision to invade Iraq, domestically as well as internationally. One famous occasion when one of the principal players in this game explicitly mentioned the importance that the link between Saddam Hussein and his presumed weapons of mass destruction on the one hand, and al-Qaeda on the other, had on the process of trying to get support for the already taken decision to invade Iraq, was when Deputy Defense Secretary Paul Wolfowitz brought it up in an interview with *Vanity Fair* during the Spring of 2003.[14]

The third main goal that the Bush administration had with the invasion of Iraq is the most multifaceted one and the one hardest to analyse. In the case of this overriding goal – in broad terms, that the invasion should contribute to the democratization as well as stabilization of first Iraq and then the whole Middle East – there have been so many exaggerations and simplifications in the public as well as policy debate that it is hard to pin down the basic goal that the Administration sought to pursue. These exaggerations have come from the Bush administration, as well as from outsiders, to such an extent that it sometimes seems hard to fathom that something like this truly was a goal that the US leadership pursued. However, there are so many signs that a goal along these lines was something that the Administration did pursue that it is impossible to ignore it.

Several indications imply that there have been two different views within the Bush administration on how to combat terrorism since 11 September, a distinction that is of importance for the analysis of what is here called the third main goal. Both within the torrent of books that has flowed ever more abundantly in the wake of the 11 September attacks and the war in Iraq, and within several more journalistic accounts, two views are identified within the Bush administration as to how terrorism should be weakened, if not eradicated, and how the Iraq invasion and its consequences should be seen in this context. One is the 'realist' view, mostly represented by Vice

President Richard Cheney and Secretary of Defense Donald Rumsfeld. For these two men the crucial thing is that the US can use military force to topple regimes that threaten the country and can threaten other countries that may seek to become competitors to Washington. The other view, called the 'neo-conservative' or the 'neo-imperialist' view, has among its most prominent adherents Deputy Secretary of Defense Paul Wolfowitz and Under Secretary of Defense for Policy Douglas Feith. Outside the Administration, some of the most important proponents are Richard Perle, Assistant Secretary of Defense under the Reagan administration, and the two influential journalists William Kristol and Robert Kagan. The visionary goals for the transformation of the Middle East emanate from this second view.

Much remains to be done in future research to identify the true nature of these divisions, but for present purposes it is assumed that something along the lines of the split described here existed within the Bush administration at least during the period when the decision to invade Iraq was made.[15]

The first two main goals identified in this chapter were the basic ones, which probably in themselves led to the taking of the decision to invade Iraq. The pursuit of these two goals taken together explain why the Bush administration decided to invade Iraq. The third main goal, elaborated later, evolved after the basic decision had already been taken.[16] If we accept the assumption that the decision to topple the regime of Saddam Hussein had been taken in principle in early 2002 at the latest, there was subsequently a wide-ranging debate about what additional goals the US ought to pursue in Iraq, within the Administration as well as more publicly. During this time, from early 2002 until the start of the invasion of Iraq in March 2003, what is here called the third main goal became ever more important in public discussion, which means that it cannot be excluded here.

No clear hierarchy exists among the more detailed objectives linked to this third overriding goal. However, it is likely that the objective of making Iraq a democratic example for the region ought to be mentioned first. As a researcher, one hesitates to highlight this objective because its achievement in practice – not least seen in the light of more than one year of low-conflict battle and terror attacks in Iraq – seems far-fetched. Still, it is hard to deny that this was truly an objective that important members of the Bush administration held, particularly those with a neo-conservative view, as well as the President himself. On this reasoning, they believed that a well-carried out military invasion, followed by fairly simple reconstruction afterwards, was something that the Administration thought it could accomplish. Realization of this objective also seems to be a precondition for the realization of the other objectives under this heading.

The view of the Bush administration was that if the objective of constructing a democratic and stable Iraq can be attained, the door will be opened for the democratization of other countries in the region. This democratization would be a good objective to realize in itself, and it would also be regarded as contributing to the stabilization of the entire region. There are speeches by, among others, Secretary of State Colin Powell and by National Security Adviser Condoleezza Rice indicating that the Bush administration was indeed also pursuing the stabilization of a broader area than just Iraq itself at an early date. There has also been, since December 2002, a 'Middle East Partnership Initiative', which further indicates an emphasis on democratizing the Middle East, even if the original sum of funds allocated was just $29 million. During the spring of 2004 there was talk of a 'Greater Middle East Initiative' that the Bush administration intended to present to the meeting of the Group of 8 (G8) in June 2004. As a result of continuing problems in Iraq, with both civilian Iraqi and US military casualties mounting and with Iraqi opinion turning against the US and its allies, the initiative has been scaled down. It was presented at the G8 meeting in early June 2004 under the awkward name 'Partnership for Progress and a Common Future with the Region of the Broader Middle East and North Africa'. The new programme appears to represent a reduction of the ambitious plans that seem to have existed within the Bush administration during the first months after the fall of Saddam Hussein, but it still represents ideas connected to those that were behind the invasion of Iraq.[17]

If the democratization and stabilization of the Middle East were successful, then the chances for reaching a third objective would be increased: diminishing the opportunities for al-Qaeda, and for organizations allied with it, to recruit new terrorists intending to plan terrorist attacks in the US or against US interests abroad. If the goals of a more democratic as well as stable Middle East were at least to come closer to fruition, then – in the view of the relevant decision-makers in the Bush administration – there would be a good chance that recruitment for al-Qaeda and its adherents would in fact diminish. In this view, it is reasonable to assume that the authoritarian and corrupt structure that is prevalent in most if not all Arab countries, prominently including the two countries from which the hijackers of the planes from 11 September came (Saudi Arabia and Egypt) is conducive to such recruitment. If more democratic, and thus more responsive, governments are installed in these countries it would make it harder for al-Qaeda to find new recruits there in the future. Again, this is a goal whose practical realization seems exceedingly unlikely, at least from a short to medium-term perspective.

The fourth objective under the third heading is that in the planning stages for the Iraq War the Bush administration regarded a democratic Iraq as bringing improved chances for a peaceful solution to the Israeli–Palestinian conflict. The planned ousting of Saddam Hussein from power was regarded as depriving the most militant Palestinians, who refused to entertain the notion of ever accepting an Israeli State, of their most important ally among the Arab states. (For example, Saddam Hussein's regime had given fairly substantial sums of money for several years to the families of the men and women who gave their lives in terrorist attacks on Israelis.) This weakening of the militant Palestinians, which the crucial members of the Bush administration saw as a natural consequence of the toppling of Saddam, was also regarded as increasing the power of those forces among the Palestinians open to negotiation with Israel.

In this connection, it should be mentioned that the fact that Bush administration was working since mid-2002 to topple Yassir Arafat from his position as leader of the Palestinian Authority can be linked to the wider goal of democratizing the Middle East. The Bush administration regarded Arafat as an undemocratic leader and as at least a passive supporter of terror attacks against the Israeli State.[18]

The oil that so many observers and private citizens have mentioned as a prime, if not the only reason for the US invasion of Iraq, to my mind comes into the equation here as one of several objectives under the main rubric of the third main goal. A quote from a central policy document from the first Gulf War, signed by President George H. W. Bush, clarifies the importance of oil at that time for the superpower:

> 1. Access to Persian Gulf Oil and the security of key friendly states in the area are vital to U.S. national security. Consistent with NSD 26 of October 2, 1989, and NSD 45 of August 20, 1990, the United States remains committed to defending its vital interests in the region, if necessary through the use of military force, against any power with interests inimical to our own.[19]

There is no reason to believe that the younger President Bush had any different view of the importance of oil for his country's national security more than ten years after the signing of this document. It ought to be obvious that in a democratized and stabilized Middle East the probability of disturbances to the flow of oil is less probable than in a region that is both authoritarian and unstable. In this sense, the Bush administration in all likelihood included access to oil and the free flow of oil to world markets in the wide-ranging discussions that were probably held before the president finally ordered the invasion of Iraq. This is, however, something very different from the explanation for the invasion that so many people have presented: 'The US is only after Iraq's oil'. This author is convinced that the superpower does not take complex security policy decisions on such simple grounds, or, to put it differently, absolve me from monocausal explanations to complex analytic problems in international relations.

My fundamental belief that most, if not all, complex decisions on foreign and security policy in Washington are taken with several goals in mind also makes me wary of single explanations. This scepticism carries over into the Iraq invasion of 2003. However, the two first main goals presented in this chapter, that of demonstrating the continued power and decisiveness of the superpower after 11 September by overthrowing the Saddam regime and that of eliminating, once and for all, any risk that Saddam's Iraq might use WMD to threaten the US, or might give such weapons to terrorists, go a very long way towards explaining why Washington chose to invade Iraq.

Conclusion

The reader of this chapter may easily get the impression that the author has seen it as his task to present the Bush administration's goals with the invasion of Iraq in the most positive light possible. There are at least two reasons why this essay may be viewed in this manner. One is that the method chosen for analyzing the goals, which may perhaps be called a rational reconstruction, tends to result in a list of goals and objectives presented as more thought-through and logical than was probably the case when the real decision was taken. It is not easy to see how this drawback can be completely avoided with the method chosen, but the reader should still be made aware of this problem.

The second explanation for why the Bush administration's strategies may appear as an idealistic expedition intended, among other things, to democratize as well as stabilize one of the world's most unstable regions, without really taking the national interests of the US into account, can be linked to a basic trait in US foreign policy. Washington often conducts a foreign policy that has two sides: one is idealistic, the other furthers US national interests. The fact that many aspects of US foreign policy reflect a kind of idealism in this way leads to an inability by many policy-makers in Washington to understand foreign criticism. These officials are genuinely convinced that the basis for their policies are in a general sense good for the country and the people that are the object of those policies. Perhaps it may be said that in the case of the invasion of Iraq the criticism from leaders and peoples outside the US is not so much about the goals pursued themselves, with the exception of the first main goal of demonstrating US power and resolve: the criticism is instead first and foremost directed at three other aspects of US policy. The first is the means used to accomplish the goals: the majority of the world's governments seem to hold the view that it was illegitimate for the US and Great Britain to topple the Iraq regime by way of a military invasion, without having an explicit mandate from the UN Security Council for this invasion. In other words, is it legitimate for one or two countries to act militarily to bring down another country's government, however noble the goals might be that the invading state or states are striving to reach? The second aspect criticized pertains to the possibilities of ever reaching the goals of democracy and stability that the US had through the use of a military invasion of a country in the Middle East. Many critics wonder if it is reasonable to assume that the invasion of Iraq can really lead to democratization and stabilization first of the Iraqi system, and then other systems

32

in the region? Isn't it more likely, the same critics ask, that a probable outcome would be destabilization of the region? The third aspect that should be mentioned is the possibility that the US government, by using the Iraq invasion as an example, may come to take unilateral decisions about invading other countries in the future as well.

The decision by the Bush administration to invade Iraq also raises the question of whether the invasion was justified, in particular as it was justified by the Administration as a necessary case of pre-emption. This has not been the focus of this analysis. This author shares many of the worries expressed by several critics of the Bush administration about what the use of military force without the approval of the UN Security Council might mean for the legitimacy of the UN and for other states as they contemplate the use of military force in various situations. An analysis of these aspects from the perspective of politics must, however, be undertaken in another context.[20] Many of these issues are analysed from the perspective of international law in Chapter 7 of this volume.

Notes

1 The US Congress declared war on Great Britain in 1812, on Mexico in 1846, on Spain in 1898, on the Central Powers in 1917, and on the Axis powers in 1941. See M. Boot, *The Savage Wars of Peace: Small Wars and the Rise of American Power*, New York: Basic Books, 2002, p. 291.

2 There are numerous analyses of these matters. One of the most typical, and still the most clarifying, is E. S. Corwin, *The President: Office and Powers*, fourth revised edition, New York: New York University Press, 1957, particularly pp. 170–262. The quote from the Constitution is from Article II, Section 1. One analysis of how US participation in many 'small wars' has contributed to executive dominance of questions of war and peace is M. Boot, *The Savage Wars of Peace*, op. cit.

3 My previous assumption on this point has now received some support from the publication of Bob Woodward's book *Plan of Attack*, New York/London: Simon & Schuster, 2004. Woodward starts his book (pp. 1–3) by describing how President George W. Bush asked Secretary of Defense Donald Rumsfeld for a new war plan on Iraq as early as November 2001. If only for the reason that the existence of a war plan is not proof that the state in question plans to invade the object of the war plan, this does not finally determine that my initial assumption of the decision to attack Iraq in principle had been made late 2001/ early 2002, but it does make more likely that this was so.

4 The division of the policy process into three stages can be seen as a simplified version of what in policy research is called 'the stages approach to the policy process' and applying this to a strategic decision in security affairs. See, for example, P. deLeon, 'The Stages Approach to the Policy Process: What Has It Done?' in P. A. Sabatier (ed.), *Theories of the Policy Process*, Boulder, CO: Westview, 1999, pp. 19–32.

5 It will be obvious to all readers of this book that there has been an immense amount of material published in English about the Iraq War during the two years before our analysis is published. In principle, our analyses stand on their

own. In the case of this chapter on the goals that the Bush administration sought to reach with its invasion of Iraq, two other works need, however, to be briefly commented upon. The first is Bob Woodward's previously mentioned *Plan of Attack*. While this book contains a wealth of interesting information for the reader interested in US security policy, it must be remembered that Woodward's starting point, perhaps more so in this book than in his previous books on US foreign and domestic policy, is that of almost a court reporter. He gains access to 'all' the relevant players and they respond more or less on the record. From the perspective of this analysis, his approach is essentially equivalent to an analysis of the public statements of the decision-makers. The second is Jeffrey Record's *Dark Victory: America's Second War Against Iraq*, Annapolis, MD: Naval Institute Press, 2004, which contains a chapter called 'War Aims' (pp. 64–77) which in many respects resembles the analysis in this chapter. I can only state that I first read this chapter very late in my working process and that its analysis has not influenced the structure of this chapter.

6 Hawaii became a state in the Union in 1959.

7 Bearing in mind the caveat about Woodward's later books stated in note 5 above, it cannot be denied that in his book *Bush at War*, New York: Simon & Schuster, 2002, Woodward gives a credible account of this process.

8 The best analysis so far of the period before the Iraq War in US domestic politics is K. M. Pollack, *The Threatening Storm: The Case for Invading Iraq*, New York: Random House, 2002.

9 John Kingdon develops his views on the policy process in the US in his influential book *Agendas, Alternatives, and Public Policies*, 2nd edn, New York: HarperCollins, 1995. The term 'policy window' and its implications are analysed particularly on pp. 165–94.

10 See Woodward, *Bush at War*, p. 49 and even more Woodward, *Plan of Attack*, particularly pp. 25–26 which indicate this.

11 It must once again be stated that the issue discussed in this chapter is different to that discussed with hindsight: whether Saddam did indeed have any WMD and how the Bush administration presented its case for the risk that these purported weapons programmes posed to the US and its allies. Even if the Bush administration had less solid evidence for the existence of these WMDs than it stated at the time, and even if it exaggerated what evidence existed, it is still possible that the decision-makers acted upon their own belief that these weapons programmes really did exist. For two different types of assessments on related issues see J. Cirincione, J. T. Mathews, G. Perkovich, with A. Orton, 'WMD in Iraq: evidence and implications', Carnegie Endowment for International Peace, January 2004, Available at http://www.ceip.org/files/pdf/Iraq3FullText.pdf (accessed 27 March 2004) and M. Massing: 'Now They Tell Us', *The New York Review of Books*, 51, 2, 26 February 2004, available at http://www.nybooks.com/articles/16922 (accessed 27 March 2004), and ' "Now They Tell Us": An Exchange, *The New York Review of Books*, 51, 5, 25 March 2004, available at http://www.nybooks.com/articles/170007 (accessed 27 March 2004), and ' "Iraq: Now They Tell Us": An Exchange', *The New York Review of Books*, 51, 6, 8 April 2004, available at http://www.nybooks.com/articles/17027 (accessed 27 March 2004). On the use of WMD as an argument for going to war see also L. Freedman, 'War in Iraq: Selling the Threat', *Survival*, 46, 2 (2004), 7–49.

12 There is a vast literature on all the military interventions the US has carried out abroad, particularly after 1898. See for example T. Smith, *America's Mission: The United States and the Worldwide Struggle for Democracy in the Twentieth Century*, Princeton, NJ: Princeton University Press, 1994; R. N. Haas,

Intervention: The Use of American Military Force in the Post Cold-War World, 2nd edn, Washington, DC: Brookings/A Carnegie Endowment Book, 1999; K. von Hippel, *Democracy by Force: US Military Intervention in the Post-Cold War World*, Cambridge: Cambridge University Press, 2000; and M. Boot, *The Savage Wars of Peace*, op. cit.

13 See for instance D. Priest and G. Kessler, 'Iraq, 9/11 Still Linked by Cheney', *Washington Post*, 29 September 2003, page A01. The head of the CIA, George Tenet, in March 2004 told the Senate Armed Services Committee that he had privately told Vice President Cheney several times that the latter had been giving 'public misstatements on intelligence'. See D. Jehl, 'C.I.A. Chief Says He's Corrected Cheney Privately', *The New York Times*, 10 March 2004.

14 The interview is available at http://www.defenselink.mil/transcripts/2003/tr20030509–depsecdef0223.html (accessed 31 March 2004).

15 Among several analyses of the neo-conservatives see, for example, A. Schlesinger, Jr. 'Eyeless in Iraq', *The New York Review of Books*, 16, 3, 23 October 2003; J. Newhouse, *Imperial America: The Bush Assault on the World Order*, New York: Knopf, 2003, in particular pp. 148–152; I. H. Daalder and J. M. Lindsay, *America Unbound: The Bush Revolution in Foreign Policy*, Washington, DC: Brookings, 2003, in particular pp. 15–16 and 46–47; G. J. Ikenberry, 'The End of the Neo-Conservative Moment', *Survival*, 46, 1 (2004) 7–22; and J. Record, op. cit., pp. 17–29. For two books that spell out versions of the neo-conservative views on relevant issues see L. F. Kaplan and W. Kristol, *The War over Iraq: Saddam's Tyranny and America's Mission*, San Francisco, CA: Encounter, 2003 and D. Frum and R. Perle, *An End to Evil: How to Win the War on Terror*, New York: Random House, 2003.

16 The fact that some senior members of the Bush administration had long focused on the threat from Iraq, and of instability in the region more generally, to the supply of oil from the Middle East to the OECD countries in general, and to the US in particular, does not mean that a transformation of the Middle East was a central goal with the Iraq invasion from the moment the decision was taken. It does mean, however, that ideas along these lines existed with the Administration, and were supported by influential voices outside it. See, for example, J. Mann, *Rise of the Vulcans: The History of Bush's War Cabinet*, New York: Viking, 2004, particularly on Paul Wolfowitz at pp. 79–83.

17 The Carnegie Endowment for International Peace in Washington publishes a series of interesting papers and reports on US policy in the Middle East. For three examples with relevance for this chapter see M. Ottaway, 'Promoting Democracy in the Middle East', *Working Papers, Middle East Series, Number 35*, March 2003, Carnegie Endowment for International Peace, available at http://www.ceip.org/files/Publications/wp35.asp?from = pubauthor (accessed 31 March 2004); M. Ottaway and T. Carothers, 'The Greater Middle East Initiative: Off to a False Start', *Policy Brief 29*, March 2004, Carnegie Endowment for International Peace, available at http://www.ceip.org/files/pdf/Policybrief29.pdf (accessed 31 March 2004); and A. Hawthorne, 'Middle Eastern Democracy: Is Civil Society the Answer?', Carnegie Papers, No. 44 (March 2004), available at http://www.ceip.org/files/pdf/CarnegiePaper44.pdf (accessed 9 June 2004).

18 President Bush gave a clear expression of this position in a speech given on 24 June 2002, when he said: 'I call on the Palestinians to elect new leaders, leaders not compromised by terror.' Available at http://www.whitehouse.gov/news/releases/2002/06/20020624–3.htm (accessed 4 April 2004).

19 National Security Directive (NSD) 54, signed by President George H. W. Bush two days before the air attacks start during the first Gulf War, Operation

Desert Storm, available at http://www.washingtonpost.com/wp-srv/inatl/
fogofwar/docdirective/htm (accessed 4 April 2004).
20 For a view by two US lawyers supporting the position of the Bush administration on the role of international law in the Iraq War see D. B. Rivkin and
L. A. Casey, 'Leashing the Dogs of War', *The National Interest*, 73, Fall 2003,
pp. 57–69.

References

Boot, M. *The Savage Wars of Peace: Small Wars and the Rise of American Power*.
New York: Basic Books, 2002.
Cirincione, J., Mathews, J. T., Perkovich, G. with A. Orton 'WMD in Iraq: Evi-
dence and Implications', Carnegie Endowment for International Peace, January
2004, available at http://www.ceip.org/files/pdf/Iraq3FullText.pdf (accessed
27 March 2004).
Corwin, E. S. *The President: Office and Powers*, 4th revised edn. New York: New
York University Press, 1957.
Daalder, I. H. and Lindsay, J. M. *America Unbound: The Bush Revolution in Foreign
Policy*. Washington, DC: Brookings, 2003.
deLeon, P. 'The Stages Approach to the Policy Process: What Has It Done?' in
P. A. Sabatier (ed.), *Theories of the Policy Process*. Boulder, CO: Westview,
1999, pp. 19–32.
Freedman, L. 'War in Iraq: Selling the Threat', *Survival*, 46, 2 (2004), 7–49.
Frum, D. and Perle, R. *An End to Evil: How to Win the War on Terror*. New York:
Random House, 2003.
Haas, R. N. *Intervention: The Use of American Military Force in the Post Cold-War
World*, 2nd edn. Washington, DC: Brookings/A Carnegie Endowment Book,
1999.
Hawthorne, A. 'Middle Eastern Democracy: Is Civil Society the Answer', *Carnegie
Papers*, No. 44 (March 2004), Carnegie Endowment for International Peace,
available at http://www.ceip.org/files/pdf/CarnegiePaper44.pdf (accessed 9 June
2004).
Ikenberry, G. J. 'The End of the Neo-Conservative Moment', *Survival*, 46, 1 (2004),
7–22.
Jehl, D. 'C.I.A. Chief Says He's Corrected Cheney Privately', *The New York Times*,
10 March 2004.
Kaplan, L. F. and Kristol, W. *The War over Iraq: Saddam's Tyranny and America's
Mission*. San Francisco, CA: Encounter, 2003.
Kingdon, J. *Agendas, Alternatives and Public Policies*, 2nd edn. New York: Harper-
Collins, 1995.
Mann, J. *Rise of the Vulcans: The History of Bush's War Cabinet*. New York:
Viking, 2004.
Massing, M. 'Now They Tell Us', *The New York Review of Books*, 51, 2, 26 February
2004, available at http://www.nybooks.com/articles/16922 (accessed 27 March
2004).
—— '"Now They Tell Us": An Exchange', *The New York Review of Books*, 51, 5,
25 March 2004.
—— '"Iraq: Now They Tell Us": An Exchange', *The New York Review of Books*, 51,
6, 8 April 2004.
Newhouse, J. *Imperial America: The Bush Assault on the World Order*. New York:
Knopf, 2003.

Ottaway, M. 'Promoting Democracy in the Middle East', *Working Papers*, Middle East Series, Number 35, March 2003, Carnegie Endowment for International Peace, available at http://www.ceip.org/files/Publications/wp35.asp?from = pubauthor (accessed 31 March 2004).

Ottaway, M. and Carothers, T. 'The Greater Middle East Initiative: Off to a False Start', *Policy Brief 29*, March 2004, Carnegie Endowment for International Peace, available at http://www.ceip.org/files/pdf/Policybrief29.pdf (accessed 31 March 2004).

Pollack, K. *The Threatening Storm: The Case for Invading Iraq*. New York: Random House, 2002.

Priest, D. and Kessler, G. 'Iraq, 9/11 Still Linked by Cheney', *Washington Post*, 29 September 2003, page A01.

Record, J. *Dark Victory: America's Second War Against Iraq*. Annapolis, MD: The Naval Institute Press, 2004.

Rivkin, D. B. and Casey, L. A. 'Leashing the Dogs of War', *The National Interest*, 73, Fall 2003.

Schlesinger, A., Jr. 'Eyeless in Iraq', *The New York Review of Books*, 16, 3, 23 October 2003.

Smith, T. *America's Mission: The United States and the Worldwide Struggle for Democracy in the Twentieth Century*. Princeton, NJ: Princeton University Press, 1994.

von Hippel, K. *Democracy by Force: US Military Intervention in the Post-Cold War World*. Cambridge: Cambridge University Press, 2000.

Woodward, B. *Bush at War*. New York: Simon & Schuster, 2002.

—— *Plan of Attack*. New York/London: Simon & Schuster, 2004.

3

THE IRAQ WAR AND THE TRANSATLANTIC RELATIONSHIP

Bo Huldt

Introduction

Through history, few alliances have been as successful and long lasting as the North Atlantic Treaty Organization (NATO); none have demonstrated the same complexity and degree of organization. When the cold war ended, with the breaking up of both the Warsaw Pact and the Soviet Union, NATO also defied the laws of history and of international relations expertise when it refused to fade away together with the enemy that had been the rationale for its creation. The allies did not (immediately) fall out among themselves, quarrelling over the spoils of victory.

Instead, NATO reinvented itself phoenix-like with new roles as bridge-maker and integrator in the relationship with the former enemies, a 'school-ing', confidence and competence-building function foreseen by few during the hard years of the 'new cold war'. By the mid-1990s, a new role was shaped with NATO as European peacekeeper in the Balkans, if not quite out of area at least on the borderline of the originally defined area.

The 1990s thus became a *seconda prima vera* for the Western Alliance, now through the Partnership for Peace Program becoming an alliance of sorts for all of Europe – also making it possible for neutral countries like Sweden to become, if not formal and *de jure* members, de facto working partners in various fields of competence building and real action.

The new threats suggested by post-cold war strategists – Russian revenge, societal collapse in Eastern and Central Europe under the burdens of recon-struction, new extra-European threats, and the final breakdown of trans-atlantic cooperation – did not materialize during the 1990s. It is true that Yugoslavia broke down in a bloody chaos, an all but inevitable disaster that everyone had expected with Tito's death in 1980 but which seemed an exaggerated threat as Yugoslavia remained standing through the 1980s. However, with the disintegration of the Soviet Union, the cohesion of Yugo-slavia also ended. Still, this did not turn out to be the pattern. Instead, the

38

transition of the 1990s turned out to be much smoother than we should have had any reason to expect; like the end of the cold war – somewhat of a miracle.

The 'West' – the 'community' of interest and cooperation between trans-atlantics, Western Europeans and Asia-Pacifics which had emerged as an accident of the histories of the two world wars and the cold war and which had survived the challenges of Soviet Marxist-Leninism, of Maoism and of decolonization – thus seemingly withstood the erosion of time and in the 1990s still appeared to provide the foundation upon which 'World Order' rested. Nonetheless, there were those in the 1990s who kept reminding us about the theory of inevitable alliance break up.[1]

Today, the 1990s appear a period of transition between 'past time' and 'future time', perhaps even justifiably referred to as a 'happy' decade between the failed Soviet counter-revolution in August 1991 and the outbreak of megaterrorism in September 2001. Today, the very term 'West' – an affilia-tion the neutral Swedes were quick to adopt with the end of the cold war – does not have the same connotations as it did in the 1990s. In 1991, the trans-atlantic and European 'architecture' presented an image of a three-piece armoured structure without chinks, intended to be stronger than any imagin-able storm: NATO was the link between the continents, holding the Americans to the Europeans and vice versa and providing for 'hard' security in emergencies. The Conference on Security and Co-operation in Europe (CSCE) was a meeting place for all Europeans and a provider not only of an outlet for crises and protests but also of norms and European standards. The projected European Union (EU) was Europe of the future, with all its various functions and mechanisms and a vision of a modern Rome but also linked to the transatlantic world, a *summa* of European history and of the achievements of the Atlantic Age.

The 1990s masked a continental drift taking place under the surface of American–European consensus and cooperation that characterized the deft management of the transatlantic relationship by the Clinton presidency.[2] The Europeans were allowed their visions while Bill Clinton pursued more down-to-earth economic and other interests with more consideration for the economy of empire than visionary concepts. At the same time, Clinton succeeded in projecting an image of his presidency as 'European' also in his exhortations to the Europeans to adapt their military resources to the needs of a new NATO, with the Partnership Program, and with the new demanding international operations of the Implementation Force (IFOR) in Bosnia, Stabilization Force (SFOR), also in Bosnia, and the Kosovo Force (KFOR) expeditionary forces that the crises in the Balkans necessi-tated from 1995 onwards.

In fact, NATO had a long and stormy history of quarrels between the United States and its European allies during the cold war. The dismantling of the European colonial empires, Suez 1956 and the gradual American take-over of the British and French positions in the Middle East did not pass without strains on the relationship. The war in Indochina was inherited by the Americans, with traditional positions on colonial issues being reversed. In 1966 a strong-headed French president took France out of NATO's military cooperation, also in other respects pursuing policies designed to demonstrate European (or at least French) rights to its own interests. Henry Kissinger talked about NATO as 'the troubled partnership' and he was not alone in his analysis.[3]

A perennial theme during the cold war had been American frustration over what was seen as a lack of European will to provide sufficient military resources, hardware and software, to the extent thought necessary in Washington for the defence of Europe (and thus also for a deterrent sufficient to hold back the Soviets). The question of burden sharing was on the agenda almost up to the moment of Soviet collapse – and then the issue reappeared with the new problems of the first Gulf War and subsequently of the Balkans. These experiences were not happy for the Europeans either. The relative lack of European capabilities for expeditionary warfare under conditions more demanding than in UN peacekeeping thus seemed an unacceptable weakness to both sides – with the Kosovo War in 1999 a clear demonstration of the problems of coalition warfare against a very inferior enemy.[4]

By then, however, a new European track had been laid out with the Maastricht treaty of 1991, which came into force in 1993 establishing the EU. In 1954 a proposal for a European army had fallen through in the French parliament and European integration had instead continued on the economic track. With Maastricht, however, and with the disastrous developments in the Balkans that proved the Europeans incapable of mastering on their own, the demand was again made for a European military capability, primarily for peace operations but also in a longer time perspective as a strategic fallback should NATO be unable to provide European security, the US being increasingly reluctant to bear the costs of engagement. The Americans did intervene in Bosnia in 1995 and again in Kosovo four years later, but a mix of US requests for a stronger European effort and European unhappiness with its own limitations when it came to fielding powerful forces – not for national and territorial self-defence but for power projection and stabilization – now created a new political climate.

In the Amsterdam treaty of 1997 the West European Union (WEU) Petersberg peace operations commitments of 1992 were brought on to the EU agenda (to no small extent thanks to Finnish and Swedish initiatives) and by December 1999 at the EU's Helsinki meeting a target was identified for 2003 and beyond (Headline Goal Process) calling for an EU force of some 50–60,000 men, including all services, ready to be in the field on two months' notice and to be kept there for up to one year. Such a force would obviously not be conjured out of the ground (or the sea) from one day to the next – but there now seemed to be no doubt about purpose and direction.[5]

This development, proceeding at the speed of light when measured by EU standards (and largely unforeseen when the Swedes had said yes to the Union in a 1994 referendum), owed much to British and French leadership and could be seen both as *European* capability-building and as a response to American burden-sharing requests. Even though concerns were voiced on the United States side over the Europeans wasting resources on the EU that should instead have gone directly into NATO efforts, by and large the Clinton administration reacted positively to the 1997–99 European initiatives. The none too happy American experience with coalition warfare in Kosovo might also have encouraged thinking along the lines of more of a distribution of work between allies, once the Soviet threat was gone.

The Bush administration reports for duty and 'America Unbound' faces a new enemy

As presidential candidate George W. Bush had made it clear from the start that an Administration led by him would do all things differently from the policies conducted by the despised predecessor. As Clinton had been generally popular in Europe this was not necessarily a declaration initiating a loving relationship. On the other hand, Bush recalling the old battle cry 'America first' sounded ironically familiar, as this had also been the declared intention of the early Clinton who in the end was able (and forced) to see a bit further than this. Clinton's catch-phrase 'It's the economy, stupid!' had turned out to be inadequate when facing the realities of international politics, not least in the Balkans. Bush started with similar ambitions to keep a low profile regarding US international commitments.

The first eight months of the Bush administration seemed characterized by a determined effort to gain additional freedom of action for the US by giving notice of termination of international agreements already entered into (the ABM Treaty) or refusing to sign on the dotted line in cases where Clinton had already committed the US (the Kyoto Protocol on climate change and the statute of the International Criminal Court (ICC)).

At the same time, Bush pushed the NATO enlargement issue energetically. The first enlargement had been decided by his predecessor (the Czech Republic, Hungary and Poland joined the alliance in 1999); in the summer of 2001 the determination to go for a 'big bang' was announced by Bush, the goal now apparently being an alliance including all of Central Europe from the Gulf of Finland to the Black Sea. Bush here had to contend with considerable European scepticism about whether such an alliance would be viable and could be upheld against real threats. Like his father on the German unification issue in 1989–90, Bush junior pushed an issue conflicting with the interests of major European actors with great determination, possibly indicating an impatient will to have this business out of the way and to move on to other things.

The combination of refusals to accept treaty or convention limitations on US freedom of movement ('treaty busting') with subsequent action on Afghanistan later in 2001 and Iraq in 2002–03, as well as the launching in September 2002 of the new national security doctrine, have led commentators and analysts to define the Bush administration as both unilateralist and imperialist from the start. Inclined towards unilateralism, yes, but, on the merit of its record of the first half year or so, the Administration would seem to be leaning more towards isolationism than to imperialism.

The academic solution to this problem of terminology is, of course, the introduction in 2003 by Ivo Daalder and James Lindsay of a new concept, *America Unbound*, which has the added attraction of recalling an earlier debate on American foreign and security policy, initiated by Stanley Hoffmann under the heading of *Gulliver's Troubles* in the late 1960s.[6] Subsequent statements by Bush administration insiders have indicated that an Iraq – and 'greater Middle Eastern' – policy aiming for 'system change' was formulated from the start, several months prior to 9/11.[7] It would not be unfair to label such a policy imperial and in the 'winter of our discontent' 2002–03 it brought the US into conflict with allies and non-allies alike. To go for a big bang NATO enlargement in the summer of 2001 against this background would seem a well taken strategic decision, securing new allies and managing Russian opposition on one issue before opening another.

The terror attacks on New York and Washington on 11 September 2001 changed the whole stage for the Bush administration which now found itself in a Pearl Harbour situation, under attack rather than being itself the aggressor. Regardless of any plans for Middle Eastern transformation that the Administration may have had prior to the attack it was now given an opportunity to strike back, carried on a wave of international sympathy.

For the Americans, 9/11 was a horrible shock with the realization of instant vulnerability. For those not hit full comprehension may not be possible, but there was no doubt about the European solidarity emerging after the attack, despite the concerns that had been growing over the policies of the Bush administration.

NATO's North Atlantic Council, under the guidance of the Secretary-General Lord Robertson, rose to the occasion and already on 12 September declared its full support and invoked Article 5 of the North Atlantic Treaty, whereby NATO member states agree 'that an armed attack against one or more of them in Europe or North America shall be considered an attack against them all'. This had never happened during the cold war, but now was the moment. The dramatic gesture was, however, made meaningless by a chilly American response – 'thank you, but no thank you' – from Defence Secretary Donald Rumsfeld who declared that 'the mission determines the coalition'. Hardly a masterpiece of psychology, this refusal could be seen by the Europeans as a confirmation of US unilateralism, although it might primarily have been an American reaction caused by the unhappy experiences in the Kosovo war. Perhaps there also lurked an American suspicion that the European eagerness to come to the rescue of the US was motivated also by a desire to exercise a measure of control over the forceful US response that the Europeans knew was coming.

The effect, however, was an impression of the US 'deserting' the Alliance rather than the usual one of the Europeans failing at burden-sharing. There is little doubt that this was not the view in Washington, where the Administration probably took NATO and the allies for granted but considered the US to be quite within its rights to choose multilateralism or unilateralism as seen fit and most practical.

The attacks of 11 September brought a totally new appreciation of the types of threats that not only the Americans but ultimately all of us are facing. The view advanced by various experts of terrorism afterwards – that there really was no change but that the danger had been there for a long time – overlooks the psychological factor. Sympathies for the Americans remained strong. Working in a systematic and measured way, much like his father during the Kuwait crisis in 1990, George W. Bush had no great difficulty in securing UN support for an armed operation against Taliban-ruled Afghanistan, base and supporter of al-Qaeda, whose members had early on been identified as the evil-doers. Negotiations with the Taliban government in Kabul led nowhere and the US, in cooperation with Britain and insurgent Afghan forces (the Northern Alliance), attacked Afghanistan. Kabul fell but the war declared on terrorism by President Bush had just begun. The struggle for the future of Afghanistan continued with efforts to root out the Taliban and al-Qaeda groupings and to rebuild and modernize the country. The US presence was thinned out, UN assistance involved and a NATO operation, the International Security Assistance Force (ISAF), launched to secure order and stability, at least in Kabul.

In 2002, however, Afghanistan had already begun to look the same dead end that it had been to previous occupiers. Afghanistan had one redeeming feature, however: at first glance, at least, it was of no great strategic value or significance per se and it did not involve great conflicting interests among the major powers. The uncomfortableness with Afghanistan was the lack of momentum and progress and the perception that the US was continuing its campaigning in other places while leaving unfinished business like mopping-up to allies, partners and international organizations.

The American administration had taken pains to inform the world that fighting terrorism was the new Manichean conflict, elevating al-Qaeda *et consortes* to a position just recently occupied by the mighty Soviet Union. In this struggle no one could be neutral or a disinterested spectator: 'Those who are not with us are against us.' The very terminology, 'war' against terrorism, created difficulties for the Europeans (not to mention Arabs and other Muslims) who could not easily fight a war against potentially suspect sections of their own societies difficult to close off and target, being already 'inside the walls' – a problem less apparent to the 'world isle', the United States. Terrorism would have to remain a police action task for America's allies and other members of the international community. For the United States the war concept came naturally, not only because of the country's global reach, but also because war was the American terminology often used in major campaigns, whether national or international, calling for a concentration of effort.

What began to emerge, as the impressions of 9/11 faded away for others than the Americans themselves, was an element of cultural *Vefremdung*, or alienation. We have already alluded to a more long-term form of 'continental drift'. It is important to underline that growing resentment against the United States in Europe did not spring either out of nothing or only out of the Iraq conflict. The events of 9/11 won the Americans sympathy and made it possible to exercise leadership over willing partners through what is described as soft power. The Bush administration's pre-9/11 record, however, was not forgotten and the jarring note from a culture clash between the European ways and Bush's personal, missionary style, as well as that of his staff, was increasingly obvious even before Iraq. Clinton had managed the cultural differences with finesse and the force of an easy going personality. These assets were no longer available – neither did it seem that the Bush administration would have cared much for such skills had it even possessed them.

The road to Iraq

As previously noted, indications are that the Bush administration may have had an agenda for the greater Middle East from the first, involving the same trouble spots that it was later assumed that Osama bin Laden had identified, although with different aims, as targets for the al-Qaeda terrorist campaign: the Iraq and Palestine conflicts. After 9/11 the American agenda gave priority to fighting terrorism but linked to this was also the unfinished business from 1990–91, Saddam Hussein's evading a final account of his weapons of mass destruction (WMD) and the possibility of linkage between Iraq, with its presumed WMD arsenal, and terrorist groups.

The logic of historical events was thus Saddam Hussein's attack on Kuwait in 1990 followed by the UN-mandated and US-led ousting of Iraqi forces from Kuwait and the weapons inspections and sanctions regime imposed by the UN on Iraq, with its accompanying story of a tug of war between the Iraqis and the inspectors. The US-led intervention against Iraq (and presence in Saudi Arabia from 1990 onwards) produced a jihad against the infidels spearheaded by al-Qaeda, which sought revenge in the attacks of 9/11, which in turn led to the US taking a more aggressive stance against terrorism and attacking Afghanistan.

Publicly, the Bush policy vis-à-vis Iraq prior to 9/11 did not appear much different from that of his predecessor. When the weapons inspectors had been thrown out of Iraq in 1998, after some six years of efforts at disarming Iraq of its WMD arsenal (much of it also being destroyed), the Clinton administration chose not to make this a *casus belli*; sanctions continued but there seemed neither a particular urgency nor obvious solution to the conflict. Bush appeared inclined to continue the past strategy of pressure on Iraq through the UN Security Council – no threat of invasion was indicated. In the background there was also a continuing lack of unity among the major powers in the Security Council – China, France and Russia were leaning towards breaking off the whole sanctions/inspections process, while Britain and the United States were looking for ways to step up the effort.

Again, after 9/11 these perspectives changed. Now the risk of Saddam Hussein providing terrorist groups with weapons out of his (supposedly) still existing WMD arsenal became a major challenge for an American Administration determined never to allow a second 9/11 to happen. By the summer of 2002, the Bush administration had turned its full attention from Afghanistan to Iraq, seeking to mobilize European and UN support for harder measures.

The American strategy was based on the window of opportunity and the still-lasting momentum created by 9/11. It also rested on the power of coercion, of applying military pressure without necessarily having to use force. However, the view that use of force for preventive or pre-emptive purposes was legitimate was clearly stated in the new American national security doctrine published in September 2002: 'The United States has long maintained the option of preemptive action to counter a sufficient threat to our national security.'[8]

While the world was contemplating the implications (and possible novelty) of this statement, two parallel developments were in motion: on the one hand a massive military build-up around and in the neighbourhood of Iraq, making both a full-scale military threat and a strategy of coercion credible; on the other hand a reopening of the issue in the UN Security Council, the US now speaking from a position of authority as a victim of terrorism flexing its muscles. The scepticism of the Chinese, French and Russians was now at least temporarily overcome and on 8 November 2002 the Security Council unanimously adopted resolution 1441 calling on Iraq for immediate delivery of full and conclusive documentation of their arsenal and/or its destruction. Here was a moment of almost heavenly harmony, and, as George Bush senior had said in 1990 about the UN facing Iraq, 'the system worked'.

Iraq delivered volumes of documentation but was still found to be vague on specifics by the reinvigorated inspectorate team led by a Swede, Dr Hans Blix. The issue now became whether one should continue to pressure Iraq for more information and more intrusive inspections – perhaps over a longer period of time – or whether the time had now come for forceful measures, the Iraqis already being found in 'material breach' of previous UN resolutions. The UN Security Council quickly divided along previous faultlines with several members, including France, Germany and Russia, calling for more inspections over months and perhaps even years while the Americans and British were willing to give Iraq only the briefest period of grace.

From the US point of view the momentum now seemed to be lost, with additional confusion having been added by the renewed inspection debate, and the British and Americans prepared a resolution that would open the way for the use of force against Iraq as in 1990–91.

Now the heavenly harmony disappeared. Vetoes were threatened by both Russia and France, the latter acting as the major opponent against all resolutions that would legitimize the use of force, and a situation presented itself in which the US and the UK could not even be sure of a simple majority. Apparently, Washington had miscalculated the reach of its power and influence. For the strongest state in the world not to be able to have its way in the UN Security Council on an issue of great national interest could only be seen as a heavy defeat. The consequences were foreseeable: the US and the UK withdrew the proposed resolution and invoked the resolutions passed by the UN during the initial conflict in the Autumn of 1990 and its follow-up during 1991 as legal ground for military intervention, Iraq being in 'material breach' of these resolutions by stalling the process for more than 12 years.[9]

After a last warning to Saddam Hussein on 17 March 2003 hostilities opened in the night of 19–20 March with an air bombardment followed by invasion. Military operations proceeded rapidly and Baghdad was taken on 7 April. Allied losses were very small; those of the Iraqis substantial but still smaller than had been expected due to the fact that the Iraqi armed forces tended to fade away rather than fight. The real problems came later.

The military build-up during 2002 had made renewed pressure on Iraq possible (as well as a military solution should diplomacy fail, as did happen) but the deployment of the forces also placed the allies in a trap of their own making: troops could not be kept in a state of high readiness forever. The many months or year(s) of renewed inspections now enthusiastically proposed by UN Security Council members and opponents of the Anglo-American draft resolution would have been costly for the allies – in more ways than one in a hot climate.[10]

An adverse vote in the Council had been avoided but a deep rift had opened up within the West. That rift was further exposed in an internal NATO crisis when Turkey asked for a preventive deployment of Patriot ground-to-air missiles to protect itself from Iraqi strikes, possibly with WMDs, in case war did break out. The French (and Germans) opposed this, and even if their blocking effort was circumvented through procedural manoeuvre it caused deep distress among the members. Secretary of State Colin Powell called the French vote 'unforgivable' and there is some reason to sympathize with him: the credibility of Alliance solidarity had been put at risk.[11]

Great power conflicts in the twenty-first century

So what then had the great quarrel over draft resolutions, continued or discontinued inspections and vetoes threatened been about? Many things, probably, including personality clashes, but definitely about three things: Iraq, the use of force and world order.

To carry the 'war against terrorism' to Iraq – with an ambitious plan of system change and societal and regional transformation on top – was a vastly more ambitious undertaking than attacking Afghanistan and highly provocative for other actors with interests and ambitions in Iraq. In the 1970s, Iraq signed a friendship treaty with the Soviet Union and Iraqi-Soviet relations, through massive military aid and arms deliveries, developed into a strategic partnership of sorts which, despite Soviet support for the international operation against Saddam Hussein in 1990–91, survived the end of both the cold war and the Soviet Union. Moscow had substantial interests, both strategic and economic, in Iraq. The same could be said for France with its involvement in the development of Iraqi competence as to nuclear technology, but also for other states – including the US – which in the past had had various close contacts with Baghdad, in some cases assisting (unknowingly or knowingly) in the Iraqi build-up of various forms of military competence, possibly including WMD technology. Through its oil resources, Iraq was also a partner of potential, even though the development of these resources was under international control at the time (through the Oil for Food Programme).

By descending on Iraq, the Anglo-American alliance thus threatened the interests of many for whom the whole notion of 'system change' and a policy of regional reconstruction did not have much immediate appeal but rather seemed like a rebuilding of the old Western stronghold in the Middle East.

On the use of force, France together with Germany, an elected member of the UN Security Council at the time, had been emphatic. Force could only be legally used against Iraq if sanctioned by the Council and the two European powers saw no need for this as long as weapons inspections could be continued. However, the French opposition to the use of force was hardly absolute – French willingness to use force and to accept heavy losses had been demonstrated in Bosnia in the 1990s and in other places during the cold war. The German attitude was complicated for historical reasons but also because Germany was at the time in the process of taking over the leadership of the ISAF operation in Afghanistan.

Robert Kagan's much-debated book *Of Paradise and Power* provides a caricature description of the Europeans as being peaceful (and soft) 'Venusians' while the Americans are 'Martians', prone to violence.[12] It gives us a picture at odds with European history but still holds a grain of truth about European legalism and preference for procedure and negotiation, learnt by centuries of hard experience. The definition of what constitutes legitimate self-defence is often hard to agree on (but had not been so on 9/11) and here the (supposed) European view and that of the United Nations majority collided with the outlook of an American government, hit by terrorism and determined to practice a strategy of preventive self-defence in a global war on terrorism. As it turned out, however, there was room for different European opinions on Iraq. Constitutionally, France and its partners in the UN Security Council stood on firm ground. The mandate of the Council rests on the UN Charter's identification of five, formally equal, great powers and their individual rights to exercise veto power. The three permanent Council members, China, France and Russia, thus prevented (or, rather, would have prevented) an Anglo-American draft resolution authorizing the use of force against Iraq from being adopted. Vetoes in the UN can be circumvented, however. During the cold war this was done through the Uniting for Peace formula of 1950, adopted in the context of the attack on South Korea. It gave the General Assembly a right to adopt resolutions *recommending* action when the Security Council was deadlocked. In connection with the Kosovo war in 1999, the West (including France) chose not to take the NATO intervention issue to the UN Security Council and instead acted within the regional framework, practising collective self-defence. Chinese and Russian vetoes were hereby avoided.

This brings us to the third theme involved in the 2002–03 controversies over Iraq, the issue of world order. Here we are on more uncertain ground but concerned with the configuration of power in the post-cold war world. The UN Security Council, with its unique legitimacy, could be seen by France, Russia and China (as well as by other member states) as a guarantee against unchecked use of power by the one remaining superpower, the US. The Security Council stands for constitutionality and moral high ground, even though the 'world community' might in any given situation be represented by a group of states whose motives may not necessarily have much to do with the benefit of that community. All UN member states uphold their interests rather than constitute a conclave of the gods, something many enthusiastic UN supporters find hard to believe.

World order is about much more than a single vote in the UN. The power position of the US inevitably gives rise to ideas of mobilizing counter power and of creating, through new alliances, a balance of power, now as always in world history (and in the future, one might venture to say). This was also apparent in different statements made in the late 1990s by both Chinese and Russian spokespeople on resistance against world hegemonism. In France, the Gaullist tradition has represented similar although, one hastens to add, less confrontational ideas.

The model to reach for, as repeatedly argued by Evgenii Primakov, former Russian prime minister, was 'multipolarity'. One might speculate about what a modern version of the European balance-of-power system of 1648–1939 would look like. In historical memory the workings of the 'model' is connected with four world wars (the Seven Years War 1756–63, the Revolutionary and Napoleonic wars 1792–1815, and the First and Second World Wars 1914–1918 and 1939–45). The attraction of this, on a truly global scale, is not self-evident. Of course, the advocates of multipolarity do not see the past as our future but rather envision a harmonious balance between several global actors, holding the US to the 'rules'.[13]

The Iraq controversy, with the deadlock at the turn of the year 2002–03, offered a possibility to bring things to a head and use the UN authority to check the Americans. As it turned out, the tactic did not work. After 9/11 the Americans were not open to guidance from others, even a majority of the great powers, setting the terms for how the UN Charter should be interpreted when the US saw itself as the defender of the world against terrorism.

Thus, the attempt to bring the Bush administration to heel seems foolish: it did not prevent the war in Iraq but it enraged the Americans. On the other hand, given the way the situation in Iraq has developed after the initial military triumph of the allies, some of the intended effect was still achieved as the American difficulties in Iraq have undoubtedly affected its status and prestige, even if not its national power base, and placed it in a more precarious position than before the war. One might also say that by denying the US and its allies legitimacy (and above all by failing to come to terms with the Iraq issue during a long decade) the UN Security Council members have contributed to creating a highly unstable situation dangerous to all. The result has been substantial damage to the UN and to the prestige of the Security Council, which after all is the source of the special and august positions held by the permanent five Council members. In other words, all lost.

Still, the Council's European opposition, France, Germany and Russia, with their historical experience going back to the League of Nations, might also argue that they had in fact saved the UN from responsibility for a risky enterprise that might have threatened its survival. Historical memories are, of course, always selective and another approach would suggest that the League failed not because of daring but because of meekness.

Either way, the ideas of countering hegemonism and building a multipolar world have no doubt survived the fracas in the UN Security Council.

Partition of Europe?

The crisis in the UN Security Council produced a Europe (and EU) divided into at least three groupings: the active opponents to the US/UK draft resolution and subsequent attack on Iraq; the US/UK supporters; and those seeking to stand apart from what could after all be seen as a traditional great power conflict, of which there was much unpleasant UN experience from the cold war.

A conspiratorial mind might have suggested that the invasion of Iraq had even more purposes than those several openly stated by Washington – disarmament of Iraq, system change, regional reconstruction of the wider Middle East, strike at terrorism – including a demonstration of the division among the Europeans and the lack of substance to the EU concept. The goals of the Bush administration in invading Iraq are discussed in Chapter 2 in this volume.

The first group, the opponents, was led by France and Germany supported by Belgium and Luxembourg. French and German ambitions and expectations were clearly to speak for and lead the EU against the UK and the US. That did, however, fall flat as the 'troops' did not follow the self-appointed leaders. On 22 January 2003, with the UN Security Council deadlocked, France and Germany, while celebrating the 1960 Elysée Treaty signed by Konrad Adenauer and Charles de Gaulle, publicly declared that a war in Iraq had to be prevented. During the following two weeks public messages were sent out by a total of 18 other European states, including Britain, together declaring loyalty to the US and their deep concern with the threat posed by Iraq.

This second group, in the end thus supporting the invasion of Iraq, was a mixed bunch. It included a number of countries with maritime background – Britain, Italy, Portugal, Spain and Denmark – but also practically all of Eastern and Central Europe, i.e. countries that had become NATO members in 1999 through the 1997 enlargement decision or were in the process of entering NATO by 2004 through the timely decision in 2002 before the Iraq War began. A third group was made up of countries transatlantically oriented but for constitutional reasons unable to accept the legality of the invasion. The non-aligned countries belonged to this group.

The former 'Eastern' states, which considered themselves to have had enough experience with dictatorship and oppression, showed no hesitation in joining the US-led alliance, in effect declaring themselves guided by their historically tested moral compasses. For this they were rewarded with scorn from French President Jacques Chirac – and open threats that their future membership of the EU could now be in danger.

This must have been a low-water mark of European performance during the pre-war phase. But it also illustrated how deeply complicated the issue of terrorism was for European governments. Already in 1990–91, the

French had tried harder and longer than anybody else to avoid a war with Iraq over the occupation of Kuwait. Many reasons were no doubt involved then as later in 2002–03, but in France, with a colonial past and a growing immigrant Muslim population and concerns about terrorism increasing, rather than being reduced, through an invasion of Iraq, the Arab connection would have played a role for any government – as in other European countries that are not only 'Venusian' but also have a large Muslim population.

European division thus produced a complicated series of movements, a contre dance involving several factors historical and political. But it did not lead to partition in the sense of a dramatic change of the European strategic map. Despite the hard words in 2003, the European Union continued its slow march towards enlargement in 2004, with ten new members. However, labour on the EU Constitution is still in process.

Those with ambitions to lead the EU may have come to the conclusion after the quarrel in early 2003 that the Union cannot be led as was possible during the long Franco-German stewardship from the 1950s to the 1990s. The effort by the French and Germans to lead on the Iraq issue could be described as a tactical mistake, as it gave warning to the others about what a Union under French and German leadership could imply. Now, the game is a different one. The Iraq War and the Central and East European 2003 demonstration of emancipation both from the East and the traditional West European great powers will in all likelihood lead to a renewed interest on the part of some old members in 'core group' designs or in notions of an 'advance guard' pointing the way, if not leading the procession into the future. Thus, partition in the sense of some members becoming more unionized than others may be an increasing challenge because of Iraq.

On the American side, an elegant effort to achieve partition was Defense Secretary Donald Rumsfeld's Alexander-like cutting of the continent into 'Old' and 'New' Europe. Old Europe was anti-American, backward-looking and with no understanding of how the new challenges, of terrorism and its supporters, the axis of evil (Iran, Iraq and North Korea), had to be handled; the New Europe, on the contrary, was the product of the cold war ending, willing to confront new dangers side by side with the United States. The description was designed to fit the line-up between a 'French' group and a 'British' one and had no purpose but to identify American supporters and opponents, good guys and bad. It reflected an old American problem: do we want a strong Europe or a weak one, one which stands on its own feet, a real ally but also someone who may be prepared to stand up against the US, or one dependent on us, whom we must prop up but who will be malleable?

The obvious answer is of course that assuming that the Europeans are with us, they should be strong; if they move against us, as France and Germany did in 2003, we would prefer them weak. With the end of the cold war this question had become more relevant insofar as European support had already been called for in international operations (in the Balkans) and that European weakness had been an embarrassment. As things developed over Iraq it became painfully evident that the US needed a Europe willing to pull at least some weight. This would mean EU takeover in the Balkans, European NATO forces in Afghanistan, and above all more of a European willingness to support the Iraq effort. The US had little to gain from European weakness and the promotion of partition, suggested by the 'Old' and 'New' concepts, quickly disappeared.

The American version of strengthening Europe through NATO enlargement had been running successfully parallel with the rising Iraq crisis. NATO's decisions in November 2002 in Prague led to membership in 2004 for those states that had loyally supported the Anglo-American cause in early 2003 (but also for some more lukewarm). Washington at the same time created pressure on the EU to admit Turkey, another actor in the Iraq game, about whom the Europeans had doubts. Despite the Americans pushing, it became obvious in 2004 that Turkey was in for a long accession process, if any. Turkey's ambiguous role in the Iraq campaign, refusing the US rights of passage and ultimately playing no role other than as watchdog against Kurdish sovereignty either outside or inside a future Iraq, again demonstrated how things did not fall into place as had been expected prior to the conflict.

The European experience was generally one of being disunited and outside the decision loop, even though the British strategy of influence through cooperation was carried through the conflict. The Iraq crisis did not create a division that was not there before – it confirmed that there were fault lines, demonstrating in early 2003 that the drama was greater than anticipated with the 'revolt of the 18' against the Franco-German position. In the end, by the turn of the year 2003–2004 the Americans saw no use in playing on the Old/New Europe theme and at the Davos World Economic Forum in January 2004 Vice President Dick Cheney emphasized the need for cooperation and for the Europeans to re-arm, again the theme of burden sharing. According to Cheney, the citizens of Europe deserved a stronger and more influential Europe.[14]

The war in Iraq – from triumph to chaos and/or exit strategy?

The Iraq War went well for the United States and its British ally, but the sequel did not. It is in the light of this process, from the summer of 2003 till the autumn of 2004, that we will now have to assess the consequences of the war, which have created the impression of the Americans now having two Afghanistans on their hands rather than being in the process of achieving a replay of the successes in Germany and Japan after the Second World War.

After the fall of Baghdad and a professionally glorious military victory, the allies lost three months failing to establish rapport with and control over Iraqi society. Not until July 2003 did the American-led Coalition Provisional Authority (CPA) succeed in establishing an Iraqi Governing Council of 25. The UN had by then installed itself in Baghdad but its representative Sergio Vieira de Mello was killed in August and the UN fled the scene – a turning point demonstrating the problems of nation-building and of raising and holding on to new allies once the war itself was over. Instead, the situation gradually deteriorated during the Autumn, with the old opponents of the war seeing little reason to be either helpful or generous.

In November 2003 President Bush did the Canossa thing by turning again to the UN and calling for its assistance as an intermediary in facilitating a process towards a transitional parliament and a formal turn-over of power by mid-2004.[15] This role was played by Lakhdar Brahimi, representative of the Secretary-General and by June 2004 – against the background of continuing disorder and full-scale uprisings in Iraq – UN Security Council resolution 1546 confirmed the procedure leading to the establishment of an interim (and not-elected) government and the fact that the UN was now, as many thought it should have been from the beginning, a major actor even if the US remained in military control.

The road to this point – 30 June 2004 – had been bloody and costly and all sorts of doubt remained (and has increased rather than diminished) as to whether this has not all been too late and in vain. The lost confidence of the Iraqis was difficult to recapture.

By the summer of 2004, however, the United States was turning towards its own presidential elections. Both presidential candidates kept the debate on Iraq out of front-line discussion and the happy make-believe of campaigning. The message implied was that a political process was under way in Iraq that would eventually overpower the violent forces trying to tear Iraq to pieces. At the same time, however, the United States Armed Forces (and its allies) were still left in the line of fire.

Conclusion

Both political processes, such as elections, and also our political analyses tend to be oriented towards the present moment and its main actors and personalities: Gorbachev, Yeltsin and Putin in the East; Clinton, Bush and Kerry in the West. It is still not impossible to imagine the American presidential elections producing a new policy and a new American strategy that modifies the Bush administration's messianic unilateralism and tendencies towards the fast lane and also reduces the importance of ideology in favour of realism.[16] At the moment of writing (and of the presidential campaign), however, it seems that this will have to be done by a chastised and reformed Bush himself rather than by his opponent, Senator John Kerry. A president on his second term may turn out wiser and more inclined to compromise. This is certainly not the way George W. Bush looks – but the fighting in Iraq continues with its rising costs both economically and to the US strategic position, and with some 100,000 plus soldiers tied down in the country and having to be rotated at regular intervals. Some of the 'magic' of the American superpower status has been lost.

The memory of European lack of unity (and of loyalty to the US) may still impact on the mind and future choices of a president more liberal than George W. Bush. It would probably be wrong to assume that Iraq is a second Vietnam from which the US can withdraw with the intention of forgetting everything. Not everything is wrong in the 'war on terrorism'.

There may be a renewed willingness on both sides of the Atlantic to co-operate in partnership – because there is no other way. The rise of Asia, notably China and India, is still but a distant rumbling on our respective horizons, but a new American presidency and the Europeans will have to confront also this new fact. The preferred scenarios of Charles Kupchan and Joseph Nye of an enlightened American 'empire' maintained through a mixture of soft power and contraction on the basis of the cooperative structures built by Franklin Roosevelt and his successors after the Second World War may also still be possible.[17]

Still, the Iraq conflict brought a crisis in the relationship between the US and the Europeans – and in the inter-European pattern of politics and integration. The Europeans discovered their second-rate status, even as a Union. Economically the EU may be a giant and rival to the US, but certainly not militarily. Thus a European sense of a 'fall', of being of less importance and 'value' is, according to some observers, the very reason for European anti-Americanism.[18] The Europeans also discovered – some may even have enjoyed it – that it was still possible to have a real quarrel among themselves; not as deadly as the balance of power games of the past, but still dramatic and emotional enough. Europe turned out to be not quite the reformed character we had supposed.

At the same time, dissension among the Europeans took place at a time when unity among them might have had an historical impact – but that seems to be what we are always saying when Europe fails short of purpose and seems irremediably small.

The Americans for their part discovered that even though the Europeans could not prevent them from going for the gun they were able to make the conditions of the shoot-out difficult and unpleasant. Instead of the happy posse that should have done the job there was an improvised coalition with quite a few strange faces.

Both sides may also have understood that long-term cultural, economic and social changes, shifting values, changing elite composition and many other factors do over time change the relationships between countries and peoples, even when in alliance. Again, these discoveries would not necessarily have come now, assuming greater skill in managing the differences – as the Clinton presidency repeatedly demonstrated. But the very alienness of the Bush profile, and I do not think this is overstating it (certainly not during the silly season of the elections), even before the war, has made the Europeans see a widening Atlantic in front of them. The vision of the US as different has always been there – a mix of attraction, emulation and repulsion – through the cold war, the Vietnam War, with the idiosyncracies of the different presidential administrations – and this vision has, from time to time, coalesced into something highly positive or the opposite. So far this has been a dynamic process – the question is whether we are now in for a real change as the Bush presidency produces a qualitatively new situation, with mutual resentment reinforcing itself.

The emergence of a new transatlantic relationship will not be the result of the Iraq War per se. With the collapse of the enemy, the Soviet Union, a new relationship had to be shaped around a new purpose. 'Securing Europe' through EU and NATO enlargement and deepening appeared a worthy enough idea, but perhaps European security is now taken too much for granted in Western eyes with enlargement processes near completion. The war against terrorism may, from an American horizon, have seemed a good standard around which to rally both Europe and the world. The aftermath of 9/11, including the Iraq War, has demonstrated difficulties with such an approach, given the complexities of all three components – terrorism, American and European interests and perceptions. When large-scale terrorism struck western Europe with the Madrid massacre in March 2004 this did *not* contribute to transatlantic unity.[19]

Far short of being able to make exact predictions about the character of transatlantic relations, we may still make some observations on the basis of the Iraq experience. In the first place, Iraq has demonstrated – and continues to do so every day – that even the power of the last superpower (or 'hyperpower') is limited. Like Xerxes, the US leadership cannot tame the seas and, like all other warriors in history, the Americans eventually run out of forces, above all infantry. Coercion is better than actual use of force, but if territory has to be conquered, controlled and pacified there is little alternative to infantry. Like the Romans before them, the Americans have to rely on *foederati* or *auxiliarii*, allied and supporting forces. A war on terrorism calls for new types of auxiliaries.

Second, the Europeans cannot stick to the assumption that they can continue to monopolize the US, not even be the first among equals among United States' partners. Having NATO's offer of support turned down by the Bush administration at the outset of what quickly became the global war of our time, at least in presidential speech-making, was a shuddering awakening for the Europeans, but in terms of potential alliance partners this world is already multipolar and a privileged European position (except, perhaps, for the British) is at an end. The war on terrorism is not a 'good' war for Europeans; it is more attractive for others. New centres of power are emerging, China foremost among them, and will call on American attention.

Third, the previous observation adds urgency to the need for the Europeans to organize themselves both mentally, politically and in terms of capabilities. Burden-sharing is still on the American agenda when it comes to deployable, modern military forces but such forces are clearly a European interest too, as is also that wide spectrum of non-military crisis management competence about which the EU countries tend to be proud; it has to be a proven capability. One blessing of the Iraq War has been the adoption in December 2003 of the European Security Strategy, which although it is not properly a strategy, combining goals and means, as much as an outline of how to think about European security, still makes us look a lot more serious than before.[20]

Fourth, Europe has so far, unashamedly, drawn advantages out of the transatlantic relationship, with European power and influence enhanced by the existence of a transatlantic link. A loss of these drawing rights, as a result of a continuing estrangement across the water, would be painful.

Fifth, the opposite transfer, Europe providing strength to the US, has not been a strong theme with the present Administration, although in his efforts at 'making nice' after the quarrelling over Iraq at Davos in January 2004 Vice President Cheney again called on the Europeans to realize their true strength and potential. Washington may still be thinking in terms of more *auxiliarii*, i.e. burden-sharing. How could Europe be even more useful?

One specific idea suggested for how the Europeans might show their true value (also to themselves) would be to advance a solution to one of the most difficult of all conflicts: 'The road to a new West goes through Jerusalem.'[21] The Middle East issue as a source of transatlantic tension might also make it a possibility for joint conflict solution. While the solution of the Palestine issue would not be sufficient for eternal peace in the region it might still be *one* necessary condition (as was the demise of the Saddam regime in the eyes of the present author) for a new start, or any start at all, for regional security and stabilization.

The problem cuts to the quick of the Iraq debacle: How could the American leadership have expected to succeed in convincing the Arabs of the blessings that would be brought by the US turning Iraq upside down, while at the same time giving not an inch on Palestine but rather supporting the Sharon administration? This, if anything, will be the 'arrogance of power' issue of this conflict.

Less useful than the idea of a European role as solution stalker for the Middle Eastern conflict is the repeated call on Europe to act as a 'counterweight' or 'force to counter' the US. The EU is economically powerful but it cannot – at least not in a very long time – function as a traditional great power, armed to the teeth, able to block the hegemony. The Union has to be able to offer resistance on specific issues, to offer advice (also unsought for) and cooperation, but this is co-power rather than anti-power. It would not be to the advantage of the Europeans, given that Europe is a postmodern community rather than a modern state, to place itself armed in Achilles' path. Europe will continue to reap the greater benefits from partnership. Offers by other powers to join 'anti-hegemonic leagues' against the US would only diminish European power and influence.

There are questions connected with America's future. The Americans themselves, as usual, raise the most crucial ones concerning both the United States' world role and that of its domestic politics and system of government. The 2000 election was a strange experience. So may this year's elections turn out but there is still every reason to believe in the self-correcting abilities and dynamics of American life, both political and economic; perhaps the latter area should worry us more than the former.

The United States' European commitment may have faded as a result of the Iraq *bagarre* but that does not mean it has collapsed. NATO enlargement has reached a logical point of at least momentary completion. The Berlin Plus agreement opening for NATO resources to be placed at EU disposal in peace operations has withstood the storm and made it possible for the Union to field Operation Concordia in Macedonia in March 2003 – a modest beginning but still significant.[21] NATO exercises and day-to-day cooperation have not been hit by the 2003 quarrels.

Memories will persist, personal animosities also, but the Iraq crisis could still serve as lessons learned in our analysis of what the US and Europe, together and separately, in a realistic frame of mind but also engaged, can achieve with different instruments for crisis management – the military ones which are sometimes indisposable, and the political ones which are always necessary.

Notes

1 O. Harries, 'The Collapse of the West', *Foreign Affairs* 72, 4 (1993), 41–53.
2 On culture factors and 'drift' see C. M. Kelleher, 'Foreign Policy Culture in the United States and Europe', in B. Huldt, S. Rudberg and E. Davidson (eds), *The Transatlantic Link: Strategic Yearbook 2002*, Stockholm: Swedish National Defence College, 2001.
3 H. Kissinger, *The Troubled Partnership: A Re-Appraisal of the Atlantic Alliance*, New York: McGraw-Hill, 1965; see also L. S. Kaplan, *The Long Entanglement: NATO's First Fifty Years*, Westport, CN: Praeger 1999.
4 W. Clark, *Waging Modern War: Bosnia, Kosovo and the Future of War*, New York: Public Affairs, 2001.
5 H.-C. Hagman, *European Crisis Management and Defence: The Search for Capabilities*, Adelphi Paper 353, London: International Institute for Strategic Studies (IISS), 2002.
6 I. Daalder and J. Lindsay, *America Unbound: The Bush Revolution in Foreign Policy*, Washington, DC: Brookings, 2003; S. Hoffmann, *Gulliver's Troubles or the Setting of American Foreign Policy*, New York: McGraw-Hill, 1968.

7 *International Herald Tribune*, 27 January 2004; also *Dagens Nyheter* and *Svenska Dagbladet* (Stockholm), 13 January 2004; all pertaining to statements by former Secretary of the Treasury Paul O'Neill.

8 *The National Security Strategy of the United States of America*, September 2002.

9 Our assessment now is that Saddam Hussein did not have the WMD arsenal that was the major motive stated for the attack in 2003 by the United States and Britain. What the inspectors had not been able to verify had in effect been destroyed by the Iraqis themselves; this is supposed to have covered all categories of weapons – there also being consensus that Iraq never had any nuclear weapons at all. However, the guarded expert view prior to the war may be better reflected in the IISS pre-war view (*IISS Strategic Dossier: Iraq's Weapons of Mass Destruction: A Net Assessment*, 10 September 2002) that Iraq had an unspecified arsenal of chemical weapons and a possible capacity to produce biological weapons but, again, no nuclear arsenal. On the other hand, given access to enriched uranium, it would have been possible to develop a capacity within a short time.

10 The credibility of the threat as a diplomatic instrument depended on demonstrated war-fighting capability and willingness to fight. This also presupposed a way to transmit readable signals – and someone able to read them. If Saddam as seems likely did not believe, until the end, that war would come, the effect was obviously lost. The 'trap' effect, with the allies running out of time because the troops could not stay for months in their forward deployment, would in principle sooner or later force them either to withdraw or attack, withdrawal also risking the collapse of renewed inspections and a return to the old cat-and-mouse game.

11 France, since 1966 outside of NATO military cooperation, had since de Gaulle been voicing suspicions about whether NATO would work for Europe, in a crisis facing the possibility of the Americans refusing to risk New York for Paris. This was the key argument behind the French *force de frappe* nuclear force. Now, whether by design or not, France had proved the point by 'vetoing' the Patriot missiles for Turkey in a supposed emergency: NATO could apparently not be relied upon! In the real world, however, Turkey did get its Patriots.

12 R. Kagan, *Of Paradise and Power: America and Europe in the New World Order*, New York: Knopf, 2003.

13 The European balance of power system is a subject well researched, to say the least; see E. V. Gulick, *Europe's Classical Balance of Power*, New York: Norton, 1967. For a grand historical perspective, also arguing the 'eternal' validity of balance of power theories, however much this world changes, see H. Kissinger, *Diplomacy*, New York: Simon & Schuster, 1994. For an argument against renewed speculations in traditional multipolarity, see D. Moïsi, 'Reinventing the West', *Foreign Affairs*, 82, 6 (2003), 67–73.

14 W. Pfaff, 'Washington Makes Nice', *International Herald Tribune*, 29 January 2004.

15 Canossa in Italy was the goal for the Emperor Henry IV in 1077 forced to humiliate himself to the pope in order to lift the ban placed on him by the Papacy. On developments in post-war Iraq see L. Diamond, 'What Went Wrong in Iraq', *Foreign Affairs*, 83, 5 (2004), 34–56.

16 On Bush's 'ideological presidency', see A. Schlesinger Jr, 'Who Rules America?', *Playboy*, September 2004.
   C. A. Kupchan, *The End of the American Era*, New York: Knopf, 2002; J. S. Nye Jr, *The Paradox of American Power*, Oxford/New York: Oxford University Press, 2002.

17 J. Vinocur, 'What Does Europe Want? Criticism of U.S. Obscures Growing Disunity on Continent', *International Herald Tribune*, 20 January 2004.
18 Neither did the handling by two Spanish governments of the terrorist attack receive much public applause by France and Germany. The perpetrators were killed, but the incoming Spanish government stood by its pre-election promises to withdraw Spanish troops from Iraq, thereby de facto yielding to the terrorists.
19 *A Secure Europe in a Better World. European Security Strategy*. Document proposed by Javier Solana and adopted by the Heads of State and Government at the European Council in Brussels on 12 December 2003.
20 D. Moïsi, 'Healing the Trans-Atlantic Split: The Road to a New West Goes Through Jerusalem', *International Herald Tribune*, 10 October 2003; see also G. Caplan, 'Ein transatlantischer Ansatz zur Lösung des Nahostkonflikts: Reichen die Gemeinsamkeiten?', KAS/*Auslandsinformationen*, October 2003.

References

Caplan, G. 'Ein transatlantischer Ansatz zur Lösung des Nahostkonflikts: Reichen die Gemeinsamkeiten?', Konrad Adenauer Stiftung/*Auslandsinformationen*, October 2003.
Clark, W. *Waging Modern War: Bosnia, Kosovo and the Future of War*, New York: Public Affairs, 2001.
Daalder, I. and Lindsay, J. *America Unbound: The Bush Revolution in Foreign Policy*, Washington, DC: Brookings Institution Press, 2003.
Diamond, L. 'What Went Wrong in Iraw', *Foreign Affairs*, 83, 5 (2004), 34–56.
Gulick, E. V. *Europe's Classical Balance of Power*, New York: Norton, 1967.
Hagman, H.-C. *European Crisis Management and Defence: The Search for Capabilities*, *Adelphi Paper* 353, London: International Institute for Strategic Studies (IISS), 2002.
Harries, O. 'The Collapse of the West', *Foreign Affairs* 72, 4 (1993), 41–53.
Hoffmann, S. *Gulliver's Troubles or the Setting of American Foreign Policy*, New York: McGraw-Hill, 1968.
Huldt, B., Rudberg, S. and Davidson, E. (eds) *The Transatlantic Link: Strategic Yearbook 2002*, Stockholm: Swedish National Defence College, 2001.
IISS Strategic Dossier: Iraq's Weapons of Mass Destruction: A Net Assessment, London: IISS, 2002.
Kagan, R. *Of Paradise and Power: America and Europe in the New World Order*, New York: Knopf, 2003.
Kaplan, L. S. *The Long Entanglement: NATO's First Fifty Years*, Westport, CN: Praeger 1999.
Kelleher, C. M. 'Foreign Policy Culture in the United States and Europe,' in B. Huldt, S. Rudberg and E. Davidson (eds) *The Transatlantic Link: Strategic Yearbook 2002*, Stockholm: Swedish National Defence College, 2001.
Kissinger, H. *The Troubled Partnership: A Re-Appraisal of the Atlantic Alliance*, New York: McGraw-Hill, 1965.
—— *Diplomacy*, New York: Simon & Schuster, 1994.
Kupchan, C. A. *The End of the American Era*, New York: Knopf, 2002.
Moisi, D. 'Reinventing the West', *Foreign Affairs*, 82, 6 (2003), 67–73.
—— 'Healing the Trans-Atlantic Split: The Road to a New West Goes Through Jerusalem', *International Herald Tribune*, 10 October 2003.
The National Security Strategy of the United States of America, Washington, DC: September 2002.

Nye, J. S. Jr *The Paradox of American Power*, Oxford/New York: Oxford University Press, 2002.

Pfaff, W. 'Washington Makes Nice', *International Herald Tribune*, 29 January 2004.

Vinocur, J. 'What Does Europe Want? Criticism of U.S. Obscures Growing Disunity on Continent', *International Herald Tribune*, 20 January 2004.

4

RUSSIA'S CHOICE

Preserve the status quo

Charlotte Wagnsson

Introduction: the Iraq question

The decision of Russian President Vladimir Putin to confront the United States over the Iraqi problem in 2003 was based on a misinterpretation of the American military mission in Iraq. In January 2003 the Russian military establishment anticipated that the US would be forced to bring the issue back to the UN Security Council in May in order to negotiate an agreement. They believed that if the Americans had already invaded Iraq, they would be required to pull back their troops. Some Russian analysts even forecast that Russia would be requested to provide military assistance to the US.[1]

This theory, suggested by Russian analysts, is only one of the many explanations offered by scholars and intellectuals in an attempt to rationalize Russia's position regarding the Iraq crisis. It is, however, unsatisfactory to view the Russian position as an isolated Kremlin perspective; rather, this stance must be viewed against the backdrop of Russian foreign policy as a whole. The tendency to interpret Russian foreign and security policy as primarily a product of day-to-day politics makes it appear variable and sometimes even incomprehensible. If it is instead examined within a broader context, it can be seen to be consistent, long-term in outlook, and easily comprehensible. Analysis should thus focus on underlying norms and political principles.

In the decision to challenge the United States' stance on Iraq, the main consideration was not the global situation in early 2003 or the activism of individual Russian lobby groups such as the military establishment. A broader perspective must be taken in order to grasp why Russia chose to oppose the US.

This chapter elaborates on two political principles that guided Russian foreign and security policy from the mid 1990s. These essential features of Russian thinking arguably go a long way toward explaining Moscow's position on the Iraq war, but other explanations are also examined here.

Russian foreign policy focus

The need to preserve the current world order – the system of sovereign, formally inviolable states – is one of the two key arguments that Russian politicians maintained in the 1990s. Russia has occupied the position of a status quo power in the international system. Russian leaders have emphasized the fact that the UN Security Council is the only actor with the legal right to make decisions about military and other types of intervention into the internal affairs of sovereign states. Russian leaders have also maintained that the UN system must be preserved to hinder the strengthening of the United States' hegemonic position in world affairs.

The other main argument presented by Russian politicians is that terrorism and separatism are evils that need to be combated using all available means. In the late 1990s in particular the leadership attempted to place these phenomena on the global policy agenda. To use a term introduced by the so-called Copenhagen School, the Russian leaders sought to 'securitize' terrorism and separatism internationally. The Copenhagen School describes 'securitization' as an extreme version of 'politicization', since it may motivate extreme acts, such as the use of military force.[2] If politicians aim to securitize a problem, they will 'speak security', using rhetorical strategies intended to elevate an issue to the status of a broadly perceived securitized problem. The recipient of the political rhetoric, the audience, determines the outcome of the securitizing move. If an issue is to be considered securitized, the audience of the security speech needs to accept the problem presented as an existential threat to a shared value so that the political leaders gain a platform from which it is possible to legitimize emergency measures.[3] The Russian leaders have attempted to gain the western world's acceptance for such a threat perception in order to use extraordinary means to combat terrorism and separatism.

Keeping these two main principles in mind – the intent to defend the world order and the campaign against terrorism and separatism – the goals of Russian diplomacy can be examined and understood. To support this argument, the chapter will examine Russia's position during the North Atlantic Treaty Organization (NATO) bombings of Serbia and Kosovo in 1999, and Russian reactions to the terrorist attacks on the US on 11 September 2001.

The analysis presented here is based on a systematic review of official statements made by the Russian president, foreign minister and defence minister. The main sources are the Russian Foreign Ministry's official bulletin *Diplomaticheskii Vestnik* (*The Diplomatic Courier*), and the news bulletin published by Radio Free Europe/Radio Liberty for the former Soviet Union. *Diplomaticheskii Vestnik* is the most comprehensive source of information on Russia's official foreign policy and covers a wide range of issues, ranging from bilateral trade agreements and historical exposés of Tsarist foreign policy to political speeches.

Kosovo 1999: from a Russian foreign policy perspective

Russian leaders strongly resented NATO's decision to launch a bombing campaign against Serbian President Slobodan Milosevic on 24 March 1999, after negotiations in Rambouillet had failed. Prime Minister Evgenii Primakov was heading for the US when, after a telephone call with the American Vice President, he ordered the plane back to Moscow. Russia immediately froze formal cooperation with the western alliance.

NATO's campaign, 'Allied Force', undermined Russia's role as a significant actor in European security politics. In the 1990s, Russian leaders had continuously and persistently suggested that the Organization for Security and Co-operation in Europe (OSCE) be the main actor in the European security arena. NATO's actions demonstrated that the US was and would remain the main actor in European security politics, indicating that the Russian campaign was a failure. Of even greater concern than the continued American involvement in Europe, in Moscow's view, were the global implications: the bombings not only threatened Russia's self-image and credibility as a global power, but also reduced the value of its veto power in the UN Security Council. In addition, the Russian leaders viewed the campaign as a serious threat to the existing global security order.

The strongest Russian protests sprang from fears of a potentially emerging new world order. The leadership argued that NATO's campaign destabilized the entire global system, resulting in chaos and anarchy. The Kosovo campaign, which in the Russian president's eyes was 'an open aggression against a sovereign state', might set a precedent for similar future actions.[4] The Russian leaders argued repeatedly that only the UN and its Security Council had a mandate to solve the conflict, and defended the principle of the territorial integrity of nation states.[5] NATO's campaign was interpreted as yet another step towards a unipolar international system completely dominated by the US. To Moscow, the motivation for the Kosovo campaign was obvious: to enforce American political, military, and economic dominance on the rest of the global community. The Foreign Minister accused NATO of 'neo-colonialism' and 'NATO-colonialism', and stated that the alliance's goal was to divide European states into some kind of protectorates.[6] As an alternative to unipolarity and American dominance Russian leaders had promoted the idea of multipolarity since 1996; during the Kosovo crisis they pleaded that this order was favourable to all 'civilized states'.

Another major argument against NATO's campaign was that it completely disregarded the real threat, namely international terrorism. The Russian leaders condemned the Kosovo Liberation Army (KLA), the Kosovar Albanians' resistance movement, for committing terrorist acts. They spoke at great length of the Russian struggle against terrorism, depicting it as just and honourable, and called upon other democratic states to align themselves with Russia in its fight against terrorism in areas such as Kosovo and Chechnya.[7]

The standpoint taken in the Kosovo crisis was manifested in the National Security Concept signed by President Putin on 10 January 2000.[8] The Concept argues that first and foremost a new global 'peace order' needs to be achieved, which is to be guaranteed by the UN and its Security Council. In addition, the Security Concept criticizes the concept of 'humanitarian interventions', describing them as excuses for using unilateral violence in the absence of Security Council mandates.

The Concept depicts a more sombre global situation than did its predecessor from December 1997. The former Security Concept stated confidently that a multipolar world was in the making. The new Concept acknowledges two contradictory tendencies: one towards multipolarity, and another towards a more unipolar world order based on unilateralism and military violence, dominated by a minority of Western states, and led by the US. The Concept also lists many international threats, including international terrorism.

The two major strands in Russian foreign policy – the endeavour to preserve the world order and the battle against terrorism – were thus already apparent at the time of the Kosovo crisis of 1999. The main argument emerging from these two lines of thought was that both terrorism and American hegemony must be contested.

11 September 2001: impacting Russian–United States relations

Russia's relationships with NATO and the US improved gradually after the Kosovo crisis, but two years after the crisis US–Russian relations were still not as good as they had been before the crisis. Because of this strained relationship, observers were surprised at Moscow's robust support of Washington after the terrorist attacks of 11 September 2001.

President Vladimir Putin was the first leader of a foreign state to express his sympathies to the American president over the telephone. The same day Putin officially stated that what had happened signified a challenge to all of humanity. He emphasized that the events reinforced the urgency of Russia's call to the international community to unite in the fight against terrorism, the 'plague of the twenty-first century'.[9]

Russia strongly demonstrated its solidarity with the US in several ways after 11 September. Putin decided to commemorate the victims of the terrorist attacks with a minute of silence in Russia on 13 September 2001. An opinion survey carried out by the Russian institute VTsIOM indicated that 85 per cent of Muscovites thought that the terrorist attacks were of concern to all of humanity.[10] Another survey showed that an overwhelming majority of the respondents, 77 per cent, expressed sympathy for the American people.[11]

On 12 September 2001, the day after the attacks, Putin called Bush to discuss the possibilities for widening cooperation to counter terrorism more effectively.[12] The Russian president also assured the US of Russia's full support in the military operation against the Taliban in Afghanistan.[13] In Moscow's view, the actions taken by the US were fully justified because of the American losses suffered on 11 September.[14] Putin's rapid initiatives were followed by intense Russian diplomacy aimed at increasing cooperation with the US.[15]

In December 2001 Putin described Russia's policy aimed at improving relations with the US as a 'strategic policy', not a 'tactical move'.[16] Russian support of the American struggle against international terrorism contributed to easing some of the tension between Russia and NATO. A NATO–Russia Council was created at the May Summit of 2002. The Council provides Russia with opportunities to participate in NATO decisions, especially those involving issues such as the struggle against terrorism, regional emergencies, and arms control.

Russian leaders pleaded that all states had to join together to work out appropriate approaches and mechanisms to use in the long-term struggle against terrorism.[17] Russia also increased cooperation with the EU in order to counter terrorism. The two parties would fight money laundering, harmonize national legislation, and develop a mutually acceptable definition of terrorism.[18]

Russia also suggested that a separate UN session should focus on terrorism as a threat to global security.[19] The Russian leaders welcomed a UN resolution against terrorism adopted in September 2001, which provided a legal basis for the struggle against terrorism and placed the UN in a leading position with regard to combating terror.[20] However, they called for an even stronger international legal framework to sustain the battle against terrorism, including developing a clearer definition of the problem.[21]

In addition, Moscow attempted to gain acceptance for its view of terrorism as a widespread phenomenon with roots in several locations. The Russian leaders emphasized the links between separatists in Chechnya, the attacks on the US and terrorists based in Afghanistan.[22] Defence Minister Sergei Ivanov described terrorism in Chechnya and Afghanistan as 'branches of the same tree'.[23] At the end of September 2001, Putin was clearly satisfied that Washington had changed its tune regarding the conflict in Chechnya.[24]

Since scepticism had characterized Russian relations with Washington after the Kosovo crisis, many observers believed that Russia's demonstration of support for the US was noteworthy. Few, however, remarked that Russia's determination to battle terrorism was anything but new. In fact, the fight against terrorism had been a principal focus of Russian foreign policy since the foundation of the Russian Federation, and leaders had made an effort to demystify old enemies and identify new threats, such as terrorism, throughout the 1990s.

In 1992 President Boris Yeltsin had already made it clear that Russia and the US were no longer enemies and would never wage war against each other. In fact, they were not only partners, but allies – *soiuzniki*. At the time, Russian leaders even went so far as state that Russia did not recognize any external enemies.[25] The new threats, they reasoned, were of quite a different nature and were often transnational and difficult to counter: terrorism, economic problems, ecological problems, fascism, extremism, communism, demographic problems and conflicts between peoples adhering to different religions, ethnicities and nationalities are all examples of new threats recognized by the Russian leadership.[26] In Moscow's view these threats were of concern both to Russia and Europe, and thus provided a uniting force.[27] Russia has a pervasive, traditional focus on threats which is born of the experience of being surrounded by potentially aggressive neighbours, so it was noteworthy that it so quickly adopted a 'modern', widened security agenda.[28]

In the years that followed, conflicts and wars occurred in Abkhazia, Nagorno-Karabakh, Yugoslavia and Chechnya. Accordingly, Russian leaders continued emphasizing the danger inherent in new threats – 'threats of a new generation' – many of which were manifest in domestic conflicts.[29] The Russian leadership also regularly condemned international terrorism and organized crime, as well as the spread of weapons of mass destruction.[30] Yeltsin repeatedly called upon the international community to cooperate against such transnational dangers.[31]

The Russian leaders were unable to gain an audience in the West for their arguments during the Kosovo crisis, but nevertheless continued their rhetorical campaign against 'new threats'. Foreign Minister Igor Ivanov criticized operation 'Allied Force', emphasizing that all states' territorial integrity had to be guaranteed, and he condemned aggressive separatism and terrorism, with explicit reference to Kosovo and Chechnya.[32] The leadership continued to call for an international campaign against new threats, above all terrorism and separatism, organized crime and the drug trade.[33] They called upon other states to support Russia in its fight against terrorism in Chechnya, describing this problem as 'stretching from the Philippines to Kosovo', threatening 'the entire civilized world'.[34]

The terrorist attacks directed at World Trade Center and the Pentagon provided Moscow with new hope that their new threat rhetoric would capture attention. A few days after the attack, Putin expressed regret that Moscow had not managed to persuade the international community of the need to create an efficient defence against international terrorism. He added that Washington had failed to predict the attacks because of American unwillingness to realize that the world had changed since the cold war.[35]

It is obvious that Russian leaders believed that their relationship with the US and Russia's status in the international arena had dramatically improved as a consequence of their support for Washington. NATO's Secretary

General, Lord George Robertson, named Russia 'NATO's first partner' in the struggle against international terrorism in December 2002.[36] The Russian Foreign Minister described the year 2001 as the year when Russia had returned to the international arena as a key player, and depicted relations with the US and NATO as radically improved. According to Ivanov, these improved relations stemmed from Russia's support for the coalition against terrorism, the growth of the Russian economy, and Putin's foreign policy.[37] It is therefore striking that Russia once more jeopardized its propitious relationship with the US over the Iraq War in 2003.

Opposing hegemony and a new world order

It may at first seem odd that Moscow did not give the US its support in the war in Iraq, given the risks that decision posed to their recently improving relationship. It might be expected that the Russian leaders would have seized the opportunity to show support; Putin instead chose to put the favourable relationship that had developed at risk, by openly opposing the US, primarily by threatening to veto a US-sponsored resolution authorizing the use of force against Iraq. It seems even more odd considering that Russia's support would have corresponded perfectly with its focus on terrorism, since the Americans justified the attack on Iraq with arguments regarding the combat against terrorism.

If we consider why Russia stands by the two basic foreign policy principles in the first place, it is clear that its determination to preserve the existing world order arose from an intention to preserve Russia's historical status and position in the international system. Its position as a superpower is gone, but few Russian politicians are willing to accept the loss of Russia's status as a great power. However, only two concrete resources remain to support this status: possession of nuclear weapons, and a seat among the five permanent members of the UN Security Council. The UN security order is therefore seen as a necessary guarantor of Russia's status as a great power.

Concerning the second principle, the battle against international terrorism serves three main purposes for Russia. First, Russia's engagement in preventing and dealing with terrorism is supposed to preserve and improve the state's status in the international community by making it stand out as a 'guardian of morality'. Russia hopes to be one of the leading states in the combat against 'the evil of our time', international terrorism.

Second, the struggle functions as a community-building activity with regards to the West. Cultivation of a common enemy is a classic method that serves to unite different parties. A common battle against terrorism may bring Russia closer to its goal of being treated as an equal partner with the US and Europe, something Russia's leaders have been striving towards throughout the 1990s.

67

Third, Russian leaders perceive terrorism as a truly serious threat. The leadership links terrorism to separatism, which threatens the Russian state's territorial integrity, which in turn has been honoured as a sacred principle in Russian politics. Russia has also suffered severely from terrorist attacks. According to official Russian statistics, 29 hostage-takings and 221 terrorist attacks occurred in 2001.[38] This high incidence of terrorism has made the population acutely aware of its susceptibility to terrorism and of the fact that it can occur anywhere at any time.

For example, in the autumn of 1999 about 300 people were the victims of bombs which destroyed apartment buildings in Moscow and several other Russian cities. One year later Russia experienced what has been called 'Russia's September 11'. On 23 October 2002, Chechen separatists, led by warlord Movsar Barayev, took over an entire Moscow theatre taking 850 people hostage. Over a hundred hostages died when special Russian forces entered the building.[39] On 5 July 2003, suicide bombers killed 13 people during a rock concert in Moscow.[40] These and other incidents have helped make terrorism a primary policy concern in Russia.

The genuine concern with terrorism is linked to the other major item on the foreign policy agenda. Terrorism threatens the current, traditional security policy and the security system Russia relies upon. If threats are no longer bilateral, but diffuse and transnational, they are more difficult to deal with and are therefore more alarming. This is particularly problematic in Russia, where the strength traditionally lies within the state. The task of the Russian central power has traditionally been to counter external threats. It is symptomatic that Putin commented on the hostage taking of October 2002 in Moscow, arguing that Russia now is 'paying the price for the weakness of the state and the consequences of its inaction'.[41]

Why then did Russian leaders choose not to prioritize the battle against terrorism in 2003? Did they set aside the anti-terrorism principle in favour of the world order principle? The somewhat paradoxical answer is that they actually did comply with both principles. The leaders did not abandon their focus on terrorism when confronting the US. Moscow never accepted the United States' definition of Iraq, Iran and North Korea as an 'axis of evil'.[42] In Russia's view, Iraq was not a threat to global security. There was no evidence of links between Iraq and al-Qaeda, or any other organizer of international terror.[43] The leaders also pointed out that the Russian military had not met with any Iraqi citizens among the combatants in Chechnya, although members of thirty to forty other nationalities were encountered.[44]

In Moscow's eyes a war in Iraq would, in fact, complicate the international arena of its combat against terror. The Russian leaders stressed that such a war would generate disagreements among the Western states and undermine the international coalition against terror.[45] There were also visible signs prior to the war that Russia would not lend Washington its support. Russian leaders had long opposed an intervention, both directly and indirectly. At the time of 11 September 2001 it was already clear that Moscow's support in fighting terrorism was neither boundless nor unconditional. Three weeks after the attacks against the US, the Russian ambassador to Iraq, Aleksandr Shein, said that if Western states attacked Iraq as a part of the 'revenge' for 11 September, Russia would react in a sharply negative way.[46]

The leaders emphasized that Russia was categorically opposed to operations not supported by international law and clearly sanctioned by the UN.[47] They pleaded that terrorism should be dealt with at the international level, ideally through a global system coordinated by the UN.[48] Russia was of the opinion that an international legal framework ought to harmonize national legislation the better to contest terrorism,[49] and Putin also argued that the international community had no right to interfere to remove the Iraqi regime.[50]

Russia clearly indicated that the US should not completely take over the fight against terrorism, since that would threaten the status quo in world politics. Obvious parallels can be seen between Russia's reactions to the Kosovo crisis and to the proposed war in Iraq. Russian leaders condemned the United States' high-handed methods, and Putin warned that international law risked being replaced by a principle of 'the law of the strongest', under which no state could feel safe.[51] In his speech to the Russian parliament on 16 May 2003, Putin indirectly criticized Washington for using the war on terrorism to expand its sphere of interest, and to remove Russia from promising markets.[52]

The Russian Defence Minister repeated that the combat against new threats ought to be centralized under the UN. He argued that the Iraq War forced the international community to consider what future system of security it wished to achieve. The Foreign Minister elaborated on his support for a global coalition against terror, founded on international law and a strong UN.[53] Concurrently, the Russian leaders made it clear that a UN without a strong Security Council would be meaningless.[54]

When the Iraq War had come to an end the Foreign Minister continued to emphasize that a new international system should be created based on international law. The new system would reflect the principles of 'multipolarity' and 'multilateral global cooperation', and would be organized as a kind of pyramid with the UN Security Council at its top, supported by regional organizations and bilateral links among states.[55]

In summary, the main reason why Russia chose to oppose the United States over Iraq is that Russia's leaders placed great importance on preserving the world order and were prepared to make sacrifices to defend it. In addition, during the Iraq War they could stand up for the status quo without breaking with their other major foreign policy principle: the determination to fight terrorism.

69

Additional motivations for opposing war in Iraq

Even though the two lines of thought described above are important to Russian foreign policy, the leadership's stance may still seem puzzling. Was it irrational to challenge the US, when the likelihood of influencing the American president's posture was quite small? Russian critics warned that it was not a good strategy to confront the US, since it was impossible to hinder the superpower from doing what it was set on doing. They were also concerned that Russia risked losing important economic advantages by criticizing or 'obstructing' American plans.[56] However, there are additional factors that may have strengthened the Russian president's resolve to oppose the US.

Perhaps the Russian leaders believed that the United States' military campaign risked failure, as suggested above. The forthcoming Russian parliamentary elections may also have had an influence on the establishment's posture. Challenging the US might have been part of their strategy in view of the Duma elections. The leaders may have calculated that it was hazardous to support the US because of anti-American feelings among the electorate.[57] Peter Lavell argues that in standing up to the US the Russian leaders used the Russian search for national identity to strengthen their position. In Lavell's interpretation to be 'anti-United States' would then mean to be 'pro-Russian', i.e. to identify with the country in a swiftly changing world.[58]

The growing Russian scepticism towards the US may in turn have been caused by Washington's poor reciprocation of the support provided by Russia after 11 September 2001. Observers pointed out that the US had abandoned the 1972 ABM treaty with Russia in December 2001 and supported the NATO enlargement, the only reward to Russia being recognition of the links between Chechen separatists and international terrorism.[59]

Another possible explanation is that supporting the US might have affected Russia's status in other parts of the world negatively. China, the EU and the Muslim world might have come to view Russia as a vassal of the US if Russia had not opposed the war in Iraq.[60] By confronting Washington, Russia gained status in the international arena, since the majority of states opposed the Iraq War.[61]

Summary and conclusion

A broad examination of the factors influencing the Russian decision not to support the US in a war against Iraq reveals that the decision was soundly in line with Russia's two main foreign policy objectives. For both domestic and international reasons it was important to mark Russia's independence from Washington, underscoring its right to make its own decisions in the international political arena. In addition it was a suitable occasion to prioritize relations with Europe, because from a long-term perspective Russia's connections with Europe are extremely valuable. The European Union accounted for 40 per cent of Russia's trade in the 1990s, and despite many problems, economic relations will probably strengthen in the future. After its enlargement, the EU will account for more than 50 per cent of Russia's trade, offering the advantage of a single set of trade rules, a single tariff and a single set of administrative procedures.

Economic considerations spill over into the security arena. For example, Dov Lynch argues that Russia seeks to draw economic advantage of the European Security and Defence Policy (ESDP), which could be achieved by offering strategic airlift capabilities to the EU.[62] Bobo Lo suggests that 11 September increased the Russian tendency to link economics and security issues: the leaders perceived a window of opportunity for gaining strategic benefits from the West in the new climate of partnership.[63] Similarly, Mette Skak proposes that the need to win European supporters for Russia's entrance into the World Trade Organization (WTO) explains why Russia sided with France and Germany in opposing the United States intervention in Iraq.[64]

To link Russia's position in the Iraqi conflict to its aspirations with regards to WTO membership is probably to overestimate the importance of economic considerations to security policy. There is, however, ample evidence that Russian leaders do link security to the promotion of development goals. The National Security Concept of 2000 states that 'Russia's national interests may be assured only on the basis of sustainable economic development.'[65] The Foreign Policy Concept of June 2000 also connects economic development and security matters (and not only traditional security goals).[66] President Putin displays an awareness of the link between a strong economy and international power and influence. In his address to the Federal Assembly in 2002, he argued that Russia had to adapt to the demands of economic globalization, to be able to fight for its place under the 'economic sun'.[67] The following year, he stated that Russia's ability to compete directly determined the country's weight in international affairs.[68]

Apart from economics, the Russian leadership had strong political incentives to emphasize the importance of Russia's relationship with Europe. The Iraq crisis presented Vladimir Putin with an opportunity to put the idea of multipolarity into practice. The Russian president named the joint statement of Russia, France, and Germany on Iraq of 11 February 2003 'the first brick in the construction of a multipolar world'.[69] The idea of Europe as a pole in a multipolar world order is not novel. Russian leaders have, for example, interpreted the ESDP as a step away from American hegemony towards multipolarity.[70] They have stressed that Russia can help the EU to become a stronger, independent centre of global power. In May 2003 Putin argued that if Europe wished to become an independent global centre of power, good relations with Russia were essential.[71] A further factor, complementing the geopolitical and economic interests, may have been Putin's favourable relationship with Germany and Chancellor Gerhard Schröder, which may have made it easier for the Russian leader to join the two traditional European centres of power in their critique of the United States' intervention.

Also, Russian leaders probably calculated that the leadership in Washington would not be overly offended by their criticism. Russia had previously managed to protest against US politics, for example during the NATO enlargement process and the Kosovo crisis, while preserving a constructive relationship with Washington. During the Iraq War, the Russian leaders emphasized that they wished to maintain good relations with the US and continue to cooperate.[72] In May, Foreign Minister Igor Ivanov pointed out that Russia had kept up constant dialogue with the US and argued that the two had not acted against each other, but 'defended differing approaches to the same problem'.[73]

In fact, Russia's relationship with Washington does not seem to have suffered much harm as a result of the disagreement over Iraq. The Summit in St Petersburg in May 2003 produced a fruitful dialogue and joint statements.[74] Putin declared that the US is Russia's most important partner, and in some ways a 'unique' one.[75] Relations with Great Britain were also normalized.[76]

All this should be viewed in light of the fact that Russia had a favourable standing vis-à-vis the US to begin with. Russia is, after all, able to contribute to the combat of new threats. Few states have so much to offer in the battle against international terrorism as does Russia, not least because its vast territory borders some of the most explosive areas where terrorism tends to thrive. For example, during the war in Afghanistan, Russia was able to play a role by using its influence in the region to support the anti-Taliban 'Northern Alliance'. The leadership also consented to the US acting from areas within what Moscow views as its sphere of influence.[77]

In summary, the Russian leaders made significant gains by taking a negative stance towards the United States' intervention in Iraq. Russia's relationship with Germany and France was strengthened, and Russia's international status was enhanced as a result of the leadership's anti-war rhetoric. They were able to maintain their good relationship with Washington despite their protests of the war. This must be a favourable accomplishment in the Russian leadership's view, since its foreign policy is primarily concerned with maintaining close relationships with both Europe and the US, while not abandoning its main principles of preserving the existing world order and combating international terrorism.

Notes

1 Yuri Federov, 'Russian Military Reform and Present Security Problems', Speech at Swedish National Defence College, 7 May 2003. Cf. Andrey Lebedev, 'The War in Iraq and Future Wars', *Izvestia*, 7 May 2003.
2 B. Buzan, O. Waever and J. de Wilde, *Security: A New Framework For Analysis.* Boulder/London: Lynne Rienner Publishers, 1998, p. 23.
3 Ibid., p. 25.
4 *Diplomaticheskii Vestnik*, number 7 1999, pp. 3–5; cf. number 6 1999, pp. 74–78.
5 *Diplomaticheskii Vestnik*, number 2 1999, pp. 15–18 (Igor Ivanov), number 4 1999, pp. 3–7 (Boris Yeltsin), pp. 12–17, 31–37 (Igor Ivanov), number 6 1999, pp. 3–5 (Boris Yeltsin), pp. 74–79 (Igor Ivanov), number 8 1999, p. 39 (Igor Ivanov), number 9 1999, p. 62 (Boris Yeltsin), number 11 1999, pp. 73–76 (Igor Ivanov).
6 *Diplomaticheskii Vestnik*, number 4 1999, pp. 25–28, 31–37 (Igor Ivanov).
7 *Diplomaticheskii Vestnik*, number 11 1999, pp. 69–71 (Igor Ivanov), cf. number 12 1999, p. 11 (Boris Yeltsin).
8 National Security Concept of the Russian Federation, adopted 17 December 1999, signed on 10 January 2000. Availabile at http://www.russiaeurope. mid.ru/RussiaEurope/russiastrat2000.html (accessed 27 October 2003).
9 *Radio Free Europe/Radio Liberty Newsline*, 12 September 2001, http://www. rferl.org/newsline/ (accessed 18 September 2003).
10 *Radio Free Europe/Radio Liberty Newsline*, 17 September 2001, http://www. rferl.org/newsline/ (accessed 22 September 2003).
11 *Radio Free Europe/Radio Liberty Newsline*, 21 September 2001, http://www. rferl.org/newsline/ (accessed 18 September 2003).
12 *Radio Free Europe/Radio Liberty Newsline*, 13 September 2001 http://www. rferl.org/newsline/ (accessed 22 September 2003).
13 *Radio Free Europe/Radio Liberty Newsline*, 9 October 2001, 11 October 2001, http://www.rferl.org/newsline/ (accessed 18 September 2003).
14 *Radio Free Europe/Radio Liberty Newsline*, 9 October 2001, http://www.rferl.org/ newsline/ (accessed 22 September 2003).
15 See for example *Radio Free Europe/Radio Liberty Newsline*, 18, 19 and 20 September 2001, 24 September 2001, 27 September 2001, 1 October 2001, 15 November 2001 and 10 December 2001, http://www.rferl.org/newsline/ (accessed 18 September 2003).
16 *Radio Free Europe/Radio Liberty Newsline*, 6 December 2001, http://www. rferl.org/newsline/ (accessed 18 September 2003).
17 *Radio Free Europe/Radio Liberty Newsline*, 18–20 September 2001, 24 September 2001, 26 September 2001, 9 October 2001, http://www.rferl.org/newsline/ (accessed 18 September 2003).
18 *Radio Free Europe/Radio Liberty Newsline*, 2 October 2001, 8 October 2001, http://www.rferl.org/newsline/ (accessed 25 September 2003). Cf. A. Safanov, 'The World Needs a Global Antiterrorist System', *International Affairs A Russian Journal of World Politics, Diplomacy and International Relations*, 49, 1, 2003.
19 *Radio Free Europe/Radio Liberty Newsline*, 25 September 2001, http://www. rferl.org/newsline/ (accessed 25 September 2003).
20 *Radio Free Europe/Radio Liberty Newsline*, 1 October 2001, http://www.rferl.org/ newsline/ (accessed 25 September 2003).
21 *Radio Free Europe/Radio Liberty Newsline*, 22 October 2001, http://www. rferl.org/newsline/ (accessed 25 September 2003).

22 *Radio Free Europe/Radio Liberty Newsline*, 18 September 2001, 25 September 2001, http://www.rferl.org/newsline/ (accessed 25 September 2003).

23 *Radio Free Europe/Radio Liberty Newsline*, 25 September 2001, http://www.rferl.org/newsline/ (accessed 25 September 2003).

24 *Radio Free Europe/Radio Liberty Newsline*, 1 October 2001, http://www.rferl.org/newsline/ (accessed 19 September 2003).

25 *Diplomaticheskii Vestnik*, number 2–3, 4–5, 6, 1992.

26 *Diplomaticheskii Vestnik*, number 1, 4–5, 6, 9–10, 15–16, 19–20, 23–24 1992.

27 *Diplomaticheskii Vestnik*, number 9–10, 15–16, 23–24, 1992.

28 A. Kortunov, 'Russian National Interests: The State of Discussion' in K. Spillman and A. Wenger (eds), *Russia's Place in Europe: A Security Debate*, Studies in Contemporary History and Security Policy. Bern: Lang, 1999, pp. 1–2.

29 *Diplomaticheskii Vestnik*, number 1–2, 3–4, 5–6, 7–8, 9–10, 13–14, 19–20, 21–22, 23–24 1993; number 5–6 1994; number 1, 4, 5, 8, 10 1995.

30 *Diplomaticheskii Vestnik*, number 3–4, 5–6, 9–10, 13–14, 21–22, 23–24; number 3–4, 9–10, 13–14, 23–24 1993.

31 *Diplomaticheskii Vestnik*, number 19–20 1994; number 11 1995.

32 *Diplomaticheskii Vestnik*, number 11, 12 1999.

33 *Diplomaticheskii Vestnik*, number 8, 10, 12 2000; number 1 2001.

34 *Diplomaticheskii Vestnik*, number 8 2000; number 1 2001.

35 *Radio Free Europe/Radio Liberty Newsline*, 17 September 2001, http://www.rferl.org/newsline/ (accessed 18 September 2003).

36 *Radio Free Europe/Radio Liberty Newsline*, 9 December 2002, http://www.rferl.org/newsline/ (accessed 25 September 2003).

37 *Radio Free Europe/Radio Liberty Newsline*, 3 January 2002. Cf. M. Skak, 'Russian Security Policy After 9/11', Paper prepared for the Joint International Convention of Central Eastern European International Studies Association and International Studies Association, Budapest, 26–28 June 2003, pp. 6–7.

38 *Radio Free Europe/Radio Liberty Newsline*, 17 October 2001, http://www.rferl.org/newsline/ (accessed 23 September 2003).

39 *Radio Free Europe/Radio Liberty Newsline*, 29 October 2002, http://www.rferl.org/newsline/ (accessed 23 September 2003).

40 *Radio Free Europe/Radio Liberty Newsline*, 7 July 2003, http://www.rferl.org/newsline/ (accessed 23 September 2003).

41 *Radio Free Europe/Radio Liberty Newsline*, 29 October 2002, http://www.rferl.org/newsline/ (accessed 23 September 2003).

42 *Radio Free Europe/Radio Liberty Newsline*, 4 February 2002, http://www.rferl.org/newsline/ (accessed 26 September 2003).

43 *Current Digest of the Post-Soviet Press*, 55 (11), 16 April 2003, http://www.currentdigest.org (accessed 22 September 2003); *Radio Free Europe/Radio Liberty Newsline*, 4 and 5 February 2002, 15 November 2002, 12 February 2003, http://www.rferl.org/newsline/ (accessed 22 September 2003).

44 *Radio Free Europe/Radio Liberty Newsline*, 15 November 2002, http://www.rferl.org/newsline/ (accessed 18 September 2003).

45 *Current Digest of the Post-Soviet Press*, 55 (4), 26 February 2003, http://www.currentdigest.org/ (accessed 19 September 2003); *Radio Free Europe/Radio Liberty Newsline*, 9 September 2002, 13 February 2003, http://www.rferl.org/newsline/ (accessed 18 September 2003).

46 *Radio Free Europe/Radio Liberty Newsline*, 3 October 2001, http://www.rferl.org/newsline/ (accessed 22 September 2003).

47 *Radio Free Europe/Radio Liberty Newsline*, 24 September 2001, 9 September 2002, http://www.rferl.org/newsline/ (accessed 22 September 2003).

48 *Radio Free Europe/Radio Liberty Newsline*, 24 and 25 September 2001, 18 November 2001, 26 March 2003, 4 April 2003, http://www.rferl.org/newsline/ (accessed 18 September 2003).
49 *Radio Free Europe/Radio Liberty Newsline*, 1 October 2001, 22 October 2001, http://www.rferl.org/newsline/ (accessed 18 September 2003).
50 *Radio Free Europe/Radio Liberty Newsline*, 4 March 2003, http://www.rferl.org/ newsline/ (accessed 26 September 2003).
51 Vladimir Putin in *Rossiiskaja Gazeta*, 21 March 2003.
52 *Radio Free Europe/Radio Liberty Newsline*, 19 May 2003, http://www.rferl.org/ newsline/ (accessed 26 September 2003).
53 *Current Digest of the Post-Soviet Press*, 55 (9), 2 April 2003, http://www. currentdigest.org/ (accessed 22 September 2003).
54 *Radio Free Europe/Radio Liberty Newsline*, 1 April 2003; Cf. *Radio Free Europe/ Radio Liberty Newsline* 4 April 2003, http://www.rferl.org/newsline/ (accessed 26 September 2003).
55 *Radio Free Europe/Radio Liberty Newsline*, 13 May 2003, http://www.rferl.org/ newsline/ (accessed 26 September 2003).
56 For example Sergei Karaganov quoted in *Radio Free Europe/Radio Liberty Newsline*, 23 April 2003. Vladimir Lukin quoted in *Current Digest of the Post-Soviet Press*, 55, 9, 2 April 2003, http://www.currentdigest.org/ (accessed 22 September 2003).
57 A. Åslund, 'The Scales have tipped towards a Resurgent Russia', *New York Times*, 29 May 2003, and P. Lavell, 'Whither Russia's Anti-Americanism?', *RFE/RL End Note* 14 April 2003.
58 Ibid.
59 A. Åslund, op. cit.
60 *Radio Free Europe/Radio Liberty Newsline*, 18 March 2003, http://www.rferl.org/ newsline/ (accessed 26 September 2003).
61 Lavell, D. Lynch, 'Russia faces Europe', *Chaillot Papers no. 60*, Paris: European Union Institute for Security Studies, 2003.
62 Lynch, B. L., *Vladimir Putin and the Evolution of Russian Foreign Policy*, Oxford: Blackwell Publishing, 2003. p. 73.
63 Lo, op. cit., pp. 121–122.
64 Skak, op. cit., p. 20.
65 Russian National Security Concept 2000, paragraph 2.
66 B. Nygren, 'Russia and Europe, or Russia in Europe?' in Y. Federov and B. Nygren (eds), *Russia and Europe: Putin's Foreign Policy*, Stockholm: Swedish National Defence College ACTA B23, 2002.
67 Annual Address by President of the Russian Federation Vladimir Putin to the Federal Assembly of the Russian Federation Moscow, 18 April 2002.
68 Annual Address by President of the Russian Federation Vladimir Putin to the Federal Assembly of the Russian Federation Moscow, 16 May 2003.
69 *Radio Free Europe/Radio Liberty Newsline*, 12 February 2003, http://www. rferl.org/newsline/ (accessed 26 September 2003).
70 *Diplomaticheskii Vestnik*, number 12, 2000; number 1 2001.
71 RFE/RL 28 March 2003, http://www.rferl.org/newsline/ (accessed 26 September 2003).
72 *Current Digest of the Post-Soviet Press*, 55, 9, 2 April 2003, http://www. currentdigest.org/, 17 September 2003. RFE/RL 5 March 2003, 17 March 2003, 31 March 2003, 4 April 2003, 21 April 2003, http://www.rferl.org/newsline/ (accessed 26 September 2003).

73 *Radio Free Europe/Radio Liberty Newsline*, 13 May 2003, http://www.rferl.org/ newsline/ (accessed 26 September 2003).
74 *Radio Free Europe/Radio Liberty Newsline*, 2 June 2003, http://www.rferl.org/ newsline/ (accessed 26 September 2003).
75 *Radio Free Europe/Radio Liberty Newsline*, 4 June 2003, http://www.rferl.org/ newsline/ (accessed 26 September 2003).
76 *Current Digest of the Post-Soviet Press*, 55, 25, 23 July 2003, http://www. currentdigest.org/ (accessed 22 September 2003).
77 A. Åslund, op. cit.

References

Annual Address by President of the Russian Federation Vladimir Putin to the Federal Assembly of the Russian Federation Moscow, 18 April 2002.
Annual Address by President of the Russian Federation Vladimir Putin to the Federal Assembly of the Russian Federation Moscow, 16 May 2003.
Åslund, A. 'The Scales Have Tipped Towards a Resurgent Russia', *New York Times* 25 May 2003.
Buzan, B., Waever, O. and De Wilde, J. *Security: A New Framework For Analysis*. Boulder/London: Lynne Rienner Publishers, 1998.
Current Digest of the Post-Soviet Press, available at http://www.currentdigest.org/.
Diplomaticheskii Vestnik, volumes 1992–1995 Moscow: Nauchnaia kniga pri Diplo- maticheskoi akadenii MID Rossii, 1999–2001.
Federov, Y. 'Russian Military Reform and Present Security Problems', Speech at the Swedish National Defence College, 7 May 2003.
Huysmans, J. 'Revisiting Copenhagen: Or, On the Creative Development of a Security Studies Agenda in Europe', *European Journal of International Relations* 4, 4 (1998) pp. 479–506.
Kortunov, A. 'Russian National Interests: The State of Discussion' in K. Spillman and A. Wenger (eds), *Russia's Place in Europe: A Security Debate*, Studies in Con- temporary History and Security Policy, Bern: Lang, 1999.
Lavell, P. 'Whither Russia's Anti-americanism?', *Radio Free Europe/Radio Liberty Newsline* 2003–04–14, http://www/rferl/org/newsline/.
Lebedev, A. 'The War in Iraq and Future Wars', *Izvestia*, 7 May 2003.
Lo, B. *Vladimir Putin and the Evolution of Russian Foreign Policy*. Oxford: Blackwell Publishing, 2003.
Lynch, D. 'Russia faces Europe', *Chaillot Papers no. 60*, Paris: European Union Institute for Security Studies, 2003.
National Security Concept of the Russian Federation, adopted 17 December 1999, signed on 10 January 2000. Availabile at http://www.russiaeurope.mid.ru/ RussiaEurope/russiastrat2000.html (accessed 27 October 2003).
Nygren, B. 'Russia and Europe, or Russia in Europe?' in Y. Federov and B. Nygren (eds), *Russia and Europe: Putin's Foreign Policy*, Stockholm: Swedish National Defence College ACTA B23, 2002.
Radio Free Europe/Radio Liberty Newsline, available at http://www.rferl.org/ newsline/.
Safanov, A. 'The World Needs a Global Antiterrorist System', *International Affairs A Russian Journal of World Politics, Diplomacy and International Relations* 49, 1 (2003) pp. 28–34.
Skak, M. 'Russian Security Policy After 9/11', Paper prepared for the joint Inter- national Convention of Central Eastern European International Studies Associa- tion and International Studies Association, Budapest, 26–28 June 2003.

5

IRAQ'S POLITICAL STRATEGY BEFORE AND DURING THE WAR

Roger Karlsson

The die is cast!

On 12 September 2002, I and about 30 other UN employees were in the cafeteria of the Canal Hotel, the UN headquarters in Baghdad. We were tense and expectant before the President of the United States, George W. Bush, spoke to the UN General Assembly, asking ourselves whether a war was inevitable and what the future would hold for the population of Iraq. The speech contained no doubts that the Iraqi regime posed a serious and growing threat to the authority of the UN and to world peace. A gleam of hope was lit in us when it was emphasized that the US had no quarrel with Iraq's population, but we wondered how this should be viewed. Iraq's population was described as being imprisoned by the regime. Saddam Hussein's regime was thus singled out as a separate problem detached from the population. Enabling the Iraqi people to live in freedom was, in itself, an independent and lofty moral objective but also, at this point, an important strategic goal for the US.[1] It was said that the Iraqi people deserved freedom and that the security of all states in the world demanded that Iraq should become a free and open society.

There was a moment of silence in the crowd before someone remarked loudly that the time had now come to dust off the evacuation plan, which existed if only in draft form, showing how an evacuation of the UN staff should be carried out in case they had to leave Iraq. This time, the UN headquarters in New York had determined that none of its international employees would be left behind as human shields. From President Bush's speech, we gathered that it was no longer an issue of whether a war would break out, but rather when it would happen. Iraq's Deputy Prime Minister Tariq Aziz expressed the same view a few days later: 'The way Mr Bush and Mr Blair are conducting their campaign against Iraq means doomed if you do, doomed if you don't.'[2]

Thesis, method, and disposition

Of course, a war would not be an even fight. On one side was a high-tech superpower and on the other a nation with armed forces that might at most put up some resistance to one of its neighbours. Iraq's military capability had probably declined to about 20 per cent of what it was in 1990. The bulk of Iraqi materiel was obsolete, poorly maintained, and in some cases even totally useless.[3] Faced with the serious threat of war against an enemy vastly superior both on the ground and in the air, the Iraqi leadership, in its planning for how to deal with the enemy, had a very limited range of available options. The purpose of this chapter is to identify Iraq's overall political strategy and attempt to understand it with the help of the concept 'soft power'.

It is reasonable to assume that for Saddam Hussein, threatened with regime change, the overarching objective was political as well as personal survival (since both were strongly intertwined). This time, having much smaller armed forces, he gave priority to defending his regime. Thus, the defence of Iraq was about the very survival of an entire government apparatus.[4] If Saddam was to stand the slightest chance of organizing successful resistance, he had to focus on thwarting the Iraq policy of the US. The main thing for Saddam's regime was to frame a political strategy that could avert the outbreak of war. It is the thesis of this chapter that, in order to prevent a war from breaking out, Iraq initially intended to stop a UN resolution by driving a wedge between the US and the other members of the Security Council. At the same time, there were Iraqi propaganda attempts to induce both Arab and American domestic opinion to help stave off a war or stop it before the regime had fallen. The first effort was a continuation of the existing strategy to get the UN's Oil for Food programme and the accompanying sanctions cancelled.

This strategy was meant to tie the Arab countries to Iraq and, at the same time, show the American public the high cost the US would incur economically and in terms of lost international respect by an attack. The obvious risk of unilateral US action worried not only the Arab world but also a majority of the Western countries.[5]

Most of the works about the Iraq conflict published so far (by the fall of 2003) are written by American and British authors, who often treat the question of Iraq's political strategy as unproblematic. They seem to take it for granted that Iraq would act as it had done earlier in similar situations. In order to contrast with this literature, I have used source material from the Iraqi media output. Since both TV and newspapers were government-controlled, they voiced only the official policy line. The material is taken from *Babil*, *Babil online*, *Iraqi Daily*, the web site of the Iraqi News Agency (INA), *All Dailies*, and *al-Thawra*, the newspaper of the Ba'ath Party. The newspapers referred to were controlled by Uday Hussein. Unfortunately for this study, most of the sources have ceased to exist for obvious reasons, and in order to supplement the material, I have drawn on other Arab media and on the newsletter issued daily by the UN Office of the Humanitarian Co-ordinator for Iraq (UNOCHI).[6] On the basis of the material, Iraq's struggle to destroy the legitimacy and credibility of the enemy's policy and to influence the political decision-making processes of the UN system and of the states involved is described and analysed in the context of the concept of 'soft power'. By legitimacy is meant here the legal and moral considerations invoked to justify a course of action. Credibility refers to the veracity of the arguments presented by the parties.

Before proceeding to the research, it is appropriate to discuss the concept of soft power briefly to explain its significance for this study. Joseph Nye and Robert Keohane argue in favour of a fundamental division of power into two categories, one consisting of behaviour and the other based on resources.[7] Behavioural power, in turn, can be divided into hard and soft power. Hard power means the ability to make others behave in a way they would not otherwise do – this is accomplished primarily by threats and punishments or by rewards. Soft power is derived from appealing assets like cultural attraction, political values and social conditions esteemed by others. This is not a new phenomenon. Historically, the US and other great powers have always tried to capitalize on their reputation and ideology. While hard power will always be the core means for a state to secure its sovereignty, soft power is gaining in importance when it comes to solving transnational problems. Policies for the advancement of democracy and human rights demand tact and serious consideration of soft power instruments.[8] Soft power encompasses the ability to influence the international political agenda and thereby shape the preferences of others. If the US manages to represent norms and values followed voluntarily by other nations, it will have less reason to use expensive hard power instruments. Soft power, then, is more than persuasion. It is, above all, the ability to encourage emulation, to a large extent founded on attractive ideals. Legitimacy and credibility are vital to soft power because the soft power of a state is strengthened when its policy is seen as legitimate by other states. If the US is to succeed in using soft power the critical factor is not whether it can present good arguments but whether it lives up to its own principles. Credibility has always been important in international politics, and it is becoming even more important as the flow of information increases. If governments are to take advantage of information, their behaviour must seem credible.[9] Accordingly, great efforts are made to create and undermine governmental credibility. This leads to a credibility contest. Governments vie with each other in increasing their own credibility and decreasing that of their adversaries. Those having access to a multitude of communication channels and enjoying strong credibility due to correct behaviour will probably have the best prospects of success with regard to soft power.[10]

79

This aspect of power, making others strive to attain what you are striving for, is central to an understanding of Iraq's strategic situation and the Iraqi political strategy before and during the war.

Saddam, the Ba'ath Party and internal security

In any serious discussion of Iraq and the war, it seems reasonable to raise the question: how did Saddam manage to hold on to power even though he had started two major wars ending in defeat?[11] The previous wars depleted Iraq's resources and drove the country into deep depression, with a national debt estimated at $40–50 billion, and prolonged isolation. Moreover, Saddam lost control of 15 of the country's 18 regions during the insurrection following the last Gulf War in 1991, but he still succeeded in regaining control over the country, with the exception of the Kurdish parts. The person best qualified to answer the question how this could happen is probably Saddam himself.[12] Nevertheless, some of the factors explaining his success will be discussed here.

The clan system

One factor is the clan system, which contributed strongly to Saddam's power base. The basic principles of clans and patriarchal forms of government have existed for a long time in Iraqi society and have created a mutual dependency and a strong sense of loyalty among clan members. Saddam strengthened the ties between himself and groups that were important to keep him in power. He rewarded them according to their performance and their importance to him. Saddam was regarded as the obvious leader of the Sunni Muslims, chosen to dominate over the more numerous Shia Muslims and the Kurdish population. High-ranking officials of the security organizations and the Republican Guard were paid in US dollars, and they also received cars and other luxuries. The underlying reason for selecting clan and family members to the highest government positions was to ensure that the closest circle was loyal to Saddam. If he were overthrown, the entire upper stratum would accompany him in the fall. Consequently, there were few incentives for the Iraqi elite to try to topple Saddam.

The Ba'ath Party

Another source of Saddam's power was the Ba'ath Party, which had about 1.5 million members. Saddam was never particularly ideologically oriented in his relations to the party but took a pragmatic approach, and this also applied to his relationship with Islam. He emphasized ideology, pan-Arabism and religion when it served his purposes.[13] Since the security of the regime was the overriding objective, party control over the army became an imperative necessity. By placing people from the clan system in important positions, Saddam could secure the loyalty of the high command of the armed forces. In consequence, the party controlled the army, and the clan controlled the party. This state of affairs made it possible for the president to bypass several layers of the command structure and give orders directly to selected commanders.

By creating a network of mutually supervising military organizations, the Ba'ath Party successfully subverted the collective identity of the military.[14] The regime thereby deliberately sacrificed the military effectiveness of units so that they would constitute no threat whatsoever to Saddam's continued rule. Under these circumstances, it became extremely difficult for any group to mobilize enough support for an attempt to overthrow Saddam. It is even doubtful whether such an attempt could be planned without the regime getting knowledge of it. Since 1968, hundreds of officers have been forced into exile, removed from their posts or retired, arrested or simply liquidated on the suspicion of being disloyal. As a result, the army consisted of officers incapable of making their own decisions or finding creative solutions to problems. The military command structure was gradually undermined by party officers, members of the various security organizations, and the 'civilian security establishment', which had gained full control over the military. The Ba'ath Party eventually destroyed the ability of the military to function independently.

Tyranny and propaganda

The image of Saddam watched over the Iraqis for such a long time that they no longer knew of anything else. Every day the residents of Baghdad passed an immense number of Saddam statues and portraits. When new offices for the Iraqi airline were built just behind Hotel Palestine, the project started with the erection of a statue of Saddam. On the government-controlled TV, the evenings were consumed in showing Saddam's meetings during the day. All of this was, of course, a carefully devised political strategy to remind people, wherever they were, of their great leader Saddam Hussein.[15]

Torture, executions, rapes, genocide and other atrocities were committed by the regime: torture was used not as a last resort but rather as a first measure. The regime kept everything and everyone under surveillance, using a force of volunteers who reported everything that looked suspicious. Rewards were offered for reports on activities that might be regarded as hostile to the regime and penalties were imposed for failure to report. Sometimes, officers of the security service feigned to be oppositional and said something unfavourable about Saddam in order to check if people would report on the incident. Children were encouraged to inform on their parents or on family friends. The regime bugged public places and buildings, and public telephone wires were tapped. In some cases, ordinary people were tailed by the security service for no apparent reason.[16] A network of informers kept the population in check. Like Stalin, Saddam thus frightened every potential political opposition into complete silence.

Internal security

During the 1990s, officials at the Pentagon worked out a series of proposals for solving the Iraq question, which some felt had been left unresolved after the Gulf War in 1991. Options ranging from attempts to instigate a coup by officers of the Iraqi armed forces to an outright military attack on Iraq were considered in the US. When in his state of the union address in January 2002 George W. Bush referred to Iraq as a country that, together with North Korea and Iran, constituted an axis of evil, the tension between the countries was highlighted again. For the US, the aim of possible intervention in Iraq was to overthrow the regime, or rather Saddam personally. The US therefore took great pains to identify individuals who might be in touch with key persons within the Iraqi armed forces. One of them was the former army chief of staff, General Nizar al-Khazraji. Another, perhaps more influential person, was General Najib al-Salhi, previously active in the Republican Guard and now head of a movement of so-called free officers. It was said that he had at his disposal a network of officers still serving in the armed forces.[17]

Well aware of the inadequacies of the opposition, Saddam pursued several political strategies to protect himself and his power base from this type of American interference, which escalated gradually in 2001–02. Arrests and executions of officers were instrumental in reducing the risk of conspiracies or coup attempts originating from the Iraqi armed forces.[18] Because of this, those who had hoped that a coup would occur were disappointed. Through corruption and terror, Saddam's regime had created such a well-functioning security system that the population feared what would happen if the regime fell. With regard to internal security, Saddam had succeeded in shaping Iraq's political milieu so that it now suited his conception of how a political and social order should be upheld. He was fully aware that what he had created resembled a Stalinist system more than anything else. It was a political system built around the person of Saddam rather than ideology.

Less concerned about the internal opposition, the regime developed a political strategy to meet the increasing external threat of military intervention.

The struggle over legitimacy

The Oil for Food Programme and the no-fly zones

Only a few weeks after taking office, President George W. Bush authorized the Pentagon to strike at targets outside the southern no-fly zone. He did so because Iraq was believed to be in the process of connecting parts of its air defence system to a newly installed network of fibre-optic cables, thereby improving opportunities to get at the American and British aircraft patrolling the two zones. On 16 February 2001, the Pentagon ordered air strikes on five targets north of the 33rd parallel (the attack killed three civilians). After the bombings, the US and Great Britain initially declared that Iraq had upgraded its air defence system but later retracted that statement, saying instead that Iraq was on the verge of doing so.[18] All Arab states except Kuwait immediately criticized the US; the general opinion among them was that the US had acted to punish Saddam for supporting the Palestinian Intifadah.

The attack drew attention to the fact that despite the sanctions Iraq had managed to modernize its air defence by introducing new technology. This was a clear warning signal to the states responsible for supplying technology to Iraq. In this particular case, China was the likely supplier. Against the background of these events, the US and Great Britain suggested to the UN that it was time to reconsider the sanctions, since they were not having the intended effect. A proposal for imposing 'smart' sanctions directed at Iraq's military capability was discussed. These sanctions would aim at preventing modernization of the Iraqi armed forces.[19] Such a solution would probably have deprived Iraq of large revenues from lucrative smuggling to neighbouring countries, and neither Syria nor Turkey were interested in it. It was estimated that 50,000 barrels of oil were smuggled out daily in 1992. During the autumn of 2002, 500 trucks loaded with 20–30 cubic metres of smuggled goods crossed the Syrian and Turkish borders every day.[20]

Iraq suffered a further setback in November 2001 when the UN Security Council adopted Resolution 1382 in which free trade with Iraq was again linked to the return to the country of a group of weapons inspectors, the UN Monitoring, Verification and Inspection Commission (UNMOVIC). At the same time, Russia had moved towards the US position. This made it more difficult for Iraq to demand that the sanctions be lifted altogether. Iraq insisted that it no longer possessed any weapons of mass destruction, but the international community had no faith in Iraq, as the resolution of the Security Council made clear.

The situation remained essentially unchanged after Operation Desert Fox (December 1998) until the meetings in the spring of 2002 between Iraq's Foreign Minister Naji Sabri, a former professor of English Literature, and UN Secretary-General Kofi Annan. During these meetings, held in Vienna and New York, Mr Sabri sought to connect the issue of letting weapons inspectors return to Iraq with the issue of having the sanctions removed and the issue of compensation for the damages caused by the American and British air raids in the no-fly zones. When Annan and Sabri met in March 2002, Annan's main interest was discussing the return of weapons inspectors and the 700 Kuwaiti war prisoners detained in Iraq since the last Gulf war, whereas Sabri wanted to discuss the lifting of sanctions, the no-fly zones, the compensation demands on the US and Great Britain and the lack of progress in the question of establishing the Middle East as a zone free of weapons of mass destruction.[21]

The Iraqi regime stuck to its line of demanding withdrawal of the sanctions right to the last, convinced that if it demonstrated the unjust nature of the sanctions and appeared accommodating towards the international community it would eventually prevail. In this context, Iraq's Permanent Representative to the United Nations Muhammed Al-Duri stressed that the only way to end the suffering of the Iraqi people was the immediate lifting of the unjust embargo on their country, and urged the UN Security Council to shoulder its responsibility in accordance with the UN Charter to lift the embargo off Iraq and end the 'no-fly zone' imposed unilaterally by the US and British. He added that the US changed this context from the technical and scientific aspects to the political aspect by demanding that Iraq prove it had no WMD, when in fact Iraq was only required to cooperate actively with the UN inspectors.[22]

Twelve years after the invasion of Kuwait and the imposition of the first sanctions, most Arabs believed the official Iraqi assertion that the US alone was responsible for the suffering of the Iraqi people under the sanctions and for the disintegration of Iraq, the once so prosperous and developed Middle East country.[23]

The importance to Iraq of pan-Arabism

As the threat of military intervention became obvious in 2001–02, Iraq paid more attention to improving its relations with neighbouring countries. For more than ten years, Iraq had levelled strong criticism – verging on abuse – against Kuwait and Saudi Arabia because they allowed US military forces to have bases on their soil. Now Iraq reversed its policy, seeking instead reconciliation and normal relations with these countries. At the meeting of the Arab League in Beirut in March 2002, Saudi Crown Prince Abdullah presented a plan for peace between Israel and the Palestinians. The plan was supported by Iraq, and in return Iraq received support from the league, which condemned the US war designs against Iraq. At the same time, the prince promised to promote normalization of the relations between Iraq and Kuwait. Saudi Arabia reopened its border with Iraq at Arar, and

Saudi companies recommenced a more extensive trade with Iraq. The Iraqi delegate at the meeting, Mr Izzat Ibrahim, and the Kuwaiti foreign minister shook hands publicly after signing a document in which Iraq officially recognized Kuwait and its right of self-determination.[24] In accordance with the spirit of the agreement and the meeting, both countries undertook to stop reporting negatively on each other in the media. In addition, they would try to find a solution to the problem of the Kuwaiti prisoners of war. Meanwhile, at a meeting in London with British Prime Minister Tony Blair, King Abdullah II of Jordan expressed great fear that a war against Iraq could open Pandora's box while the Israeli–Palestinian conflict was still unsolved.[25]

More importantly, the meeting of the Arab League adopted a statement implying that an attack against an Arab country would be considered an attack against all members of the league. Many Iraqi articles about the meeting urged the Arab countries to cooperate. One appeared in *al-Thawra* on 1 March 2003.

> Iraqi Foreign Minister Dr Naji Sabri said that the Arab League's ministerial meeting had approved a draft decision concerning the US threats against Iraq and the Arab world. He added in a statement to the INA correspondent that the decision also stresses Arab countries' rejection of plans aimed at interfering in their domestic affairs and the need to free the region of weapons of mass destruction. He stressed that the Arab role is big and very important in strengthening world rejection against the aggressive colonization schemes.[26]

With this statement he hoped to win support among the other Arab states. In other words, Saddam did not hesitate to use religion as a uniting solidarity factor, despite the fact that his secularized Ba'ath Party governed Iraq.

Iraq's relations with the international community

Now Iraq concentrated on improving its relations with Russia and France, both permanent members of the UN Security Council. Iraq was indebted to these countries for $10 billion and $7 billion respectively after weapons purchases in the 1980s. They therefore had an interest in having the UN sanctions lifted so that Iraq could once again become one of the world's largest oil producers. In the autumn of 2002, Iraq also made an agreement with Russia enabling Russian companies to operate in Iraq as soon as the sanctions were lifted.[27] Furthermore, great efforts were made to ensure that China, also a permanent member of the Security Council, would act in favour of abolishing the sanctions.

The 7 September 2002 Saturday edition of *Babil* contained an article by Dr Abd-al-Razzaq al-Dulaymi which highlights Iraq's diplomatic path. Its title was 'The successful diplomatic offensive'. Below is an excerpt from the article.

> We moved in the direction of China, Russia and Germany, played a splendid role in Johannesburg, and succeeded in the Arab League. But all this does not cancel or reduce the arrogance and superciliousness of the US administration, which, if it was determined to pursue its hostile plan, would pay no attention to anyone, as it does not respect any pact or pledge to begin with. . . . The only thing that the evil US administration considers is the material and human losses and their effect on weakening, and in fact destroying, US prestige, as well as on the forthcoming US elections, as they could strengthen Bush's opponent and blow up the bases of the new order, which this administration has been publicizing. More important, this administration cannot find, up to now, any of what it terms justifications and excuses to launch an aggression against Iraq . . . What we are proud of is our political and diplomatic success in rallying around us all the righteous people in this world, especially the Arabs.[28]

Iraq concluded new trade agreements with its creditors Russia and France. It also struck a deal with Iran and, perhaps more important, agreed to sell oil to Turkey, Syria and Jordan. The latter countries realized that if Iraq was attacked, their vulnerable economies might be affected very negatively.[29]

Iraq repeatedly pointed out the preposterousness of the United States' acting without a UN mandate. As might have been expected, this position was stated before the UN Security Council by Iraq's UN Ambassador Dr Muhammad al-Duri. One of his statements was summarized in *al-Thawra*, the newspaper of the Ba'ath Party, on 8 September 2002.

> Iraq's permanent representative to the UN has said that the UN Security Council and UN Secretary-General are legally responsible in accordance with the UN Charter for preventing any aggression against any UN member state. He said this would preserve international peace and security. He added Iraq made important initiatives to promote and maintain dialogue with the UN so as to arrive at a comprehensive settlement. Dr al-Duri stressed Iraq's categorical rejection of the language of threats because it does not achieve security and peace in the region. He said Iraq believes in the language of dialogue and resolving differences through peaceful means. He added that Iraq has good relations with neighbouring states.[30]

In late August 2002, an article in *Babil* by Dr Abd-al-Razzaq al-Dulaymi entitled 'When they deprive the United Nations of its role' called the legitimacy of the behaviour of the US into question. Eventually, the language of the Iraqi press hardened. On 24 February 2003, the article 'American hysteria' was published in *Babil*.

> Why this American hysteria to issue a new resolution despite the previous resolution that is still there and is being implemented with clear effectiveness? Iraq hopes for the continued steadfastness of the defenders of peace and those who care for the prestige, neutrality and position of the Security Council . . . Iraq also trusts all just and good people in the world and particularly the Security Council member states, some of which did not fear to declare honestly their opposition to any new resolution of the Security Council, contradicting evil US policies . . . We say to whom it may concern that when the United Nations avoids US pressures and rejects the victory of the logic of US usurpation at the Security Council, it is a victory for the entire humanity and a victory for international legitimacy and laws.[31]

The struggle over legitimacy: advantage Iraq

Saddam's position was that Iraq had no weapons of mass destruction and that all sanctions should be withdrawn immediately. His strategy involved a diplomatic charm offensive at the meeting of the Arab League in Beirut in March 2002. At the meeting, a declaration protesting against a possible US-led attack on Iraq and demanding withdrawal of the UN sanctions was adopted. The meeting also welcomed Iraq back as a full member of the Arab community.[32] This strategy was aimed at tying the neighbouring countries together by economic agreements so that they would suffer economically if an attack was carried out. At the same time, a wedge was to be driven between the US and its allies, a strategy already employed during the previous Gulf War.

Unable to match the military capability of the US, Russia, France, China and Germany 'blocked' a second UN resolution. Consequently, the US failed to obtain legitimacy for its Iraq policy. The Turkish parliament also denied the US legitimacy when it refused to let the 4th US infantry division use Turkish territory to attack Iraq from the north. The US inability or failure to apply soft instruments of power meant that the US options were limited to the use of hard power instruments.[33] Meanwhile, opinion polls showed that the American people was prepared to support a war with Iraq *if* it was sanctioned by a joint UN resolution.[34] If the US policy had appeared as legitimate, American soft power would have been stronger.

Now the US had to take the consequences of its failure to get a second UN resolution adopted.

The struggle over credibility

The real mission of the weapons inspectors

The international community hoped that Iraq would make some concessions on the issue of weapons inspections and the Iraqi leadership realized that it had to initiate talks at least about this demand. Removal of the UN sanctions seemed to be at hand and it was very important to the Saddam regime to influence the terms of removal. The Saddam regime made several attempts to refute the US allegation that Iraq still had weapons of mass destruction. According to a spokesman of the Iraqi Foreign Ministry, cited in *All Dailies* on 3 September 2002, the United States made 'misleading and fallacious allegations on the presence of weapons of mass destruction in Iraq without extending any hard evidence'. Statements of leading representatives of the Bush administration constantly undermined the credibility of the weapons inspectors.

To prove his case, the spokesman stated that the United Nations Special Committee (UNSCOM) and the inspection team of the International Atomic Energy Agency (IAEA) had found no materials or activities prohibited by the UN Security Council. Specifically, the IAEA had confirmed the non-existence of an Iraqi nuclear programme. *All Dailies* further reported:

> The spokesman said that the Iraqi National Assembly invited members of the US Senate and House of Representatives to escort experts in chemical, biological and nuclear weapons to visit Iraq and search any locations suspected by the US administration of producing weapons of mass destruction. However, the US administration turned down this initiative. Earlier, Iraq also called on British Prime Minister Tony Blair, who said he is positive that Iraq developed nuclear and other mass destruction weapons, to send a team of British experts to tell the world about the locations used for developing and producing such weapons. Concluding, the Foreign Ministry spokesman said that the international public opinion is dismayed at the insistence of the US administration, which claims that it is the pioneer of democracy in the world, on its crazy obsession with the fabrication of cheap and fallacious excuses one after another. He said that this obsession with such excuses is a reckless effort that seeks to convince the world and the American people of the US evil intentions against Iraq, Palestine and the other Arab and Islamic states.[35]

At first, Iraq questioned whether UNMOVIC was capable of conducting new weapons inspections objectively and without American interference. Would the commission spy on Iraq on behalf of the US or could it be trusted? After Ambassador Rolf Ekéus admitted in an interview that UNSCOM indeed had spied on behalf of the US, on 1 August 2002 *All Dailies* suggested that Iraq's concerns, conveyed to Kofi Annan in the spring, were sound and legitimate.[36] Eventually, the Iraqi regime veered on the issue and became more accommodating towards UNMOVIC and its inspections. By cooperating with the weapons inspectors the Iraqis were, in their own opinion, demonstrating that they were telling the truth when they insisted that they no longer had any weapons of mass destruction. On 9 February 2003, the Iraqi satellite TV station broadcast a feature showing how willingly the Iraqis helped the weapons inspectors.

> Iraq's opening of the 'Al-Mu'taasim' Missile Plant, south-west of Baghdad, for foreign journalists and news agency correspondents, so that they could see first hand that the allegations and fabrications made by US Secretary of State Colin Powell before the UN Security Council on Wednesday [5 February] were baseless. The journalists made sure that all assets of the plant were stamped by the inspection teams, thus constituting categorical evidence that the inspection teams inspected the plant in its entirety when they visited the site 10 days ago.[37]

Did the Iraqi moves make a difference? Among several analysts, General Wesley Clark (retired) contends that it did not matter at all whether the Saddam regime acted in accordance with UN resolution 1441 or not. No cooperation in the world could change the Bush administration's stand except, perhaps, strong American domestic opinion.[38] Saddam, for his part, assessed the situation on the basis of previous experience and his own conviction that the US, no matter what measures he took to cooperate with UNMOVIC, would try to engineer a regime change in Iraq.

The underlying US motives for war

In August 2002, a Gallup poll showed that the American people's support of a war against Iraq had dropped from 88 per cent in November 2001 to 53 per cent. Even more disturbing for the Bush administration was the finding that only 20 per cent were in favour of war if the US prosecuted it alone and that 75 per cent were directly opposed to unilateral action. To this should be added the fact that France and Germany would not support an attack that was not sanctioned by the UN. A breach in the Western coalition had opened, and Saddam moved quickly to take advantage of it. He wanted to drive a wedge even deeper between the members of the UN Security Council (Germany had been a member since January 2002).[39]

Saddam's move was to expose what he felt were the underlying US motives for starting a war against Iraq. This was made clear in *All Dailies* on 3 September 2002.

> The oil in the Middle East constitutes 65 percent of the world oil reserves. According to the Iraqi President, 'when America becomes the oil holder, fixing its prices and the amount this or that oil-consuming country should take, this means it will determine the economic growth level of various countries.' The President hailed the European shift of policy adding that its current position reflects solidarity with Iraq not only for humanitarian and legal reasons, but also in defence of the future, independence, freedom and interests of Europe in the face of the 'US monster's scheme.' By controlling oil – and if they get Iraq out of their way – the Americans want to control the social and cultural life in every country. 'Iraq's battle, therefore, is no longer only national and pan-Arab, but also a human battle,' the Iraqi President said.[40]

Iraq's permanent UN representative Dr Muhammad Al-Duri expressed the same view, that the US administration did not aim at weapons of mass destruction but used that issue as a cover and a pretext to launch an aggression against Iraq for the sake of oil and for controlling the region. Speaking to the INA correspondent at the UN, Al-Duri said 'that of all world countries, only the United States and Britain want to launch war against Iraq. He said that all other countries, including permanent UN Security Council (UNSC) member states, want a peaceful solution'.[41] The Iraqi regime saw some signs that its strategy was successful, as noted in a news item on INA's homepage, 'In 1991 Iraq was attacked and nobody commented on that battle. But at the present, there are protests in Germany, the United States, Britain and other states.'[42]

The struggle over credibility: a draw

Bush succeeded in the sense that the US Congress, the American public and a number of allied governments supported his decision to go to war against Iraq. But did he succeed in the sense of fashioning a credible policy? When the Bush administration associated a 'private' terrorist network like al-Qaeda with a UN member state, an issue which had certainly been on the agenda for more than ten years but for completely different reasons, the weakness of the US argument became manifest. One of the most important grounds for going to war presented by the Administration was that Saddam's regime might provide al-Qaeda with weapons of mass destruction, but the claims about links between Saddam and al-Qaeda were tenuous. The US administration's officials continued to make misleading and fallacious allegations on the presence of WMD in Iraq without offering any hard evidence of their claims. A serious flaw in the US reasoning on the alleged Iraqi possession of WMD was the unwillingness to take important facts into consideration: instead, the US leadership lapsed into rhetoric. Both the legitimacy of acting outside the UN and American credibility were seriously questioned.[43]

Saddam stressed that Iraq fulfilled its commitments as prescribed by the UN Security Council resolutions. The inspection teams of the United Nations Special Committee (UNSCOM) and the International Atomic Energy Agency (IAEA), which worked in Iraq from 1991 to 1998, failed to prove the US allegations on the presence of prohibited materials or activities although they conducted 13,648 inspection tours all over Iraq.

Saddam's efforts to bring Iraq back into the international community and at the same time ward off the threat of an American invasion without undermining his continued rule proved to be a difficult balancing act.[44] The great difficulty lay in trying to direct such a process, particularly in view of the international community's long-standing lack of confidence in Saddam.

The struggle over the decision-making process

Attempts to influence world opinion

All television in the Arab world was owned and controlled by governments until Qatar permitted an independent TV station, al-Jazeera, to broadcast.[45] Its uncensored pictures of Osama bin Laden addressing Tony Blair made a strong political impact after 11 September 2001, and bin Laden's ability to gain sympathy in the Arab world increased his influence. One can imagine that Iraq would have been more likely to have been met with understanding for its invasion of Kuwait if CNN had chosen to describe it from the viewpoint of the Iraqi regime.[46] However, access to soft power enabled the US, not Iraq, to define the political situation.

A principal element of the Iraqi attempt to direct world opinion, especially that of the US and Great Britain, was to invite congressmen and members of parliament to visit the country. During the months before the outbreak of the war, several Western politicians and other moulders of public opinion visited Iraq. The idea was that on returning home they would influence domestic opinion and the political decision-making process. As a matter of course, the UN system was also included in this endeavour. As early as August 2002, *Iraqi Daily* reported:

> Meanwhile, former US attorney Ramsey Clark urged the United Nations to act to prevent an assault on Iraq, saying that a military

attack on Baghdad could breed more violence. Earlier, Clark said that a strike against Iraq would be a massive crime against all international law. 'The United Nations must act to prevent an attack by the United States against Iraq,' Clark told a news conference in Baghdad. 'If the UN is unable to restrain the US it should at least express publicly opposition to any attack,' he said. Clark has been a vocal opponent of US policy on Iraq and the UN sanctions imposed on Iraq. He arrived in Baghdad earlier this week. 'My message to President Bush is: we have absolutely no right to attack the people of Iraq . . . You shouldn't and must not do it,' Clark said. 'We are here to urge the people of the world to stand up and say we don't want a superpower beating up on a small nation.'[47]

Opening Pandora's box

The Iraqi leadership had long held the view that American public opinion would not tolerate a large number of killed or wounded US soldiers. The spectacular media display of 18 killed American soldiers in Mogadishu in 1993 and the suicide bombing of the US military quarters in Beirut in 1983 both resulted in a pull-out of American troops. Iraqi leaders were therefore convinced that Iraq, despite its inferiority, stood a chance of holding its ground against the US. Giving the media relatively free scope could play into the hands of the Iraqi regime. During Operation Iraqi Freedom, there was a free press and TV in the area. Al-Jazeera and about 20 other stations operated freely and constituted strong competitors of the CNN for transmitting news, to the Arab audience in particular.[48]

Before the war, several analysts predicted that the forces of the US-led coalition would have to fight mainly in cities under intensive media coverage. If the Iraqis concentrated their defence in built-up areas, they might avoid a battle reminiscent of the static defence lines that had been enveloped and defeated during the last Gulf War, and if they forced the coalition to fight in such areas, the speed of attack would decrease, since the coalition forces would have to take the civilian population and the infrastructure into account.[49] Moreover, urban warfare is almost exclusively to the advantage of the defender. Both *Babil online* and INA carried articles on the subject. One appeared on INA's web site on 6 March 2003.

The head of Iraq's delegation to the extraordinary summit of the Organization of Islamic Conference, Izzat Ibrahim, has said in his speech that Iraqi people, army and leadership will fight to defend their country. He added that the Iraqi army of 7 million now is completely trained and is deployed all over the country. He stressed in his speech that Iraq will be tough for the invaders, that the land of

Iraq be their cemetery and that the Iraqi people will teach them a lesson never to be forgotten.[50]

Because the US had resolved to overthrow the regime, the safety of Saddam and his closest aides became a more urgent matter for the Iraqi side. One important stratagem to protect them was to have them move around between palaces and underground command centres.[51] This was done even in normal circumstances before the war, but the practice was intensified when the war started. The beginning of the war was therefore a staggering blow to Saddam, because it involved precision bombing of the building where he reportedly resided. An already paranoid Saddam was naturally alarmed when he realized that someone close to him had probably betrayed him: the event prompted increased control. At the same time, the regime hastened to counteract its effect on Iraqi morale. Three hours after the bombs had been dropped, Saddam appeared live on Iraqi TV, dressed in a green uniform. Later in the day, Iraq's information minister appeared, as he would do during the remainder of the war.[52]

The Iraqi information minister appears

The Iraqi Information Ministry made a concerted effort to establish a system for handling contacts with the media. The Iraqi information minister and the head of al-Jazeera held several preparatory meetings to discuss the role the media were to play in a coming war. As soon as the bombings began the media would show killed and wounded civilians. Pictures of five American prisoners of war, originating from an al-Jazeera broadcast, circulated widely in world media during a couple of days. The purpose was of course to influence public opinion to stop the war before the fall of the regime. Several days later, Iraqi state television also broadcast a feature about two Iraqi women who had carried out a suicide attack against American soldiers. The message was that Iraqis were ready to fight the coalition even if it meant suicide attacks.[53] The most tangible effect of the suicide attack in Najaf was that the coalition soldiers became more tense and nervous in encounters with civilians.

Meanwhile, a continuous information operation to confuse the Iraqi leadership was in place. As Air Marshal Brian Burrige put it: 'we had to make the Iraqi leadership believe they were losing, if possible faster than they actually did'.[54] Iraq's information minister had a difficult task: when he appeared in front of the assembled international press and asserted that the coalition forces still had a long way to go before reaching Baghdad, he was probably presenting the situation corresponding to the information he had.[55]

The struggle over the decision process: advantage the United States

Seized by momentary euphoria, Saddam told *All Dailies* in an interview published on 13 February 2003 that 'the US has not started the actual war, yet they have lost the battle of media and politics against Iraq'.[56] The reality was different. Despite all efforts to influence world opinion, Iraq failed to obtain sufficient support, in part because the international community had lost confidence in Saddam but mainly because the regime could not withstand the US media superiority. One fruitful innovation used by the coalition forces was the so-called embedded journalists who accompanied the front line units. Their reports undermined Saddam's strategy of attempting to create international opinion against the coalition by spreading accounts to the effect that coalition soldiers were deliberately shooting at civilian targets and killing innocent civilians.[57] Apart from the enormous difference in firepower between the warring parties, information, or rather Iraq's lack of it, decided the outcome of the war as the US military directed the information, first through the journalists travelling with the units and later through its press conferences.

Conclusion

Having suppressed internal threats constantly throughout the 1990s, the Iraqi leadership was less concerned about domestic opposition and turned to developing a political strategy to meet the increasing threat of military intervention. This strategy comprised a spectrum of measures more varied than implied by the thesis put forward in the introduction to the chapter. It can be summed up as follows.

The Iraqi political strategy consisted of three elements. The first was an offensive diplomacy aimed at driving a wedge between the US and its allies, an approach practised during the last Gulf War. Iraq went to considerable lengths to question the legitimacy of American behaviour. At the same time, Iraq worked to tie the Arab countries together by negotiating trade agreements and by emphasizing a religious and cultural community, pan-Arabism. The short-term purpose was to deny the US access to bases in the area, a vital necessity if American forces were to overthrow the Saddam regime. The more long-term goal was to put the Iraqi economy in order.

The second element was a campaign to undermine the credibility of US arguments and behaviour. The underlying motives of the US for initiating a war against Iraq were deeply flawed. Iraq also asserted that the results of the inspectors' visits prove the credibility of Iraq and the lies of both Washington and London.

The third element of Iraq's political strategy was an effort to foster international opposition against starting an attack on Iraq or, if it was launched, against pursuing it. Emphasis was given to an attempt to influence the decision-making process of the UN system, but Iraq also attempted to induce American public opinion to act in Iraq's favour. Invoking the prospect of large casualties for the coalition, the Saddam regime characterized an attack as the opening of a Pandora's box. The regime also advanced the argument that a war would create more terrorists, since an attack on Iraq would be considered an attack on Islam as a whole. To mobilize the sympathy of other actors such as the peace movement and humanitarian aid organizations, the regime cited the large number of innocent civilians affected by an invasion.

In conclusion, one could say that great powers like the US have an advantage in the matter of soft power, yet in spite of this, their governments have some difficulty in handling the matter. According to Nye, soft power is becoming more significant vis-à-vis compelling hard power, because credibility is now one of the most important power bases of governments and organizations. Power in the coming decades will probably be a mixture of hard and soft ingredients.

Notes

1 M. L. Sifry and C. Cerf, *The Iraq War Reader: History, Documents, Opinions*, New York: Touchstone, 2003, pp. 316–317.
2 Ibid., p. 281.
3 S. Beck and M. Downing (eds), *BBC News: The Battle for Iraq*, London: BBC Press Ltd, 2003, p. 109.
4 T. Dodge, 'Cake Walk, Coup or Urban Warfare: The Battle for Iraq', in T. Dodge and S. Simon (eds), *Iraq at the Crossroads: State and Society in the Shadow of Regime Change*, Adelphi Paper no. 354, Oxford: Oxford University Press, 2002, p. 64.
5 C. Tripp, *A History of Iraq*, 2nd edn, Cambridge: Cambridge University Press, 2002, p. 290.
6 A selection of Iraqi press articles translated to English.
7 J. S. Nye and R. O. Keohane, *Power and Interdependence*, 3rd edn, New York: Longman, 2001, pp. 220–223.
8 B. W. Jentleson, *American Foreign Policy: The Dynamics of Choice in the 21st Century*, New York: W. W. Norton, 2000, p. 403.
9 Nye and Keohane, op. cit., pp. 223–246.
10 J. S. Nye, *The Paradox of American Power: Why the World's Only Superpower Can't Go It Alone*, New York: Oxford University Press, 2002, p. 69.
11 K. M. Pollack, *The Threatening Storm: The United States and Iraq, the Crisis, the Strategy, and the Prospects after Saddam*, New York: Random House, 2002, pp. 111–147.
12 Ibid., p. 112.
13 Ibid., pp. 114–123.
14 T. Dodge, op. cit., pp. 59–61.
15 S. Beck and M. Downing, op. cit., p. 121.
16 K. M. Pollack, op. cit., p. 124.
17 C. Tripp, op. cit., p. 267.
18 D. Hiro, *Iraq: A Report from the Inside*, London: Granta Books, 2003, p. 136.

19 C. Tripp, op. cit., p. 282.
20 C. Coughlin, *Saddam: The Secret Life*, London: Pan Macmillan, 2003, p. 290.
21 D. Hiro, op. cit., p. 185.
22 Headlines Today, 2002–2003. *From the Office of the Humanitarian Coordinator for Iraq*. Iraqi press summaries 1 August 2002–17 March 2003. *All Dailies*, 20 February 2003.
23 J. S. Yaphe, 'America's War on Iraq: Myths and Opportunities', in T. Dodge and S. Simon (eds) *Iraq at the Crossroads*, pp. 23–44.
24 D. Hiro, op. cit., p. 289.
25 Ibid., p. 212.
26 Headlines Today, 1 March 2003.
27 C. Tripp, op. cit., p. 262.
28 Headlines Today, 7 September 2002.
29 J. S. Yaphe, op. cit., p. 28.
30 Headlines Today, 8 September 2002.
31 Ibid. 24 February 2003
32 J. S. Yaphe, op. cit., p. 28.
33 J. S. Nye, 'U.S. Power and Strategy', *Foreign Affairs*, 82, 4 (2003), pp. 60–73.
34 T. Dodge and S. Simon, op. cit., p. 15.
35 Headlines Today, 3 September 2002.
36 Ibid., 1 August 2002.
37 Ibid., 9 February 2003.
38 W. K. Clark, *Winning Modern Wars: Iraq, Terrorism, and the American Empire*, New York: Public Affairs, 2003, p. 147.
39 D. Hiro, op. cit., p. 221.
40 Headlines Today, 3 September 2002.
41 Ibid., 9 February 2003.
42 Ibid., 23 February 2003.
43 D. Hiro, op. cit., p. 213.
44 C. Tripp, op. cit., p. 290.
45 B. Katovsky and T. Carlson, *Embedded: The Media at War in Iraq, an Oral History*, Stonington, Guildford, CN: The Lyons Press, 2003, pp. 179–184.
46 J. S. Nye, op. cit., pp. 66–70.
47 Headlines Today, 31 August 2002.
48 D. Hiro, op. cit., p. 195.
49 D. Ochmanek, 'A Possible US-led Campaign Against Iraq: Key Factors and an Assessment', in T. Dodge and S. Simon, op. cit., p. 48.
50 Headlines Today, 6 March 2003.
51 T. Dodge, op. cit., p. 71.
52 S. Beck and M. Downing, op. cit., p. 125.
53 R. Ramesh (ed.) *The War We Could Not Stop: The Real Story of the Battle for Iraq*, London: Faber and Faber, 2003, p. 142.
54 S. Beck and M. Downing, op. cit., p. 108.
55 In early April, the coalition eavesdropped the communication between several senior officers. The conversations revealed that Saddam's younger son Qusay still led the Iraqi resistance. However, it turned out that the commanders were so frightened of Qusay that they fabricated situation reports indicating that the enemy was beaten back and had suffered heavy losses. See *Daily Telegraph* (2003), p. 15.
56 Headlines Today, 13 February 2003.
57 J. S. Nye, 'U.S. Power and Strategy', p. 67.

References

Beck, S. and Downing, M. (ed.) *BBC News: The Battle for Iraq*. London: BBC Press Ltd, 2003.

Clark, W. K. *Winning Modern Wars: Iraq, Terrorism, and the American Empire.* New York: Public Affairs, 2003.

Coughlin, C. *Saddam: The Secret Life*. London: Pan Macmillian, 2003.

Dodge, T. 'Cake Walk, Coup or Urban Warfare: the Battle for Iraq' in T. Dodge and S. Simon (eds) *Iraq at the Crossroads: State and society in the shadow of regime change*, Adelphi Paper no. 354. Oxford: Oxford University Press 2002, pp. 59–76.

Dodge, T. and Simon, S. 'Introduction' in T. Dodge and S. Simon (eds) *Iraq at the Crossroads: State and Society in the Shadow of Regime Change*, Adelphi Paper no. 354. Oxford: Oxford University Press, 2002, pp. 8–20.

Headlines Today, 2002–2003. *From the Office of the Humanitarian Coordinator for Iraq*. Iraqi press summaries between 1 August 2002–17 March 2003.

Hiro, D. *Iraq: a Report From the Inside*. London: Granta Books, 2003.

Jentleson, B. W. *American Foreign Policy: the Dynamics of Choice in the 21st Century*. New York: W. W. Norton, 2000.

Katovsky, B. and Carlson, T. *Embedded: The Media at War in Iraq, An Oral History*. Guildford, CN: The Lyons Press, 2003.

Nye J. S. *The Paradox of American Power, Why the World's Only Superpower Can't Go It Alone*. New York: Oxford University Press, 2002.

—— 'U.S. Power and Strategy', *Foreign Affairs*, 82, 4 (2003), 60–73.

Nye, J. S. and Keohane, R. O. *Power and Interdependence*, 3rd edn. New York: Longman, 2001.

Ochmanek, D. 'A Possible US-Led Campaign Against Iraq: Key Factors and an Assessment', in T. Dodge and S. Simon (eds) *Iraq at the Crossroads: State and Society in the Shadow of Regime Change*, Adelphi Paper no. 354. Oxford: Oxford University Press 2002, pp. 45–58.

Pollack, K. M. *The Threatening Storm: The United States and Iraq, the Crisis, the Strategy, and the Prospects after Saddam*. New York: Random House, 2002.

Ramesh, R. (ed.) *The War We Could Not Stop: The Real Story of the Battle for Iraq*. London: Faber and Faber, 2003.

Sifry, M. L. and Cerf, C. *The Iraq War Reader: History, Documents, Opinions*. New York: Touchstone, 2003.

The Daily Telegraph, *War On Saddam*, London: Robinson, 2003.

Tripp, C. *A History of Iraq*, 2nd edn. Cambridge: Cambridge University Press, 2002.

Yaphe, J. S. 'America's War on Iraq: Myths and Opportunities' in T. Dodge and S. Simon (eds) *Iraq at the Crossroads*, Adelphi Paper no. 354. Oxford: Oxford University Press, 2002. pp. 23–44.

6

SWEDEN, THE WESTERN WORLD AND THE WAR THAT SAW THE BIRTH OF IRAQ

Implications of the events in 1914–1921 for the present conflict

Lars Ericson

Introduction

When the war in Iraq broke out in the spring of 2003, with British soldiers participating alongside the US troops, many Iraqis as well as British probably felt as if they were watching an old film, although the actors, their equipment and the motives for their actions were new. Basically, they had seen it before.

Some 85 years earlier, British soldiers were also fighting their opponents in Kirkuk, Baghdad and above all Basra. The conflict in those days was at least as entangled in broader international relations as was that of 2003. The general course of the invasion and occupation of Iraq in 2003 was strikingly reminiscent of the events in 1914–1921. But the similarities do not end there. In both cases, the occupiers had a political and cultural mission and had difficulties in winning the local population over to their ideas. The Western world, mainly represented by British military units, contributed to create the new nation of Iraq and to drawing its borders on the map. It also tried to instill a kind of Iraqi national consciousness. In the new Iraq War the assumptions and motives of the actors were very different, but history was very much alive for the actors involved.

Iraq: creation of the state

It is certainly not only in the Arab–Israeli conflict that history, and the memory of conflicts in the past, plays a central and often very destructive role. As an example, it may be enough to mention the fact that Saddam Hussein very often appeared in public on a white horse trying to impersonate

Salah ad Din. This Kurdish (sic!) Emir of Egypt, more widely known as Saladin, is the great hero of the Muslims, who defeated the army of the Christian crusaders at Hattin in 1187 and recaptured Jerusalem from the Christians. From this perspective the living memory of what happened in the 1910s is a short one, and it is no coincidence that during the spring of 2003 British units had the main responsibility for Basra, a city where British military units carried out substantial operations during the war that created Iraq.

Both before and during the operations explicit historical links were made by the different actors. In today's situation, with Western, Christian units occupying Iraq, these historical experiences and antagonisms are used in different ways.

In the light of this there are very good reasons to look in the historical mirror at the events that occurred in Iraq 85 years ago. These events not only resulted in the creation of the modern state of Iraq, but were also the cause of much of the animosity threatening stability in Iraq today: between Shia and Sunni Muslims, between Arabs, Persians, Kurds, Armenians and Turkmens, as well as between Iraqis and Westerners.

This chapter focuses on Iraq, but it will also cover Syria and Lebanon. I will discuss the region using the present state names, although I am well aware that this is somewhat incorrect for the period before the creation of these states, i.e. the period around 1920.

The Ottoman empire falls apart stage by stage

Turkey, or the Ottoman empire, had, ever since it conquered Christian Constantinople in 1453 and changed it into the main Muslim stronghold on the edge of Europe, been regarded as a major and deadly threat by the Christian states of Europe. The Turkish armies were not stopped until they reached the gates of Vienna in 1683. The border had been established in the north-western Balkans, alongside the southern border of the Habsburg Empire. Today's borders between Croatia and Bosnia-Hercegovina on the one hand, and Serbia on the other, reflect this borderline between the Austrian Habsburg Empire and Turkey. Sharp animosity towards the Turks did not prevent European states from enlisting Turkish assistance in the European political game, and France and Sweden in particular tried to use Turkey as an ally against their main adversaries, Austria and Russia.

During the nineteenth century old-fashioned, inefficient and corrupt Turkey began to be regarded more and more as 'the sick man of Europe'. The Ottoman empire was crumbling. In 1875 the Muslims in Bosnia-Hercegovina started a rebellion against what they saw as a heavy tax burden, and they were soon followed by the Christian Bulgarians. Constantinople regained control over these areas and also managed to defeat the autonomous state of Serbia, which had taken the opportunity to declare war on

Turkey. In 1877, however, Russia intervened. The Turks were defeated several times and forced to sue for peace, although Constantinople was supported by Great Britain, which feared that Russia would gain too much influence in the Balkans. The result of the war was that Serbia, Montenegro and Romania became independent, while Bulgaria still had a certain dependence on Turkey. Areas of eastern Anatolia were annexed into the Tsarist empire. At the same time Austria-Hungary took over the administration of Bosnia-Hercegovina (formally still a part of the Ottoman empire) and the British took control over Cyprus.

How were these events connected to Iraq? When the new borders were drawn on the maps at a conference in Berlin in 1878, the European powers began to share Turkey between themselves. Only one country, Germany, did not participate in this race to hive off parts from the Turkish empire. This experience led to Constantinople regarding Germany as its only friend, something that was to have decisive importance for Turkey's allegiance when the First World War broke out in 1914. In 1903 a German consortium was granted the task of extending the Berlin–Constantinople railway line through Anatolia and Iraq down to Baghdad and finally to the harbour in Basra, but when war broke out in 1914, the railway only ran as far as the Taurus mountains.

In Constantinople attempts to reform the political system were initiated by the grand vizier Midhat Pasha, who had been governor of Iraq before he rose to the highest political level in the Ottoman empire. This, however, was not enough, and more reformist groups, commonly referred to as 'Young Turks', began to form opposition groups to which Arab nationalist forces within the Empire were linked. In Syria and Lebanon a pan-Arab movement dominated the opposition arena, while in Egypt it was Islam that fuelled the opposition movement.

It is notable that Islamic-inspired Arab nationalism was primarily directed against Christian groups; relations with the Jewish minority can be described as relatively free of tension.[1] As early as the 1840s animosity between Christian Maronites and Muslims had begun to escalate in Lebanon, and was exacerbated by European diplomats and Ottoman civil servants. Open fighting broke out and in 1860 thousands of Maronites were killed in battle or died of starvation, while about 100,000 fled their homes. In Damascus between 5,000 and 10,000 Christians were massacred and anti-Christian riots spread to, among other places, Aleppo and Nablus.

Ottoman Sultan Abdülhamid was dethroned by reformist Young Turk officers in 1908–09. The reform policy of the new regime included attempts to make the different parts of the Empire more Turkish. The Armenians were to suffer most from this. Their efforts to achieve some kind of independence had resulted in pogroms and the murder of some 100,000 Armenians as early as 1897. This was the first genocide of the modern world, and it was to be followed in 1915 by much worse atrocities when up to two million Armenians were murdered by Turkish troops and civilian mobs or just died of starvation. As a result of the Turkification policy, even the Arabs eventually became alienated from their former allies, the Young Turks. In 1911 the organization al-Fatat ('the Young Arabs') was formed, with the explicit goal to create an Arab state including Iraq, Syria, Lebanon and Palestine.[2]

Not even the Young Turk government managed to defend the borders of the Empire. In 1911–12 Italian troops conquered Libya, Rhodes and the Dodecanese, while an alliance of Balkan states in the first Balkan war of 1912 almost threw Turkey out of the Balkan peninsula and the European continent.[3] After these experiences it was hardly surprising that after the outbreak of the First World War in 1914 Turkey joined forces with Germany, which it regarded as its only friend in international politics. By taking this step, however, Turkey also made itself and its positions in the Middle East legitimate targets for allied military operations.

During the decades before 1914 international competition for the region that was to become Iraq steadily grew. A number of reports talked about promising prospects of large oil findings in the region which, of course, was tempting for many of the great powers. From 1912 onwards the Turkish Petroleum Company, owned by German, Dutch (Shell) and Turkish interests, was active in Iraq. The Turkish part of the company was, ironically enough, owned by the Turkish National Bank, a British-controlled bank that had been created to promote British interests in Turkey. Very soon after the race for Iraqi oil began, powerful Armenian business interests bought up parts of Turkish Petroleum. The Turkish Petroleum Company was regarded in London as the key opponent of British interests in the region.

Tales from the Babylonian kingdom several thousand years earlier feature descriptions of burning oil wells in the ground, and geological reports in the first years of the twentieth century gave good hopes of large findings of oil. It was not until 15 October 1917, however, that the first oil well was discovered during drilling close to Kirkuk. The hunt and struggle for the Iraqi oil had begun.[4]

The First World War in the Middle East[5]

Western involvement in the Arab parts of the Ottoman empire had started around 1840, but with the outbreak of the First World War unprecented opportunities for London and Paris were opened up.

After a number of declarations of war during the 'black week' in late July/ early August 1914 the First World War broke out. Turkey stood outside the formal alliance systems but had its close connection with Germany, and on 15 November 1914 Turkey joined the central powers, Germany and Austria-Hungary, with a formal declaration of war against the entente cordiale

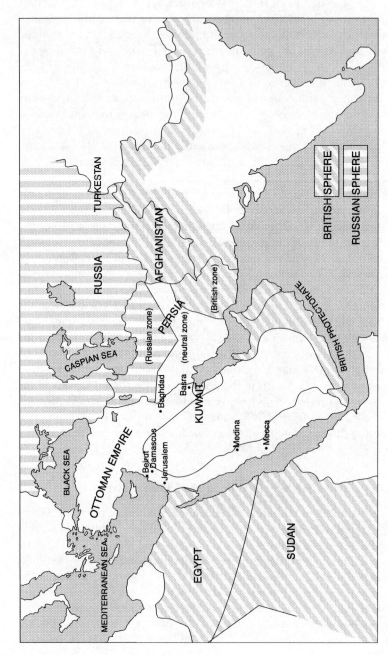

Figure 6.1 The Middle East 1914.

powers (Great Britain, France and Russia). Consequently, four new theatres of war were established: the Dardanelles (against the two Western powers), the Caucasus (against Russia) and Iraq and Egypt (against Great Britain).

The Turks immediately launched an offensive in the Caucasus, but this first operation ended in a military disaster. At the same time Great Britain annexed Cyprus which, although still formally Turkish, had been under British military control since 1878. In Egypt, British and French interests had steadily grown stronger since the later part of the nineteenth century, despite the fact that this area too formally belonged to Turkey. An Arab nationalist rebellion against 'the rule of the strangers' was suppressed by British troops in 1882. After these events the British forces stayed in Egypt and the administration of the country was gradually taken over by the British. On 18 December 1914, one month after the Turkish declaration of war, it was announced that Egypt had been transformed into a British protectorate. The following day the last ties between Egypt and Constantinople were broken when the Turkish sultan's governor of Egypt, the Khediv Abbas Hilmi, was declared removed from office.

The main front for the Turks was of course the Dardanelles, where the Western powers tried to secure free passage for their ships to the Black Sea and their hard-pressed Russian ally. The struggle culminated with the large British and French force landing on the Gallipoli peninsula in 1915. This resulted in terrible casualties for these units, and after several months of unsuccessful attacks on the Turkish positions the Allied forces withdrew from the Dardanelles.

Meanwhile, in October 1915, an Anglo-French 'Army of the Orient' landed in Salonika, with the main task of fighting against Bulgaria, which had joined the war on the German and Turkish side. The following year the remains of the Serbian army had to evacuate to Corfu in order to escape severe pressure from the overwhelming force of the central powers. After reorganization, Serbian troops were sent to the front in Greece. The battles in the Balkans and at Gallipoli required the bulk of Turkey's increasingly strained military resources, and made it possible for Russian forces to advance on the Caucasian front: at the beginning of 1916 they conquered Erzerum from the Turks.

Directly after the outbreak of the war and in 1916, in an attempt to ease the severe pressure on the central areas of their empire, the Turks launched offensives from their bases in Palestine against British positions in Egypt, from where important sea lines of communications were established by the British to Gallipoli and Greece. The offensives were, however, repelled by the British across the Suez Canal. After the Turkish setback the initiative passed more and more to the British side.

At this juncture, the British command in Egypt decided to try to split the Turkish empire. In 1917 London in the so-called Balfour Declaration promised a national home for the Jews in Palestine in order to win their support in the struggle against Turkey. At the same time, similar promises were given to Arab nationalists.

At the outbreak of the war, the Englishman T. E. Lawrence was fully occupied with archeological excavations in Syria. Possessing deep knowledge of the Arab world, he was soon used by the British army as an adviser to the Bedouin leader Faysal, who had begun a rebellion against the Turkish rule in the deserts of the Arab peninsula. In June 1916 Faysal's father, the Emir of Mecca Hussein Ibn Ali, had raised the flag of rebellion against the Turks and was recognized as King of Hidjaz, an area along the west coast of the present Saudi Arabia. Increasingly escalated activity followed, as Faysal and his British adviser Lawrence mustered steadily larger numbers of mounted troops and attacked vulnerable Turkish positions along the railway lines on the Arabian peninsula. Lawrence soon acquired an almost mythical reputation as 'Lawrence of Arabia'.[6]

During 1916, British units began slowly but methodically to advance through the Sinai peninsula. In March and April 1917 two failed attempts to break through the Turkish defence lines along the southern borders of Palestine were made. During the first and second battles of Gaza, the defenders were able to withstand the attacks, but in June 1917 General Edmund Allenby took command of the British troops. The forces were reorganized and reinforced with Faysal's and Lawrence's camel and cavalry units. In the third battle of Gaza, from 31 October to 6 November 1917, the British won a total victory and on 11 December Allenby's forces marched into Jerusalem. The British advance then continued northwards through Palestine and at the beginning of October 1918 Allenby's forces reached their goal, Damascus.[7]

By then Turkey's will to fight was broken. On 14 October 1918 a newly formed Turkish government asked for an armistice and on 30 October an armistice agreement was signed enjoining the Turkish forces in Syria and Iraq to lay down their arms. Little more than a week later, on 11 November, Turkey's ally Germany had to give up the fight.

Turkey's losses amounted to some 300,000 killed or missing in action and 400,000 wounded during the war. The whole empire collapsed. Arab areas were literally torn from the motherland and several hopeful Arab nationalists arrived at the peace conference in Versailles in 1919. They were all to be disappointed, however. The promises of the Western powers proved to be more and more shallow as the peace negotiations dragged on. France established its own power in the newly formed states of Lebanon and Syria, while the British took control of Palestine. Arab as well as Jewish nationalists had every reason to feel deserted and cheated by their former allies. An embittered Lawrence left the Versailles conference before it ended. All Kurdish hopes for a national state were also extinguished at Versailles.

After Arab forces had taken part in the conquest of Damascus just before the end of the war, Faysal was elected King of Syria in March 1920, but he was forced by French troops to leave the city as early as July the same year. A conference in San Remo with the supreme council of the allies (British, French and Italians) decided that Syria should be a French protectorate and it was not until the collapse of France in 1940 that Syria became free, only to be occupied by the British in 1941 in order to prevent Nazi-German infiltration of the country.

The British were eager to stop all French eastward and southward expansion in the Middle East, and at the same time they tried to avoid any open confrontation with their former ally from the First World War. Secretary of State for the Colonies (and later Prime Minister) Winston Churchill developed considerable diplomatic skill and dexterity in these matters during 1921.[8]

Dethroned by the French, Faysal received a warm welcome when he arrived in Amman. This worried the British and Churchill, who like the French did not want to see a larger connected state under Arab control, began to act. The British quickly created a new state in the southern parts of Syria, called Transjordan (i.e. the area on the other, eastern side of the river Jordan, today's Jordan). The throne of this new state, which had Amman as its capital, was offered to Abdullah, a second son of King Hussein in Hidjaz. The new king was made legitimate by his kinship to the family that guarded the holy cities of Mecca and Medina and also claimed a direct descent from the Prophet himself.

In 1922 the newly established League of Nations gave the British a mandate to rule over Palestine (the land west of the river Jordan and north of Sinai). Before the end of the war, this area had formed what the Turks called Southern Syria. Abdullah's Transjordan achieved independence in 1923, although it kept close connections to Britain. The armed forces of the Jordanian king, the so called Arab Legion, was organized and trained by British officers. During Israel's war of birth in 1947–48 the Legion was the most efficient Arab military force and became the basis for today's Jordanian armed forces.[9]

At about the same time, in 1922, Egypt too became a sovereign kingdom, although British influence remained considerable until the Suez War in 1956. On the Arabian peninsula, where the nation-building process had started with Hussein's declaration of independence and Faysal's rebellion against the Turks, new fighting broke out in 1924 between forces loyal to King Hussein and the Emir Abd-el-Azez of Nejd. Hussein prevailed and united both kingdoms in what in 1932 came to be known as the kingdom of Saudi Arabia. An attempt in 1934 to incorporate Yemen with the Saudi kingdom failed, however.

What, then, happened to Faysal, the man who fought the Turks with the support of Lawrence of Arabia, only to be driven away from Damascus by the French and prevented by the British from placing himself on the throne in Amman? In this game of great power politics, where people, geographical areas and state formations were moved like chess pieces, Faysal was moved eastwards. After Churchill had given Abdullah the throne of Transjordan, his brother, Faysal, was offered another throne in the newly created Iraq. Faysal accepted the offer – hence kings from the Hashemite family had been placed on the thrones both in Amman and Baghdad. Faysal came to a country where British troops had fought Turkish and German forces as well as Arab warriors for several years, and these fights are described in the following sections of this chapter.

The fight for the future Iraq

Even if the name 'Iraq' is old, it was never used as a label for the Turkish area that today forms the state known as Iraq. The area was divided into provinces or subordinated territories: Baghdad, Basra, Mosul, Kirkuk and, sometimes, also Sulaimanijja. The northern part of Iraq was at times ruled by the governor of Diyarbakir, today a centre in the Kurdish-dominated south-eastern part of Turkey. The fact that the governor of Baghdad was at times given control over most parts of what was to become Iraq was mainly for practical reasons. It was economically wise to link Baghdad and Basra to each other, at the same time achieving a united administration that made surveillance of the areas bordering Persia (Iran) somewhat easier.The provinces in the area lacked a common geographical identiy. In European terminology the word 'Mesopotamia' was used, but it actually referred to the ancient cultural districts between the rivers Tigris and the Euphrates. The British, for their part, sometimes used the word 'Turkish Arabia', which emphasize that they did not see any fundamental difference between the areas inhabited by Arabs.

Geographically the area of Iraq consisted of the mountains in the north and the east and the flat plains in the west and south. The Zagros mountains formed a natural barrier against Persia, although border skirmishes and disputes sometimes occurred. Persian troops occupied Basra in 1775–79, but in 1847 a border treaty between the Ottoman empire and Persia was signed in Erzerum.

Only in Baghdad and Kirkuk were there substantial Turkish-speaking ethnic groups. Kurds dominated the mountainous areas in the north and Arabs the plains in the south. Iraq was the only area within the Ottoman empire where Shia Muslims dominated over the Sunni, although the latter were, and still are, the vast majority in the Muslim world. The Shi'ites were particularly dominant in the area south of Baghdad, with their holy cities of Karbala and Najaf. In Baghdad itself as early as 1800 a sharp border was created between the Sunni-dominated right bank of the Tigris and the left bank where the Shiites dominated. Unlike neighbouring Syria, Iraq had a relatively small non-Muslim minority, but Jews played an important role in business and administration, while Armenian Christians held a strong position in the business life of Mosul.

A political struggle between, on the one hand, Ottoman civil servants and, on the other, local tribal chiefs, sheikhs and religious leaders lasted throughout the nineteenth century. Constantinople gave priority to the defence of the easten border facing Iran, while it sometimes loosened its internal grip. Reforms within defence and bureaucracy changed the situation during the nineteenth century, however. Conscription was introduced in the Mosul province in 1826 and in southern Iraq in 1870, which led to the Turkish 6th army in Iraq having more locally recruited if one considers the recruitment of NCOs and soldiers, while the officer corps became more and more Turkish. The 6th army was, however, not 'Arabized' as quickly as, for instance, the 5th army in Syria. Iraqis also tended to dominate among the Arab officers in the Ottoman empire.[10]

With Persia so close, relations with this neighbour were of course always of the utmost importance. The eastern border of Iraq was also the eastern border of both the Arab world and the Ottoman empire. During the nineteenth century Russia expanded south-eastwards in what was to become its central Asian provinces, while Great Britain from its positions in India advanced towards the west and the north. British incursions into Afghanistan failed, but Persia tended to show the same symptoms of weakness as the Ottoman empire. Internal strife in Persia (which changed its name to Iran as recently as 1935) opened up possibilities for growing Russian and British influence. German businessmen and diplomats also gained influence in Persia between 1907 and the outbreak of war in 1914.[11]

When the disorder in Persia increased, Great Britain and Russia argued for neutral intervention. The result was that from 1911 to 1915 Swedish officers came to serve in Persia, mainly to organize and train a Persian gendarmerie. A total of 36 Swedish officers trained over 7,000 Persian gendarmes and took part in combat against guerrilla units as well as gangs of bandits. Four Swedes were killed and several were wounded during this mission.[12] After 1915 both the British and the Russians tried to prevent Persian alignment with Germany, and this resulted in fighting with Turkish forces and irregular Persian units along the border region between Persia and Iraq.[13]

At the outbreak of the war in 1914 Great Britain declared Kuwait to be independent under British protection – the city had been founded in the eighteenth century as an important trading post on the route between Turkey and India. With the declaration British forces acquired a base for further operations northwards, into Iraq.[14]

In Kuwait, as well as in the region around Basra and further towards the east and the Persian border, popular sentiment was substantially pro-British. This could probably be explained by the need for a functioning trade with

British India. It is generally assumed that at the time of the First World War popular sentiment in the main part of Iraq was more or less pro-Ottoman. Among the Shi'ite marsh Arabs in the south some unrest directed against Constantinople had occurred, but this did not mean that the Shi'ites in the area were ready to subject themselves to another foreign power.

In November 1914, directly after the Turkish declaration of war, Indian troops landed at Shatt-el-Arab, and the British relatively easily took positions on the Faw peninsula and in the city of Basra. But the British refused to promise local independence, and hence friendly neutrality among the Arab population soon changed to hostility. A pattern developed where tribal warriors at twilight raised ritual war cries, beat their war drums and performed war dances before they went out to fire against the British troops. Responding with grenade fire, the British usually made the warriors withdraw. British supply depots were particularly exposed to attacks in which tribal warriors sneaked under the barbed wire and left with a variety of goods, including horses. Looting and stealing rose to dramatic levels as poverty and starvation spread in the Basra region during 1915 and 1916.

At the outbreak of the war the Turks in Iraq had at their disposal some 10,000 regular soldiers, mainly in the 38th infantry division, four border guard battalions, six gendarmerie battalions, and some 20,000 tribal warriors. Minor naval units comprising the gunboat *Marmaris*, six armed motor boats and six river boats were also in place.

From the start of the campaign, the British attached importance to the oil wells, especially those on the Persian side of the border, in Arabistan, where an independent sheikh allied himself with Britain. At the beginning of 1915 a holy war, Jihad, was declared against the British. Large troop formations in the form of six battalions of Iraqi soldiers, two cavalry regiments and about 5,000 tribal warriors were sent against the British positions. Soon it became evident that Britain's local allies in Arabistan neither could nor would defend the pipelines from attacks, so British and Indian troops had to be sent there in extreme haste to secure the oil supplies. The British suffered large casualties before the Ottoman offensive could be thrown back.

The next large Ottoman offensive was launched from 11–13 April 1915, directly against the British troops in Basra. Some 6,000 men, mainly Iraqi infantry, had been assembled under the command of Lieutenant-Colonel Sulayman Askari and were reinforced by 12,000 irregular Arab and Kurdish warriors. The British defenders were pressed very hard and a squadron from the 7th Hariana Lancers was crushed by the irregular warriors. But the British managed to withstand the pressure and hold their positions. The Turks ordered a retreat and in that situation the tribal warriors turned their weapons against the regular Turkish units, some of whom were massacred; their commander, Sulayman Askari, commited suicide. Turkish attempts to rely on support from tribal warriors ended, and the British also developed mistrust towards the local population and the tribal warriors.

The British units now began to push northwards towards Baghdad and for a while had the city within their reach, but when irregulars attacked them in the rear on 13–14 July 1915 they were forced to withdraw to Nasariyah. The region formed a somewhat confusing scene of swamps and canals, populated by tribes who were as keen to attack the British as they were to fire against regular Turkish troops. The campaign began to develop into a severe problem for the British, who lacked sufficient quantities of reliable maps of the area and had no clear idea of which tribes they could rely on. In the local British command a split emerged between those who wanted to firmly put down all tendencies towards Arab nationalism and more politically-minded officers and civil servants who tried more and more desperately to gain local support for their campaign against the Turks. Moreover, the British war machine had limited use of technical assets like artillery and machine guns and quantative superiority in the confusing marsh lands.

Large forces of irregular Arab cavalry moved alongside the Turkish main force, making it possible for the Turks to outflank the advancing British troops in the battle of Ctesiphon. Turkish reinforcements surprised the British General Charles Townshend with their stubborn defence. On 22 November 1915 the British troops were forced to retreat to Kut el-Amara, some 140 kilometres southwards along the banks of Tigris. The British lost 4,600 men. At Kut el-Amara the British forces were surrounded by Turkish troops reinforced by German and Austrian units. Here for the first time in history an attempt was made to supply an encircled military force from the air, although the airlift failed to fulfil the needs of the British garrison. Meanwhile, the relief forces trying to fight their way to the surrounded troops had to halt after suffering severe casualties.

After a long siege, the surviving British troops had to surrender on 29 April 1916. Five generals, 476 officers and 13,330 NCOs and privates were taken into Turkish-German captivity. This was a disaster for the British army, and one that the Iraqi propaganda referred to with relish exactly 87 years later. Kut el-Amara had the same devastating effect on British morale in 1916 that the fall of Singapore had in 1942.[15] General Townshend had his revenge two-and-a-half years later, however. In October 1918 when Turkey started to negotiate with the allies for an armistice, Townshend was released from captivity close to Constantinople and took part in the negotiations held on the British battleship *Agamemnon*.[16]

The locally recruited police troops that the British had organized fought loyally to the bitter end in Kut el-Amara, but after the fall of the city their loyalty vanished. The remaining British troops in southern Iraq were now attacked by irregular forces including former police units, in a growing number of incidents during the rest of 1916, although major fighting had stopped in this area.

It was not until February 1917 that the British managed to start a new offensive, turning the tide. The British force in Iraq that in 1915–16 had

109

numbered at most 28,000–30,000 men was brought up to 147,000 men in early 1917. This almost immediately produced a spectacular result. On 11 March British troops conquered Baghdad. Now great efforts were made to win the support of the local population, even if Great Britain could not bring itself to make a declaration in favour of Arab independence. The new British commander-in-chief, General William Marshal, encouraged tribal warriors to attack the Turkish lines of communication, but success was limited. Attacks by the irregulars, the so-called budhoos, on British units continued. In an attempt to stop this increasing violence the British established a local police force in 1915. This *shabana* consisted mainly of Arabs but also included some Kurds; during 1916 the force exceeded 2,000 men. Its officers were former Ottoman civil servants. Other local units were led by British officers, primarily Major Eadie's Muntafiq Scouts and the Kurdish Horse organized by Major Sloane in the mountains around Khanaqin.

One main reason for the difficulties facing the allied forces in Iraq was the large German and Austrian military involvement in the Middle East. Roughly 25,000 German soldiers and 200 aeroplanes supported the Turkish war effort in the region from Sinai to Iraq. German commanders such as Colmar von der Goltz (who died in 1916) and Hans von Seeckt led the defence of Iraq with substantial success, although their own forces were limited, while Britain had to send more and more troops to Iraq. By the summer of 1918, the German and Austrian forces in Iraq, now assembled in the 6th army, had been reduced to minor transport and special units together with two flying units. A final effort was made at the beginning of October 1918 during a Turkish counterattack at Kirkuk, but after that all German military activity ended in the area. On 22 October the Turkish general staff issued an order that all German units should leave Iraq and be transported to Constantinople.

On the Ottoman side Kurds formed the army's most reliable irregular units. They fought mainly against Russian troops occupying Kurdish areas in both Iraq and Iran during 1916 and 1917. When the Russian forces were withdrawn after the revolution in Russia in 1917 they first massacred large numbers of Kurds and Azeris, which resulted in hatred among the population of the Russians and their British allies. The quest for revenge was also turned against the Christians in the region, Armenians, Assyrians and Nestorians.

The fighting continued even after the Turks had agreed to an armistice and in 1919 2,000 Assyrians helped the British to defend Mosul against attacks from combined Kurdish and Turkish forces. But British promises of support for the independence of Christian groups in north-western Iran and northern Iraq could never be realized.

The Mosul region became particularly embattled. The city of Mosul was held by Turkish troops when the armistice came into force and only British threats of continued warfare in the north could make these troops withdraw. The British had finally won the fight for Iraq, but at a cost of entirely disproportionate losses. There were around 100,000 casualties, with about a third killed.[17]

Promises were issued frequently, more in Syria than in Iraq, but during the first months after the end of the war the British perpetrated some deceits, to some extent brought about by necessity. Defeated Turkey rose in 1919 and continued to fight.

Under the leadership of General Mustafa Kemal Pasha, soon to be known as Kemal Atatürk ('the father of the Turks'), Turkish units in Anatolia refused to demobilize and instead turned their arms against the government of the Sultan in Constantinople. A peace treaty whereby Turkey gave up its territories, except Asia Minor and a small area around Constantinople, was signed in August 1920 in Sèvres. Greek forces had by then taken control of a large area around Smyrna (called Izmir after 1929) in western Asia Minor, where there was a large Greek population. The peace of 1920 was never realized: instead the fighting between Greek and Turkish units continued deep into Asia Minor, before a Turkish counter-offensive forced the Greeks back towards the Aegean sea. In September 1922 Atatürk's troops entered Smyrna at the same time as a devastating fire struck the city. These two events marked the traumatic culmination of a war which Greece lost, and hundreds of thousands of Greek civilians fled the mainland in a panic to escape the advancing Turkish troops.

The Sultan's government was thrown out of the Topkapi palace in Constantinople and replaced with a Republican Government under Atatürk, based in Ankara. This new government was able to use its military successes to force a new peace treaty in Lausanne in July 1923. Turkey regained the areas in Europe and Asia Minor which the country had been forced to hand over to Greece three years earlier and the Turkish parts of Armenia were also returned to Turkey. What the Turks actually ceded was the Arabian provinces that had been parts of the empire at the time of the outbreak of war in 1914. Atatürk did not want to cede the Mosul region in Iraq, but the League of Nations decided in 1925 that the region should belong to the new state of Iraq. Thus the border between Turkey and Iraq was settled.

A new state is born out of the flames – Iraq after 1918[18]

It was not obvious from the beginning that Great Britain would be the only Western power in the Iraqi arena. On the contrary, France demanded control over the Mosul region, which could easily be linked to the French-controlled areas in Syria. But during a meeting in London in early December 1918, the prime ministers Georges Clemenceau and David Lloyd George recognized each other's supremacy over Syria and Iraq, respectively. The

French retreat from the claims to Mosul was compensated for by French access to a share of the oil coming from the Mosul area.[19]

After the end of the war Great Britain had to keep large military units in Iraq in order to fight a rebellion that broke out in 1920: 17,000 British and 85,000 Indian soldiers fought against rebellious Iraqi forces. In addition, the Royal Air Force carried out an air campaign against the Iraqis between 1922 and 1925.[20]

The former Turkish provinces in Iraq were mandated to Great Britain in 1920. In 1921 the victorious Western powers created the new kingdom of Iraq and put Faysal on the throne. King Faysal strove to reduce the influence of London in his country and had achieved at least formal Iraqi independence before he died suddenly in 1933. In October 1932 Iraq became a member of the League of Nations and the British mandate came to an end.

However, British influence did not disappear after 1932. During the Second World War London called upon Baghdad to break off all relations with the Axis powers. When Iraq did not comply, British troops attacked and in May–June 1941 heavy fighting between British and Iraqi forces took place before British supremacy in the air decided the outcome of this short war.

In 1947 Great Britain withdrew the main part of its military units from Iraq while holding onto one or two minor air force bases. An alliance was formed between Great Britain and Iraq. The alliance led to violent riots in Baghdad, and in 1952 new riots took place. In 1958 the kingdom was overthrown in a coup d'état by officers with links to the Arab socialist Ba'ath party – one of their supporters was the young Saddam Hussein. British influence in Iraq had finally come to an end.[21]

Our man in Constantinople – the events in Iraq seen with the eyes of a Swedish diplomat

As a digression, it is interesting to note how the events in Iraq were viewed by informed observers. The Swedish military attaché in Constantinople, Captain Einar af Wirsén, sent numerous insightful reports back to Stockholm, as did Johannes Kolmodin, the First Secretary at the Swedish embassy a man with very good contacts in the circles close to Atatürk.[22] Einar af Wirsén seemed to have had very good contacts with the chief of the Turkish general staff during the war[23] and continually reported on the development on the different fronts, including that of Iraq.[24] He underlined the importance of German as well as irregular Arab troops in the operations against the British.[25]

Despite his good contacts with the Turkish supreme command the Swedish attaché had no high regard for Turkish capabilities, military or administrative. When Baghdad fell in March 1917 he noted that the event 'had caused considerable worry in the government, mainly because of internal politics'.[26] He did not believe the Turks had the ability to retake Baghdad and was obviously satisfied with the outcome of the events: 'Because of this Mesopotamia is lost for ever for Turkey – for the benefit of mankind and civilisation.'[27] But af Wirsén did not overlook the difficulties that the British encountered in Iraq after the end of the war.

> It would have been an easy task for the Entente to gain the friendship of the Arabs, but their mentality was not understood, and without a deep knowledge of the way of reasoning of the Orientals, you can't get anywhere with them. Treating the Arabs, who regard themselves as the most noble people on earth and who have a national pride that can hardly be compared with that of any other people, as minors and making this treatment is insulting, it will definitely make all the Arab tribes hostile.[28]

Concluding remarks

The British managed to throw out Iraq's Turkish rulers of 400 years, but they also contributed to forming a picture of the new state, both inside and outside Iraq. Mesopotamia, the country between the Tigris and the Euphrates, is an important part of the cradle of human civilization. In 1854 the British consul in Basra arranged excavations on behalf of the British Museum at the hill Tell al Muqayyar in southern Mesopotamia. This was the place where the biblical city of Ur was once situated, the place where Abraham was born. Immediately after the war in 1919 both British and French archeologists started new excavations to uncover Iraq's ancient history.[29] Their finds were important in the process of creating a new identity for the new Iraqi state and 'providing' it with a long history.

An important role in this process was played by Père Anastase al-Karmali, who originated from a Syrian family and had deep knowledge of Arabic literature and culture. In 1919 the British commissioned al-Karmali to write a history book that only dealt with the area of present-day Iraq. The book was written in Arabic and printed in Basra the same year. It took the reader all the way through Iraq's long history up to 1919, and it finished (hardly surprisingly) with a description of the advantages and the civilizing aspects of British occupation.[30]

Nevertheless, the British had great difficulties in creating an Iraqi national consciousness. Their difficulties were compounded by a lack of understanding of the local culture. Illuminating in this respect is probably the best known book with Iraq as a motif, Dame Agatha Christie's detective novel *Murder in Mesopotamia*, which was published in 1936. The writer was married to a British archeologist and accompanied him on excavations in Iraq. One of her key figures in the novel is sitting in the Tigris Palace Hotel in Baghdad writing home to England, describing a world far from the scenes in *A Thousand and One Nights*[31]: 'The dirt and disorder in Baghdad is totally unbelievable – and not romantic at all.'

One can say without any doubt that the British policy was successful to the extent that Iraqi national consciousness – although very mixed with Arab-nationalistic and Islamic feelings – grew very quickly among the Arab population of Iraq. At the same time, however, one can of course ask oneself if this national consciousness was perhaps directed against the foreign occupiers – Turkish or British – rather than signifying a true Iraqi affinity. In the Kurdish regions this was obviously so. Anti-Turkish feelings were, and still are, much stronger there than any feeling of affinity with Arabs, Turkmens and Assyrians within the borders of Iraq. In this we can see traces of the events in 1914–18 and the years thereafter. This also applies to the areas north of the Iraqi border settled in 1925. Today one can read formulations in official Turkish publications showing that the Mosul region is still regarded as a part of Turkey's core area.[32]

History thus plays a role for many of today's actors on the Iraqi scene, a role that is both stronger and more manifest than we often imagine today. When Iraq's new dictator Abdel Karim Qasim celebrated the second anniversary of the overthrow of the monarchy on 14 July 1960 with a massive parade in Baghdad, descriptions of Iraq's glorious history including pictures of Niniveh and Nimrod, the Tower of Babel and the Ishtar Gate, were mixed with models of modern multistorey buildings and an atomic bomb.[33] Thus far the British had been very successful in creating an Iraqi national consciousness. But this success also backfired. As a result, the events of 1914–21 still recur today in some form or other, influencing today's protagonists, their thinking and priorities, whether they like it or not.

Notes

1 M. E. Yapp, *The Making of the Modern Near East, 1792–1923*. London: Longman, 1991, pp. 133–137.
2 M. Nordberg, *Asiens historia: Från forntiden till 1914*. Stockholm: Natur och Kultur, 1971 pp. 401–404.
3 R. C. Hall, *The Balkan Wars 1912–1913: Prelude to the First World War*. London and New York: Routledge, 2000.
4 D. Yergin, *The Prize: The Epic Quest for Oil, Money and Power*. London: Simon & Schuster, 1991, pp. 184–206.
5 R. Prior and T. Wilson, *The First World War*. London: Cassell, 1999, pp. 88–95.
6 D. Nicolle and R. Hook, *Lawrence of Arabia*. Oxford: Osprey, 1989.
7 C. Falls and A. F. Becke, *History of the Great War: Military Operations: Egypt and Palestine from June 1917 to the End of the War*. London: His Majesty's Stationery Office, 1930 and D. L. Bullock, *Allenby's War: The Palestinian–Arabian Campaigns, 1916–1918*. London: Blandford Press, 1988.
8 D. A. Fromkin, *A Peace to End All Peace: The Fall of the Ottoman Empire and the Creation of the Modern Middle East*. New York: Avon Books, 1989.

9 J. Hunt, *The Arab Legion, 1923–1957*. London: Constable, 1999 and E. Karsh, *The Arab–Israeli Conflict: The Palestine War 1948*. Essential Histories 28. London: Osprey, 2002.

10 C. Tripp, *A History of Iraq*. Cambridge: Cambridge University Press, 2002 and Yapp, op. cit., pp. 137–145.

11 E. Abrahamian, *Iran Between Two Revolutions*. Princeton, NJ: Princeton University Press, 1983.

12 L. Ericson, *Svenska frivilliga: Militära uppdrag I utlandet under 1800- och 1900-talen*. Lund: Historiska Media, 1996, pp. 143–155 and M. Ineichen, *Die schwedischen Offiziere in Persien (1911–1916): Friedensengel, Weltgendarmen oder Handelsagenten einer Kleinmacht im ausgehenden Zeitalter des Imperialismus*. Geist und werke der Zeiten. Arbeiten aus dem Historischen Seminar der Universität Zürich, no 96. Bern: Peter Land, 2002.

13 *Operations in Persia 1914–1919*. Facsimile Edition with Introduction by Dr G. M. Bayliss. Imperial War Museum, London: Her Majesty's Stationery Office, 1987 (a first limited edition was published in 1929).

14 A good introduction to the operations in Iraq in 1914–1918 is given in S. C. C. Tucker (ed.) *The European Powers in the First World War. An Encyclopedia*. New York and London: Garland Publishing, 1996 pp. 476–478. Important works are also Sir F. J. Moberly, *Official History of the Great War: The Campaign in Mesopotamia 1914–1918*, vols 1–4. London: His Majesty's Stationery Office, 1923–1930 and A. J. Barker, *The Neglected War: Mesopotamia, 1914–1918*. London: Faber & Faber, 1967.

15 B. Perett, *The Battle Book: Crucial Conflicts in History from 1469 BC to the Present*. London: Brockhampton Press, 1996, p. 164.

16 M. Gilbert, *First World War*. London: Weidenfeld and Nicolson, 1994, p. 484.

17 D. Nicolle and R. Hook, *Lawrence of Arabia*. Oxford: Osprey, 1989 and H. W. Neulen, *Adler und Halbmomd: Das deutsch–türkische Bündniss 1914–1918*. Frankfurt a/M and Berlin: Ullstein, 1994, chapters XIX–XX.

18 C. Tripp, op. cit., passim.

19 Yergin, op. cit., p. 184.

20 D. E. Omissi, *Air Power and Colonial Control: The RAF 1919–39*. Manchester: Manchester University Press, 1990 pp. 9–11, 24. See also 'Planners of 1941 Dodgy Dossier Tangled with BBC', in *The Times*, 25 July 2003, p. 3.

21 M. E. Yapp, *The Near East since the First World War*. London: Longman, 1991, Chapters 2 and 9.

22 G. Jarring, 'Den första svenska diplomatiska rapporteringen om Atatürk', in *Svenska Forskningsinstitutet i Istanbul. Meddelanden no 6*, 1981, pp. 51–58.

23 See, for instance, af Wirséns report of April 21, 1916 in *Generalstabens f d hemliga arkiv, Utrikesavdelningen* E I a, Turkey volume 1, 1915–1916, Military Archives, Stockholm.

24 See, for instance, reports of 3 March and 8 August 1916 both in *Generalstabens f d hemliga arkiv 1915–1916*, op. cit.

25 Report of 8 December 1915 *Generalstabens f d hemliga arkiv 1915–1916*, op. cit.

26 Report of 26 March 1917 in *Generalstabens f d hemliga arkiv, Utrikesavdelningen* E I a, Turkey volume 2, 1917–1933, Military Archives, Stockholm.

27 Report of March 3, 1917 in *Generalstabens f d hemliga arkiv 1917–1933*, op. cit.

28 E. af Wirsén, *Minnen från fred och krig*. Stockholm: Albert Bonniers förlag, 1942, p. 343.

29 S. Lloyd, *The Archaeology of Mesopotamia: From the Old Stone Age to the Persian Conquest*. London: Thames and Hudson 1987 and L. Woolley, *Fynd i*

jorden: En arkeolog berättar (*Discoveries in Earth: An Archaeologist Tells Us*). Stockholm: Natur och Kultur 1954, especially chapter IV.
30 Y. M. Choueiri, *Modern Arab Historiography: Historical Discourse and the Nation-State*. London: Routledge, 2003, pp. 68–69.
31 A. Christie, *Mord i Mesopotamien* (*Murder in Mesopotamia*). Stockholm: Bonnier pocket, 1986, p. 4.
32 Turkish General Staff, *Atatürk and the Turkish Revolution*. Publications of the General Staff. Military History and Strategic Studies. Ankara: Turkish General Staff, 1999, p. 19.
33 S. Kahle, *Jag valde mitt liv*. Stockholm: Bonniers, 2003, pp. 518–520.

References

Abrahamian, E. *Iran Between Two Revolutions*. Princeton, NJ: Princeton University Press, 1983.
Barker, A. J. *The Neglected War: Mesopotamia, 1914–1918*. London: Faber & Faber, 1967.
Bullock, D. L. *Allenby's War: The Palestinian–Arabian Campaigns, 1916–1918*. London: Blandford Press, 1988.
Choueiri, M. *Modern Arab Historiography: Historical Discourse and the Nation-State*. London: Routledge, 2003.
Christie, A. *Mord i Mesopotamien (Murder in Mesopotamia)*. Stockholm: Bonnier pocket, 1986.
Ericson, L. *Svenska frivilliga: Militära uppdrag I utlandet under 1800- och 1900-talen*. Lund: Historiska Media, 1996.
Falls, C. and Becke, A. F. *History of the Great War: Military Operations: Egypt and Palestine from June 1917 to the End of the War*. London: His Majesty's Stationery Office, 1930.
Fromkin, D. A. *A Peace to end all Peace: The Fall of the Ottoman Empire and the Creation of the Modern Middle East*. New York: Avon Books, 1989.
Generalstabens f d hemliga arkiv, Utrikesavdelningen. E I a, Turkey volume 1, 1915–1916, Stockholm: Military Archives.
Gilbert, M. *First World War*. London: Weidenfeld and Nicolson, 1994.
Hall, R. C. *The Balkan Wars 1912–1913: Prelude to the First World War*. London and New York: Routledge, 2000.
Hunt, J. *The Arab Legion, 1923–1957*. London: Constable, 1999.
Ineichen, M. *Die schwedischen Offiziere in Persien (1911–1916): Friedensengel, Weltgendarmen oder Handelsagenten einer Kleinmacht im ausgehenden Zeitalter des Imperialismus*. Geist und werke der Zeiten. Arbeiten aus dem Historischen Seminar der Universität Zürich, no 96. Bern: Peter Land, 2002.
Jarring, G.'Den första svenska diplomatiska rapporteringen om Atatürk', in *Svenska Forskningsinstitutet i Istanbil. Meddelanden* no 6, 1981.
Kahle, S. *Jag valde mitt liv*. Stockholms: Bonniers, 2003.
Karsh, E. *The Arab–Israeli Conflict: The Palestine War 1948*. Essential Histories 28. London: Osprey, 2002.
Lloyd, S. *The Archaeology of Mesopotamia: From the Old Stone Age to the Persian Conquest*. London: Thames and Hudson, 1987.
Moberly, Sir F. J. *Official History of the Great War: The Campaign in Mesopotamia 1914–1918*, vols 1–4. London: His Majesty's Stationery Office, 1923–1930.
Neulen, H. W. *Adler und Halbmomd: Das deutsch–türkische Bündniss 1914–1918*. Frankfurt a/M and Berlin: Ullstein, 1994.
Nicolle, D. and Hook, R. *Lawrence of Arabia*. Oxford: Osprey, 1989.

Nordberg, M. *Asiens historia: Från forntiden till 1914*. Stockholm: Natur och Kultur, 1971.

Omissi, D. E. *Air Power and Colonial Control: The RAF 1919–39*. Manchester: Manchester University Press, 1990.

Operations in Persia 1914–1919. Facsimile Edition with Introduction by Dr G. M. Bayliss. Imperial War Museum. London: Her Majesty's Stationery Office, 1987 (a first limited edition was published in 1929).

Perett, P. *The Battle Book: Crucial Conflicts in History from 1469 BC to the Present*. London: Brockhampton Press, 1996.

Prior, R. and Wilson, T. *The First World War*. London: Cassell, 1999.

Tripp, C. *A History of Iraq*. Cambridge: Cambridge University Press, 2002.

Tucker, S. C. C. (ed.) *The European Powers in the First World War. An Encyclopedia*. New York and London: Garland Publishing, 1996.

Turkish General Staff. *Atatürk and the Turkish Revolution*. Publications of the General Staff. Military History and Strategic Studies. Ankara: Turkish General Staff, 1999.

Wirsén, E. af *Minnen från fred och krig*. Stockholm: Albert Bonniers förlag, 1942.

Woolley, L. *Fynd i jorden: En arkeolog berättar* (*Discoveries in Earth: An Archaeologist Tells Us*). Stockholm: Natur och Kultur, 1954.

Yapp, M. E. *The Near East since the First World War*. London: Longman, 1991.

—— *The Making of the Modern Near East, 1792–1923*. London: Longman, 1991.

Yergin, D. *The Prize: The Epic Quest for Oil, Money and Power*. London: Simon & Schuster, 1991.

7

THE IRAQ WAR AND INTERNATIONAL LAW

From Hugo Grotius to George W. Bush

Ove Bring and Per Broström

> War should only be used to uphold that which is right and once
> started must be waged within the bounds of justice and honesty.
> Hugo Grotius (1583–1645)[1]

Introduction

This chapter looks at the Iraq war in terms of international law, from a
double perspective. It follows two lines of legal thought which have been
in existence ever since the Dutchman Hugo Grotius, often called the father
of international law, published his book in three volumes, *On the Law of
War and Peace*, in 1625. This work, *De Jure Belli ac Pacis*, was presented
at the book fair in Frankfurt that year and was a great success with the
educated public of the day. Grotius died in 1645 but his work was reprinted
frequently and to a degree is still alive today. This applies in particular to the
two international law perspectives that he utilized to assess the legality of
military operations.

The first question concerns whether the Iraq war as such was legal;
whether in the circumstances at the time there was a just cause for war
under the legal regime of *jus ad bellum*. President Bush and his colleagues
argued prior to the attack on Iraq that this question could be answered in
the positive. We will investigate this assertion. The second question is independent of the first, and regards whether the military (and administrative)
behaviour during the course of the armed conflict was consistent with
humanitarian rules of warfare and with the rules of occupation that belong
to the same norm system. Here the question concerns the implementation of
international humanitarian law applicable in armed conflict, the *jus in bello*.
We will offer some comment on the warfare of both the coalition and the
Iraqis, and will focus particularly on the allied occupation of Iraq, against
the background of the rules of occupation.

Jus ad bellum: the law of the UN Charter

In his writings, Grotius developed further a medieval scholastic doctrine on the just war, *bellum justum*. Wars of conquest and unprovoked wars of aggression could never be justified; they were incompatible with the prevailing thinking, which was based on natural law and reason. However there were many other situations, as St Thomas Aquinas argued as early as the eleventh century, when a right to commence military operations must be accepted. Grotius' list of permissible reasons for war was relatively generous and extensive. For instance it included all situations where a state had not been compensated for damage or injustice it had suffered, i.e. cases which now require peaceful solutions according to the UN Charter.

As clear cases of just war, he also listed cases that we recognize from modern-day debates in international law, in particular self-defence in the case of an armed attack (Article 51 of the UN Charter), as well as more controversial instances, which might possibly be accepted by modern international law, in exceptional cases. Here we have in mind anticipatory self-defence against states and structures that constitute an imminent security threat, as well as armed humanitarian intervention in countries where people are subject to tyrannical oppression, ethnic cleansing or genocide. In the latter instance Grotius wrote – and here one thinks of Saddam Hussein – that intervention must be possible 'against men who are like beasts'.[2]

A modern form of *bellum justum*, which Grotius did not foresee, is when an international organization for collective security decides on armed intervention in accordance with its statutes. The Council of the League of Nations, according to the 1920 Covenant of the League, had the power to recommend armed force against an aggressor, just as since 1945 the more ambitious Chapter VII of the UN Charter authorizes some use of force to maintain international peace and security.

Prior to and during the 2003 Iraq War, three possible justifications for the Anglo-American war effort were discussed:

1 that the war was legal as result of the Chapter VII resolutions that the UN Security Council had passed since 1990;
2 that the war was legal as a form of preventive self-defence against international terrorism; and
3 that the war was legal because it would liberate the Iraqi people from oppression: a form of humanitarian intervention in line with the aims of the UN Charter.

The UN resolutions

The first justification, concerning the Security Council's enabling resolutions, was the one officially presented by Washington and London, in particular by the British Foreign and Commonwealth Office (FCO), where greater effort was devoted to a coherent legal argumentation than what was considered necessary in the White House and the State Department. The more elaborated British line was first presented by the Attorney General, Lord Goldsmith. In a response to a question in Parliament he argued that the military action was legal against the backdrop of Resolution 678 (1990), which authorized the use of force against Iraq to drive its troops from Kuwait and restore 'peace and security in the area'. When the Security Council, after the end of the 1991 Gulf War, adopted the cease fire resolution, number 687 (1991), the Council suspended but did not nullify the mandate to use force. The objective of this mandate was namely not only the liberation of Kuwait but also security in the region as such, hence the demands directed at Iraq in Resolution 687 for the total phasing out of weapons of mass destruction and the ban on conventional weapons exceeding a particular range.

This resolution (687) – 'the mother of all resolutions' – had two main characteristics: first, it presented a unilateral decree from the UN for a cessation of hostilities; second, it entailed an agreement between the UN coalition and Iraq on a ceasefire on certain conditions. The disarmament by Iraq of her weapons of mass destruction was one of those conditions. When Iraq did not present evidence of this disarmament the country was found to be in material breach of the resolution and the ceasefire agreement. This serious breach released the coalition from their obligation to respect the ceasefire.[3] In connection with the renewed and more stringent mandate granted to the weapons control body United Nations Monitoring, Verification, and Inspection Commission (UNMOVIC), under Hans Blix, for the resumption of inspections in Iraq in autumn 2002, it was confirmed that Iraq was in material breach of relevant disarmament obligations under the terms of Security Council Resolution 1441 (2002). As a result the mandate authorizing the use of force in Resolution 678 was renewed and the situation was 'back to square one'. Consequently war was once again legitimized. This line of reasoning is based completely on Chapter VII of the UN Charter. As soon as the Security Council, under the Chapter's introductory article (Article 39), has found that a threat exists against international peace and security, the Council can impose sanctions against a state, including military action. The Council itself decides how long and under which conditions a mandate to use force applies. The British argumentation attempted to prove that the rules of the UN Charter were followed and respected – including during the three-week Iraq War of 2003.

The concept of 'material breach' is not mentioned in Resolution 687, but was introduced first in Resolution 707 (1991), which the Security Council approved unanimously in August of that year. The Council condemned Iraq in strong terms for its failure to comply with 687, regarding the required cooperation with United Nations Special Committee (UNSCOM), the weapons inspection body at the time. The concept of 'material breach' has particular significance in international law: it indicates a right held by the party affected in a treaty relationship to suspend its obligations under the treaty. Provisions describing this are found in Article 60 of the 1969 Vienna Convention on the Law of Treaties.

It is true that there is no doubt that the so-called war resolution, number 678 from 1990, can be 'revived'. This would require that a majority of the Security Council, including its permanent, veto-holding members, can agree on such an interpretation. A joint interpretation can be manifest in a number of ways and does not necessarily have to take the form of a new resolution. When in November 2002 the Council agreed to a compromise within the framework of Resolution 1441, where Iraq was threatened with 'serious consequences' if actual disarmament was not documented, it was however clear that there was no agreement on the question of the interpretation. The Council had not agreed on the formula 'all necessary means', i.e. the code words for military force. The permanent members – France, Russia and China – were all, as was Germany, of the opinion that the Council had to approve a new resolution describing how the warning of 'serious consequences' was to be followed up – should a follow-up be necessary. Thus, Resolution 1441 was confirmation that the Council did *not* agree to return to 'square one'.

The Anglo-American line appears to have been that Resolution 1441 was actually not necessary, since in accordance with Security Council practice it was already clear that Iraq's material breach allowed a return to Resolution 678. This line of reasoning had been used by the US and the UK in conjunction with the bombing of military targets in Iraq in December 1998, although there had been no unified view on the matter in the Council at the time. The so-called December bombings were a result of Saddam Hussein expelling UNSCOM from the country. Iraq had thus broken the ceasefire resolution, committed a material breach and – as the reasoning went – put itself in a position that revived the mandate to use force from November 1990. The line of argument was the same as previously in spring 2003, but had the same shortcoming. It did not have the support of all of the permanent members of the Security Council.[4] It is true that the US/UK position sought to handle this deficiency with the argument that since Iraq had not fulfilled its obligations to disarm, this entitled *individual* members of the Council to take action without the need for collective approval. But, as Hans Blix has concluded:

> It was not reasonable to maintain that individual members of the Security Council had the right to take armed action to uphold decisions of the Council when a majority of the Council was not yet ready to authorize that action.[5]

The self-defence argument

After the Iraq War began on 19 March 2003, the world expected that stock-piles of chemical or biological weapons would be found, or at least that archives and laboratories would emerge, proving that Iraq had retained a capacity to quickly produce weapons of mass destruction. This did not turn out to be the case.

Consequently, the argumentation along the UN resolutions line, which was based on the requirement to surrender weapons of mass destruction, fell into disrepute. In Washington the argument regarding self-defence against international terrorism now started to be put forward. This approach of extended self-defence had obviously gained considerable support after 11 September 2001 and in particular after the bombing of targets in Afghani-stan had commenced on 7 October that year. After the Anglo-American attack on Iraq had started, President Bush referred in general to the United States' right to self-defence, against the background of 'the nature and type of threat posed by Iraq'.[6]

Centuries earlier, Hugo Grotius recognized a far-reaching right to self-defence, which made it possible for a state to use armed force to defend not only its *territory* but also its *rights*, the latter of both economic and non-economic nature. All instances that could be grouped under this exten-sive right to self-defence were considered just wars, or *bellum justum*. Grotius also accepted self-defence against imminent threats, but not armed force aimed at eliminating future potential threats. In other words, 'anticipatory self-defence' was acceptable, but not 'pre-emptive action'. Grotius' thinking would hold sway for at least 200 years.

A more detailed customary-law description of the right to self-defence occurred later, by way of some well-known correspondence in the field of international diplomacy. It was in 1842 that the Anglo-American dispute now referred to as the Caroline case gave rise to a line of reasoning that has become classic in international law. The *Caroline* was an American steam-ship, which in 1837 was used by a private network to support a rebel move-ment in Canada, then a British colony. The American authorities tried to stop the activities, but failed. A British force entered American territory in Lake Erie, boarded the *Caroline* amid a certain amount of shooting, set the vessel alight and sent it over the Niagara Falls. Washington protested, and London replied that the British expedition was considered legitimate and necessary self-defence. The diplomatic correspondence ended when the British envoy combined an apology for the incursion into American territory with an assertion that the right to self-defence applied. Previously, in a state-ment that would become classic, the American Secretary of State Webster had maintained that a legitimate right to self-defence must be limited to situations where 'the necessity of that self-defence is instant, overwhelming, and leaving no choice of means, and no moment for deliberation'.[7]

The note went on, setting out the so-called principle of proportionality. The idea was that Great Britain had to prove that the British force 'did nothing unreasonable or excessive, since the act (of intrusion), justified by the necessity of self-defence, must be limited by that necessity and kept clearly within it'.[8]

Webster's formula, which won general approval and which was perceived as a correct description of applicable international law, concluded by laying down three criteria for legitimate self-defence: (1) the necessity of the action, (2) the imminence of the threat, and (3) the proportionality of the reaction. One could say that this formula confirmed Grotius' thesis that anticipatory self-defence in the face of an imminent threat is acceptable, while preemptive self-defence against a distant threat is not.

When the UN Charter was adopted in 1945, Article 51 referred to 'the inherent right' of self-defence which is considered to incorporate traditional customary law in the area, for instance the principle of proportionality, as well as some right to anticipatory self-defence when the necessity of this is imminent. At the same time, the wording of Article 51 is particularly limiting, as it assumes an armed attack in conjunction with the exercise of self-defence. Article 51 begins as follows:

> Nothing in the present Charter shall impair the inherent right of individual or collective self-defence if an armed attack occurs against a Member of the United Nations, until the Security Council has taken measures necessary to maintain international peace and security.

The traditional interpretation of this provision rules out military action in self-defence following an armed attack that is no longer in progress. Various forms of hit-and-run actions have been considered 'incidents' and not 'attacks' with regard to the UN Charter. Nor has the traditional interpretation of Article 51 viewed terrorist attacks as attacks on a state as such. Consequently the right to self-defence has not become an issue, only the matter of police countermeasures within the framework of international cooperation. September 11 changed this view. The attacks on the World Trade Center and the Pentagon were seen by the UN as *large-scale* terrorist attacks that legitimized military action in self-defence against states that cooperated with terrorist networks. In this way the Anglo-American attacks against targets in Afghanistan, which were reported to the Security Council on 8 October 2001, gained approval from the international community as a new form of self-defence; preventive self-defence aimed at preventing new attacks. It was a broadening, in practice, of the application of Article 51: a new Article $51\frac{1}{2}$.[9]

When the 2003 Iraq War had gone on for a time, it became tempting for the Bush administration to attempt to legitimize it with the new right to self-defence against international terrorism. A number of semi-official murmurings to this effect were heard at press conferences in Washington.

At the beginning of the Iraq crisis, Washington had realized the difficulty of citing the right to self-defence. At that time it did not claim that Saddam Hussein had contact with al-Qaeda or that there was a risk of Iraqi territory being used as a base for terrorist attacks against the United States. No evidence, circumstantial or otherwise, had been found to corroborate either of these two possibilities. Prior to the war in Afghanistan, the US staged a round of travelling diplomacy, where various national capitals were shown proof and evidence that al-Qaeda was behind the attacks of 11 September and that the network had its headquarters in Afghanistan. This argumentation was central to the acceptance of the extended right to self-defence. As for the war on Iraq, it was not possible to repeat such a diplomatic offensive because the evidence was not there. However, if it had been possible to prove that Iraq, through contacts with al-Qaeda, constituted a genuine threat against US security, then the Afghan precedent would have been a legitimizing factor from the perspective of international law.

Now it can be argued that the Bush administration was less interested in legitimacy in terms of international law than in its own security strategy from September 2002. The central point of this National Security Strategy, the so-called Bush Doctrine, is that the threat from 'rogue states' and terrorists overlap and that it must be handled by way of action and not only through deterrence. The US must therefore act proactively and preemptively in the face of real threats.[10] As President Bush later expressed it, in relation to the traditional reactive right to self-defence: '. . . responding to such enemies only after they have struck first is not self-defense, it is suicide'.[11] The Bush Doctrine is not necessarily on a collision course with international law in every respect, but insofar as it presents the invasion of Iraq as politically legitimate, we can declare that this is the case.[12] The case in support of pre-emptive self-defence under international law fails due to insufficient evidence.

The case for humanitarian intervention

When the fighting was over, many Iraqis greeted the American and British troops as liberators. Numerous international aid workers have reported that the Iraqi people express their gratitude that they are rid of Saddam, at the same time as they hope that the foreign troops will leave the country soon.

The argument about the need for regime change in Iraq was never practicable in the UN Security Council, nor in the EU capitals when the crisis was discussed prior to the invasion. Not until Basra and Baghdad were taken was the question of Saddam Hussein's tyranny presented as a legitimizing factor.

The continual absence of human rights in Iraq for over two decades, and the fact that democratic developments could at last begin, now stood out as grounds for justification of the war. It was a justification that gave the invasion a degree of 'political legitimacy', in terms of human values and hope for the future. It was still not a question of a legal/formal legitimacy, since neither the majority of the Security Council (Russia, China, France, Germany etc.) nor the minority (the US, the UK) had argued that the protection of human rights was a reason for armed action against Iraq. The discussion surrounding Resolution 1441 was always centred on weapons of mass destruction (WMD) and not human rights.

Whatever line of approach was taken the US and Great Britain would always have needed the support of the Security Council, since only acts of war in self-defence are legitimate without the approval of the Security Council. If the political will had existed, the Council could very well have presented tyranny and the persecution of Kurds and Shia Muslims as a threat against international peace and security, and therefore as grounds for armed action in accordance with Chapter VII of the UN Charter. This did not happen – and an explanation was most certainly the strong position of the principle of sovereignty of the UN Charter. That principle has given rise to a legal expectation among the UN member states that governments in office may be criticized but not overthrown. The idea of UN-authorized regime change is a bitter pill to swallow.

However, many commentators argued, if the UN Security Council does not take its responsibility and protect human rights, then individual states must be able to conduct a humanitarian intervention against a tyrannical regime in the interest of the population. This is what happened in Kosovo, at least with the tacit approval of the international community. If international law was now making a distinction between Kosovo and Iraq, there must be something essentially wrong with international law. What the world needed was 'less international law and more human rights law'. That was basically how the discussion went in many quarters.

First it has to be said that the system of international law, as it has developed in state practice and international treaties, is not and cannot be 100 per cent *idealistic*. It is also based on realpolitik, and has to be, in order to be able to function as an instrument between sovereign states. At the same time the system aims to strike a balance between progressive development and the restraining effect of national politics. In this way, human rights has developed within the system of international law; it is not outside it as a separate phenomenon – and cannot be outside it. The practice of states and their positioning are an important part of the process towards achieving humanitarian results. Human rights are to a large extent characterized by a compromise between far-reaching protective norms on a fundamental level and less far-reaching mechanisms to guarantee fundamental protection. Hopefully international law can evolve in a direction that shifts the current balance from a great emphasis on the rights of states to more emphasis on the rights of individuals.

It is true that the principle of humanitarian intervention played a politically legitimizing role in Kosovo. The explanation for this is that, even if there is no scope under current international law (*lex lata*) for individual states to intervene on humanitarian grounds when the Security Council is unable to agree on the matter, ever since the days of Thomas Aquinas and Grotius the formulation of a doctrine on the right of intervention on humanitarian grounds has been taking place which today can be said to represent the law as many of us would want it to be (*lex ferenda*). The ethnic cleansing that took place in Bosnia had the dimensions of crimes against humanity and in 1999 the same thing was about to be repeated against the Kosovo Albanians. The belief that something had to be done to protect the persecuted Muslims in Kosovo existed both in the West and in the Muslim world, hence the political support and legitimacy that NATO's armed intervention enjoyed as long as it continued.

A humanitarian intervention against Saddam Hussein's Iraq could (and should) have taken place in 1988 when the massacres of the Kurds in Northern Iraq (including some 5,000 in Halabja) reached the level of 'crime against humanity'. In 2003 the situation in Iraq was different. Oppression and torture occurred as before, but did not reach the level of humanitarian catastrophe that the academic doctrine on humanitarian intervention presupposes in this context. A report, sponsored by the Canadian government, entitled *The Responsibility to Protect* (2001), published by the International Commission on Intervention and State Sovereignty, refers to 'large scale loss of life' and 'large scale "ethnic cleansing."'[13] The humanitarian crisis in Iraq in the spring of 2003 did not reach this level and therefore the argument for humanitarian intervention would have been problematic. This does not mean that if the US and the UK had pursued this line of argumentation from the very outset, got 'No' from the Security Council, carried out the invasion and called it 'the liberation of Iraq', then probably a substantial amount of political legitimacy, much greater than today, could have been harvested from the international community.[14]

In any case, none of the three possible bases for justification have proved sufficient. Legality under *jus ad bellum* was conspicuous by its absence. Political legitimacy was, to a degree, realized when the Ba'athist dictatorship fell, but the amount that exists today requires continual supplementing in the form of progress in the social reconstruction, including an increased role for the UN in this work. The capture of Saddam Hussein was a success for the occupation forces, but since then the worsening of the security situation in the country tends to erode whatever political legitimacy has been achieved.

Jus in bello: the law of warfare

Below we discuss the question of whether the actions during the armed conflict were in accordance with international humanitarian law on war and occupation, *jus in bello*. To simplify the presentation, the air and ground wars have been treated separately, followed by a section on the occupation.

The air and missile war

On March 20, 2003 at 05:34 Baghdad time, the US-led coalition started the war on Iraq by firing the first bomb at Saddam Hussein himself.[15] The objective was probably to achieve an early system collapse, which would make it easier for the coalition forces to gain quick control of Iraq. If so, the strategy was in line with what the US Secretary of Defense Donald Rumsfeld called 'Shock and Awe',[16] where Rapid Dominance was one criterion of success, involving a minimum of friendly losses and collateral damage.[17] The initial near miss on Saddam Hussein signalled the beginning of the numerous attacks against the senior Iraqi leadership over the following days. The coalition continued to aim its missiles at Saddam Hussein's residences and the regime's symbols in the form of presidential palaces and government buildings. For the world, the results were difficult to interpret but there were reports of numerous civilian deaths and injuries, as well as extensive damage to civilian property.

By applying the concept of Rapid Dominance, the operational capability to conduct joint operations would increase, its founders maintain, but it also assumes access to a sophisticated technological network of sensors for intelligence and analysis, which would be able to provide real-time, relevant information to the operator.[18] In this case, what is crucial to the fulfilment of the duties under international law is not whether the intelligence sensors are technical or human, but whether the intelligence can constitute reliable information for the military commander when determining the aim, means and method prior to a decision to take action. Consequently, a question that should probably be asked is whether the concept of Rapid Dominance made it easier for the coalition to realize its obligations under international law. The US, the UK and other coalition states became aggressors[18] the moment the first bomb fell. This also marked the start of their responsibility under international humanitarian law (IHL)[20] where we find the fundamental principles of distinction and proportionality.

The requirements of international humanitarian law are that each armed action must be directed at military targets, and when choosing means and method of attack the effect of the action must not result in injuries to civilians and damage to civilian property that are not in proportion to the military advantage. Therefore the legal consequences are that if there is doubt as to the legitimacy of the target, the attack may not be executed, just as in cases where the unintended (collateral) damage to civilians and civilian property can be feared to be excessive in relation to the military advantage of the attack. Thus, each individual action must be assessed based on these principles, not the actions of the campaign as a whole. If one tests this line of argument on the concept of Rapid Dominance, which is supposed to ensure a short war and consequently fewer deaths and limited collateral damage, the conclusion can be that failure to observe the rules of IHL in the individual case can jeopardize the legitimacy of the whole operation, since virtually every action in modern-day international armed conflicts soon becomes known to the world.

Thus, the reports that on 7 April Saddam Hussein was located in a building at 11 al-Saa Street in the Mansur district of Baghdad should have included information on other conditions at the site, i.e. on the risks of collateral damage to civilians and civilian property. The result of the action was that Saddam Hussein escaped but 14 civilians were killed when residential buildings were struck by four 900–kg bombs that were guided to the target.[21] It is indisputable that Saddam Hussein, in his capacity of supreme commander of the Iraqi forces constituted a legitimate military target, but the protection provided for the civilian residential blocks under IHL remained. The lesson here is that new technology with rapid intelligence and precision weapons can contribute substantially to the observance of IHL, provided that the intelligence also includes information enabling the implementation of the principles of distinction and proportionality once the legitimate target has been established.

On 4 March, prior to the attack on Iraq, the Chairman of the Joint Chiefs of Staff, General Richard Myers, said:

> If asked to go into conflict in Iraq, what you'd like to do is have it be a short, short conflict. The best way to do that is to have such a shock on the system, the Iraqi regime would have to assume early on the end is inevitable.[22]

The strategy was clear but very soon the course of events changed, which led Harlan Ullman, one of the founders of the 'Shock and Awe' strategy, to say – while the campaign was ongoing – that 'The current campaign does not appear to correspond to what we envisioned.'[23] Apparently something had happened that affected the concept for success. We might never find out exactly what, but according to officials in the Pentagon one of the reasons was the civilian casualties, which became a political liability.[24]

The ground war

A day or so after the first bombings, the coalition began the ground offensive. They soon met resistance, especially in the areas around the port city of Basra, where the main force advanced. Initially the fighting was described as heavy, but still the coalition forces advanced quickly and it was not long before the taking of prisoners of war on both sides was reported in the media. Prior to the impending war, some 600 journalists from selected news agencies had been given the opportunity to work as so-called 'embedded journalists'[25] i.e. gain status under international law as 'civilians accompanying armed forces'. This means that as long as they did not participate in the fighting, the journalists were viewed as civilians but they enjoyed the physical protection offered by the coalition forces.[26] In the war zone there were also 'journalists on dangerous assignments'. According to international law, these must also be considered civilians if they are not conducting activities that can be prejudicial to this status. However, this rule became clouded in the war on Iraq, as neither the US nor Iraq has ratified[27] the 1997 Additional Protocol I of the 1949 Geneva Conventions where this is regulated.[28] On the other hand, the United States' coalition partners, the UK and Australia, are bound by the rules and it might be against this background, and the desire to win the media war, that the US chose to offer the news agency workers the status of embedded journalists.

The capacity of the media to report the events in an ongoing war is, of course, important for everyone who for whatever reason has an interest in the outcome of the war. The manner of reporting can affect the will and morale of one's own side as well as that of the enemy. Some of the first images from the ground war to reach the outside world via Arabic-language television showed a number of American prisoners of war being held in Iraqi custody. The images were very close-up and they upset many people, in particular the American command, who pointed out that this was a breach of the rules of the Geneva Convention III regarding the treatment of prisoners of war.[29] On 25 March, shortly after this incident, the White House press spokesman said: 'we have always treated people humanely, consistent with international agreements. In the case of the fight in Iraq, there's no question that it's being done in accordance with the Geneva Conventions'.[30]

We can only speculate as to the reason why the Iraqis did not treat the prisoners of war in full accordance with the rules, but the effect was that the eyes of the world, including those of the coalition's embedded journalists, focused on the content of the laws of war, and in doing so realized fully the significance of the media war and the importance of a correct application of the rules of international law.

On 26 March the coalition announced from its headquarters in Qatar that it had attacked Iraq's largest TV station in Baghdad, with the aim of damaging Iraq's ability to lead its military forces. Thus, the coalition perceived the propaganda of the Iraq regime as a component in the warfare, a form of information operations, which gave legitimacy to the attack of an otherwise protected civilian object.[31] For a civilian object to be able to become a legitimate military target, it must contribute efficiently to the military operations and its destruction in the individual instance must bring a clear military advantage. Whether this was so in the case of the television station can certainly be debated, but the coalition was obliged to use proportional force and if possible to give advance warning, in order to minimize civilian casualties.[32]

So, by way of their reporting, the war correspondents and the 'journalists on dangerous assignments' can constitute both an integrated part of a belligerent's operations, and can also be an important instrument to ensure that international law is observed. However, many will maintain that it is the victors who decide which occurrences will lead to legal investigations after a war. Of course this can be debated, especially when a belligerent does not want to accord jurisdiction over its own citizens to anything but its own state organ.[33] It could be so, that states which have placed themselves outside the system of the permanent International Criminal Court (ICC) wish to highlight their position by increasingly prosecuting cases where their own citizens are suspected of committing war crimes. If so, this is completely in line with the principle established in international law, namely *aut dedere aut judicare*, i.e. 'either prosecute or extradite' suspected war criminals. Therefore it is worth noting the action that the American authorities brought against eight Marine Corps soldiers in October, who were suspected of murdering a prisoner of war during the war in Iraq.[34] On the other hand there are instances where the abuse of Iraqi prisoners of war did not result in legal action, but only in expulsion from the US Armed Forces.[35]

During the relatively brief ground offensive that was required to gain control of Iraqi territory a number of incidents were reported as suspected war crimes. For instance, Iraqi soldiers on numerous occasions behaved treacherously. By feigning surrender or a desire to negotiate, or by disguising themselves as civilians, they managed to get closer to the coalition forces, and subsequently opened fire on them. This is considered a serious breach of the rules of international law.[36] An aggravating circumstance is that this behaviour was encouraged by the Iraqi command in the media.

On 28 March, 58 civilian Iraqis were killed in a market in Baghdad. It has not been established who fired the grenades. The reason could be technical fault or some other occurrence, excusable in war, with tragic results, but it could also be that one of the belligerents did not apply the general principles of precaution, proportionality and distinction as prescribed under international law. By analysing images it has been found that during the war the United States 3rd Infantry Division and the United States Marine Artillery used submunitions, also called 'dual-purpose grenades', fired from (among other things) multiple launch rocket systems. The system of using numerous submunitions is useful for good coverage of an impact area but the failure rate is argued to average as much as 17 per cent.[37] A volley consists normally of 12 rockets, each containing 644 submunitions. Over an area of approximately 120 sq km this would result in some 1,200 unexploded munitions. If these are not cleared, they remain in place, with a function similar to that of an anti-personnel landmine.[38] If these munitions are used in urban environments, which in their entirety do not constitute military targets, it is difficult to argue that one is observing the requirements of international law.

The occupation

On 9 April, after three weeks of war, the United States troops took the capital, Baghdad. Three days earlier, British forces had gained control of the strategically important port city of Basra, after relatively heavy fighting. The coalition forces now controlled most of Iraq. What would happen now? Was the war over or was it just entering a new phase? To answer these questions one has to return to the time before the war broke out.

Above we have described in detail the legal arguments used by the US and its coalition partners to justify their right to attack Iraq. When the strength of the case under international law faded, the requirements of national security of those countries became the justification for the action taken. At an early stage there was a plan for how the situation in Iraq would be handled if Saddam Hussein did not comply with the Security Council's resolutions. The plan was based on occupying Iraq and overthrowing its regime. The US did nothing to hide its agenda. In a letter dated 30 September 2002 from the Congressional Budget Office (CBO) to the Senate and Congress budget committees, the American intentions are presented. It included a clear account of the estimated costs of an occupation of Iraq: 'the incremental cost of an occupation following combat operations could vary from about $1 billion to $4 billion a month'.[39] The letter also presents the costs of transporting the troops home. Thus, the aim of the occupation has been to gain military control of Iraq's territory for a time, while exercising some form of administrative rule over the Iraqi people.

Since the result of an armed conflict often leads to an occupation of territory, rules of international law have been established for these cases.[40] Important questions that require answers include, in particular, what conditions constitute an occupation. International law says that an occupation is when enemy forces have supremacy over the territory and exercise control.[41] It is also clear that geographically the occupation only extends as far as the occupying forces can control, i.e. the whole or parts of a country can be occupied.[42] When the fighting to gain control of an area is still underway, and the outcome is uncertain, the territory is considered to be invaded, but not occupied.[43] For the civilian population and others who do not actively participate in the fighting, this can lead to considerable hardship before one of the belligerents has established its control of the territory. Thus, the actual control of a territory is important, as it is through this state of affairs that one party can derive the right to exercise jurisdiction.

Without control of a territory one cannot exercise jurisdiction there, and consequently one cannot be held responsible for what takes place. In the case of Iraq, there was a responsibility under occupation law once the coalition forces managed to establish control. It took somewhat longer for the British forces to gain control of Basra than for the Americans to gain control of Baghdad. This might be the reason why the residents of Basra had to suffer hardships in the form of a lack of basic necessities and health care.

Once the occupying power is established, it acquires a number of responsibilities with respect to the population. The primary and most important task for an occupying power is to 'take all the measures in his power to restore, and ensure, as far as possible, public order and safety, while respecting, unless absolutely prevented, the laws in force in the country'.[44]

The fact that President Bush announced the end of major combat operations on 1 May was probably intended more for rhetorical purposes than as a comment on laws of occupation. Military operations can still take place on occupied territory, in which case the law of warfare applies. The statement could have been a way for the occupying forces to indicate that the focus was now shifting from military to police-related operations.

What did it mean for the coalition forces, that they had occupied a number of Iraqi cities? In Baghdad, a city of several million, parts of the infrastructure were in ruins, police and security forces were scattered or were taken as prisoners of war, and the population displayed a hesitant attitude towards the 'liberators'. What measures were the occupying forces obliged to take, in order to stop the looting that had already broken out? The question one should ask is, What preparations had been made to fulfil their duties under occupation law? Considering the fact that the US had been planning an invasion as early as September 2002, they had at least six months to analyse the task and decide the criteria for recruitment of suitable personnel, in order to be able to be the efficient occupying force they wanted to be. Now, after the fact, when observing how difficult it was for the coalition forces to maintain any form of law and order, one can also see the inadequacy of the preparations.

For decades the people of Iraq lived under a brutal regime, more recently having to endure three large wars as well as being subjected to tough sanctions from the outside world. Weapons were everywhere and there was deep mistrust as to the real intentions of the occupying power. It was therefore clear that the occupying forces would have a very difficult task restoring general order and normal public life without first building the trust of the population. For this, they had to use many interpreters and police officers or military personnel experienced in handling police duties.[45]

An additional serious factor was that the occupying force was not only responsible for maintaining law and order but also had to be able to deal with the remaining armed resistance which had evolved into a sort of low-intensity violence which had to be countered with military forces, not with police. During the planning stage there were comparative analyses available and here one can conclude that to succeed, the size of the occupying force must be proportional to the population.[46]

Three different scenarios are presented, where the first one estimates that 2.2 police officers/security guards are needed per 1,000 residents in order to maintain general security. This corresponds to the level that applied for personnel in the UN mission in Cambodia (UNTAC) 1992–93. The second level presents a ratio of four to ten police officers/security guards per 1,000 residents and as a comparison it mentions the United States' intervention in the Dominican Republic in 1965 where the task was to prevent a civil war. For the third level the ratio is 20 police officers/security guards per 1,000 residents and here the comparison is to the British forces in Northern Ireland who not only are assigned to separate the warring factions but also must be able to defend themselves against armed groups that view the British forces as an occupying power. In many respects this scenario resembles the situation in Iraq and with a ratio equal to the one in Northern Ireland, the estimated requirement for Iraq is 480,000 soldiers. This figure appeared in the American debate just prior to the coalition's attack on Iraq. Both the Army Chief of Staff, General Eric Shinseki and the Secretary of the Army, Thomas White, argued that this level was required, but without success. Instead they were publicly rebuked by Secretary of Defense Donald Rumsfeld. They resigned shortly after the start of the war. One solid reason why the US did not send more troops is said to be that it did not have any more available: 480,000 troops corresponds to the total number that the US Army has in active service and then it is not possible to rotate the personnel over time, in addition to the fact that the country is involved in many other parts of the world, such as Bosnia-Hercegovina and Afghanistan. Also, one source at the Pentagon is reported as saying that 'We don't have the infantry to hold Iraq for the regime change.'[47] The same source also said earlier that 'original war plans called for a 10-year occupation'.[48]

The conclusion to be drawn from this discussion is that there exists an obligation under international law to restore general order and normal public life within the territory that has been occupied, but that this obligation presupposes that it is possible to carry out the task.[49] So did the coalition actually take all the measures it was required to take? With the total number of forces that were available, all were devoted to offensive units. The strategy on which the operation rested supports this. However, the result was that they could not provide security in the power vacuum that arose when the Saddam regime fell. There is also much evidence that the population's attitude to a US-led occupying force was misjudged. So, can the occupying power be criticized? The fact that the occupying power consists of the armed forces of several states means that there is reason for criticism that it did not manage to establish stability more quickly.

Another interesting observation is that not all of the states that make up the occupying forces are bound by the same international law obligations, even if several of them can be viewed as having the status of customary law. The 1977 Additional Protocol I of the 1949 Geneva Conventions contains far more obligations for an occupying power than the 1907 Hague Convention IV or the 1949 Geneva Convention IV. In this instance, the UK and Australia are bound by the Additional Protocol I, but not the US. Therefore it is quite possible that certain obligations regarding the population apply in one part of the Iraqi territory but not in others. However, a co-belligerent can never evade responsibility by citing the fact that the dominant occupying partner is not bound by a particular rule. In the case of Basra, it was some time before the situation stabilized and the lack of basic necessities was a problem for a very long time. For this reason one can direct some criticism at the British forces for not helping the people more quickly and better. One can also question the extent of the assistance required under the obligations. Is there a duty to repair electricity or water networks that worked poorly even before the war? In this respect there is no real guiding rule, but the laws of occupation expresses throughout that the occupying power in cooperation with national and local authorities, in the fullest extent of the means available, has the duty of ensuring and maintaining e.g. food and medical supplies and public health and hygiene.[50] An occupying power with considerable national resources should thus have more far-reaching obligations than a poor state that occupies another country. Even here, certain new and unclear situations can arise as a result of the occupying forces consisting of more than one state, of which all are not bound by the same rules under international law.

In conclusion, we will also touch on a few of the rights of an occupying power. In order to fulfil the obligation to provide for the people and to cover the costs of administering the occupied area, the occupying power can take possession of cash, funds and property liable to requisition that constitute state property. The occupying power may also collect taxes and fees, if these benefit the state and are used for the administration of the occupied area to the same degree as the lawful government had been obliged to do.[51] In connection with this, a question that was raised prior to the invasion was what would happen to Iraq's oil resources. Could the occupying power dispose of them as it wished, or would the oil exports remain under the control of the UN under the Oil for Food Programme?[52] The second part of the question was answered as early as 22 May 2003, three weeks after President Bush had announced the end of more major combat operations. By way of Resolution 1483 the Security Council decided to lift the sanctions on Iraq and to phase out the Oil for Food Programme.[53] However, the answer to the first part of the question is unclear. Generally, natural resources are viewed as real property and if they belong to the state, e.g. forests and land, the occupying power can avail itself of the proceeds.[54] Sources of oil on the other hand do not constitute so-called renewable resources in the same obvious way. It has been stated that Iraq's oil resources would last for more than 127 years at the extraction rate that existed prior to the sanctions. A limited extraction with the obvious aim of contributing to the reconstruction of Iraq would thus be permitted, according to some. Others have argued that the oil resources, much of which is privately owned, may not be used by the occupying power. Resolution 1483 can to a degree be said to support the first view, since the UN gives the occupying power a mandate to control the oil exports.[55]

No one wanted the war on Iraq to happen; still it seems it was unavoidable. There were shortcomings in *jus ad bellum* as well as *jus in bello*, but perhaps somewhere lessons can be learned from past mistakes and can inspire new ways to improve the protection of the victims of war. Thoughts on the hardships of war inspired Hugo Grotius to write the book *De Jure Belli ac Pacis* and perhaps he was inspired in turn by the Dutch humanist Desiderius Erasmus (1466–1536), who is said to have remarked the following:

> The consequences of war are harsh for the people, even of a war that ends most victoriously and which was founded on the most righteous principles. The common people and the poor become its innocent victims.

Post scriptum

The tragic revelations of torture and degrading treatment of Iraqi detainees/prisoners in the Abu Ghraib detention facilities outside Baghdad (and other places) now has to be added to the picture. In May 2004, a US court-martial proceeding in Baghdad sentenced US-soldier Jeremy Sivits to one year in prison for his actions in breach of US Armed Forces Regulations in the subject matter. Other court proceedings will follow.

Notes

1 Hugo Grotius, *De Jure Belli ac Pacis*, 1625.
2 Translation by F. W. Kelsey in the series *Classics of International Law*, 3, II, Oxford: Clarendon Press; London: Humphrey Milford, 1925, p. 102.
3 Professor John Yoo, who in 2003 was on the staff of the US Department of Justice, claims that the attack on Iraq was justified 'under the law governing armistices' and as a result of the 'interaction between Resolutions 678 and 687' which are relevant in this context. Yoo, 'International Law and the War in Iraq', *American Journal of International Law*, 97, 3, 2003, p. 569–70.
4 The American line of argument, however, is based on the fact that 'all agreed that a Council determination that Iraq had committed a material breach would authorize individual member states to use force to secure compliance with the Council's resolutions'. William H. Taft IV and T. F. Buchwald (Legal

Advisers, State Department), 'Pre-emption, Iraq, and International Law', *American Journal of International Law*, 97, 3, 2003, p. 560. This official line allocates the law a role in the circumstances and implies that international law in regard to the UN Charter has been respected. Another 'realistic' interpretation has been put forward by Michael J. Glennon, 'Why the Security Council Failed', *Foreign Affairs*, 82, 3 (2003) 16–35. Glennon talks of the 'Death of a law' and believes that the UN's regime of non-violence 'can only be said to have collapsed'.

5 Hans Blix, *Disarming Iraq, The Search for Weapons of Mass Destruction*, London: Bloomsbury Publishing, 2004, p. 274.

6 D. M. Ackerman, 'International Law and the Preemptive Use of Force Against Iraq', CRS Report for Congress (Congressional Research Service, The Library of Congress), Received through the CRS Web, Updated 11 April 2003.

7 Quote from Robert Y. Jenning's article 'The *Caroline* and McLeod Cases' in the *American Journal of International Law*, 32 (1938), p. 89. The case is discussed by O. Bring in *FN-stadgan och världspolitiken, Om folkrättens roll i en föränderlig värld*, 4th edn, Stockholm: Norstedts Juridik 2002, pp. 150–152.

8 R. Jennings, op. cit., p. 89.

9 See O. Bring, 'En rätt till väpnat självförsvar mot internationell terrorism?', *Kungl. Krigsvetenskapsakademins Handlingar och Tidskrift*, 6th Booklet 2001, 153–164.

10 The National Security Strategy of the United States of America (17 September 2002), available at http://www.whitehouse.gov/nsc/nss.pdf. See also e.g. Wilhelm Agrell, 'Nya krig – nya världar. Några perspektiv på säkerhetspolitiska förändringar efter den 11 september 2001', *Kungl. Krigsvetenskapsakademins Handlingar och Tidskrift*, 2nd Booklet 2003, p. 52.

11 See http://www.whitehouse.gov/news/releases/2003/03/20030317–7.html (accessed 15 October 2003).

12 American international lawyers seek to legitimize the attack on Iraq by citing President Kennedy's handling of the 1962 Cuba crisis. The armed blockade/ 'quarantine' of Cuba 'was not in response to an armed attack, within the central language of Article 51, or even in response to a concrete Soviet war plan, but in recognition of the danger of a sudden change in capability'. Ruth Wedgwood, 'The Fall of Saddam Hussein: Security Council Mandates and Preemptive Self-Defense', *American Journal of International Law*, 97, 3 (2003) 584.

13 *The Responsibility to Protect*, Report of the International Commission on Intervention and State Sovereignty (ICISS), Ottawa, December 2001, p. 32.

14 The possibility of regime change within the framework of an expanded doctrine on humanitarian discussion is discussed (and rejected) by Richard Falk in his article, 'What Future for the UN Charter System of War Prevention?', *American Journal of International Law*, 97, 3, 2003, 596 f.

15 CNN.com/WORLD, 'U.S. launches cruise missiles at Saddam', http:// edition.cnn.com/2003/WORLD/meast/03/19/sprj.irh.main/index.html (accessed 15 October 2003).

16 H. K. Ullman and J. P. Wade *et al.*, *Shock and Awe – Achieving Rapid Dominance*, Washington, DC: Institute for National Strategic Studies, National Defence University, 1996 (last update: 23 January 2003), Appendix A, *Thoughts on Rapid Dominance* by Admiral Bud Edney, USN (Retired).

17 Ibid., p. 2.

18 Ibid.

19 See Common Article 2 in the 1949 Geneva Conventions I–IV.

20 See ICRC Treaty database, http://www.icrc.org/ihl (accessed 15 October 2003).

21 EXPRESSEN.SE/TT, 'Underrättelsemiss räddade Saddam' [Intelligence mistake saved Saddam], available at http://www.expressen.se/expressen/jsp/polopoly. jsp?d = 442&a = 32374 (accessed 5 July 2003).
22 Paul Sperry, 'No Shock, No Awe: It Never Happened', WorldNetDaily Exclusive, 3 April 2003, http//:www.worldnetdaily.com/news/article.asp?ARTICLE_ID = 31858 (accessed 15 October 2003).
23 Ibid.
24 Supra, footnote 16.
25 U.S. Department of Defense, 'Embedding Release for Iraq 2003', RELEASE, INDEMNIFICATION, AND HOLD HARMLESS AGREEMENT AND AGREEMENT NOT TO SUE, available at http://www.journalism.org/ resources/tools/ethics/wartime/embedding.asp (accessed 15 October 2003).
26 See article 13(4) in the 1949 Geneva Conventions I and II, and article 4(4) in the 1949 Geneva Convention III.
27 The US signed the 1977 Supplementary Protocol I on 12 December 1977 but has not ratified the document.
28 See article 79 in the 1977 Supplementary Protocol I of the 1949 Geneva Conventions.
29 See the 1949 Geneva Convention III – Relative to the Treatment of Prisoners of War.
30 Alex Halavais, 'Embedded Blowback', News Archives, 23 March 2003, available at http://alex.halavais.net/news/archives/000353.html (accessed 15 October 2003).
31 Human Rights Watch Press Release, 'Iraq: Coalition Attack on TV Station May Be Unlawful', New York, 26 March 2003, available at http://hrw.org/press/2003/ 03/iraqtv032603.htm (accessed 15 October 2003).
32 The rules ought to constitute customary law. See also articles 43, 52 and 57 in the 1977 Supplementary Protocol I and footnote 17.
33 Neither the US nor Iraq recognise the jurisdiction of the International Criminal Court (ICC).
34 CBS News, Iraq POW Death Leads To Charges, Los Angeles, 18 October 2003, available at http://www.cbsnews.com/stories/2003/06/11/iraq/main558095.shtml (accessed 18 October 2003).
35 *Aftonbladet*, 'Slog fångar – tre får sparken', available at http://www.aftonbladet. se/vss/nyheter/story/0,2789,414996,00.html (accessed 6 January 2004).
36 The rule is considered as customary law and is found e.g. in article 23 b) of the Annex to the 1907 Hague Convention IV, Respecting the Laws and Customs of War on Land.
37 Human Rights Watch Press release, 'US Using Cluster Munitions In Iraq', Washington, DC, 1 April 2003, available at http://hrw.org/press/2003/04/ us040103.htm (accessed 15 October 2003).
38 Ibid.
39 US Congress, Congressional Budget Office, 'Letter to the Honorable Kent Conrad and John M. Spratt Jr. regarding estimated costs of a potential conflict with Iraq', September 2002, available at http://www.cbo.gov/showdoc.cfm?index = 3822& sequence = 0 (accessed 15 October 2003).
40 See the 1907 Hague Convention IV, the 1949 Geneva Conventions I–IV, the 1977 Supplementary Protocol I and the 1954 Convention on the Protection of Cultural Property in the Event of Armed Conflict. See also the 1948 Universal Declaration on Human Rights and the 1966 International Covenant on Civil and Political Rights.
41 Article 42 of the Annex to the 1907 Hague Convention IV.

42 For example the section of Syrian territory on the Golan Heights that is occupied by Israel.
43 Supra, n. 41.
44 Article 43 of the Annex to the 1907 Hague Convention IV.
45 Paul Sperry, Operation: Iraqi Freedom, 'US Miscalculations Left Troops Vulnerable', WorldNetDaily Exclusive, 10 July 2003, available at http://www.worldnetdaily.com/news/article.asp?ARTICLE_ID = 33505 (accessed 15 October 2003).
46 James T. Quinlivan, 'Force Requirements in Stability Operations', *Parameters, Army War College's quarterly*, 1995, pp. 59–69, available at http://carlisle-www.army.mil/usawc/parameters/1995/quinliv.htm (accessed 15 October 2003).
47 Supra, n. 43.
48 Ibid.
49 Supra, n. 44.
50 See for example Article 56, 1949 Geneva Convention IV concerning protection for civilians in war.
51 Articles 48, 55 and 56 of the 1949 Geneva Convention IV and article 53 of the Annex to the 1907 Hague Convention IV.
52 On 14 April 1995 the UN Security Council decided by way of Resolution 986 to introduce a mechanism to relieve the population's lack of food and medicine as a result of the sanctions on Iraq. This new order came to be called the Oil for Food Programme and it meant that Iraq was permitted to export oil in order to import basic necessities for the population. The oil proceeds were administered by a special UN body.
53 UN/S/RES/1483 (2003), para 16, 18–20.
54 Article 55 of the Annex to the 1907 Hague Convention IV.
55 R. Dobie Langenkamp, 'What Happens to the Oil?: International Law and the Occupation of Iraq', University of Tulsa College of Law, 17 January 2003, s.19, available at http://www.energy.uh.edu/documents/behind_the_gas_pump/Langenkamp_FullPaper.pdf (accessed 7 January 2004).

References

Aftonbladet, 'Slog fångar – tre får sparken', Availaible at http://www.aftonbladet.se/vss/nyheter/story/0,2789,414996,00.html (accessed 6 January 2004).
Agrell, W. 'Nya krig – nya världar. Några perspektiv på säkerhetspolitiska förändringar efter den 11 september 2001', *Kungl. Krigsvetenskapsakademiens Handlingar och Tidskrift*, 2nd Booklet 2003, 45–57.
Blix, H. *Disarming Iraq, The Search for Weapons of Mass Destruction*, London: Bloomsbury Publishing, 2004.
Bring, O. 'En rätt till väpnat självförsvar mot internationell terrorism', *Kungl. Krigsvetenskapsakademiens Handlingar och Tidskrift*, 6th Booklet 2001, 153–165.
Bring, O. *FN-stadgan och världspolitiken, Om folkrättens roll i en föränderlig värld* Stockholm: Norstedts Juridik, 2002.
Bring, O. and Körlof, A. *Folkrätt för totalförsvaret, En handbok*, Stockholm: Norstedts Juridik, 2002, pp. 255–272.
CBS News, 'Iraq POW Death Leads To Charges', Los Angeles, 18 October 2003, available at http://www.cbsnews.com/stories/2003/06/11/iraq/main558095.shtml (accessed 18 October 2003).
CNN.com/WORLD, 'U.S. launches cruise missiles at Saddam', http://edition.cnn.com/2003/WORLD/meast/03/19/sprj.irh.main/index.html (accessed 15 October 2003).

Edney, B. 'Thoughts on Rapid Dominance', Appendix A in H. K. Ullman, J. P. Wade
et al., *Shock and Awe – Achieving Rapid Dominance*, 1996 (last update: 23 January
2003), USA: Institute for National Strategic Studies.
EXPRESSEN.SE/TT 'Underrättelsemiss räddade Saddam' [Intelligence mistake
saved Saddam], available at http://www.expressen.se/expressen/jsp/polopoly.
sp?d = 442&a = 32374 (accessed 5 July 2003).
Försvarsdepartementet 'Folkrättsliga konventioner gällande under krig, neutralitet
och ockupation', *Krigets lagar*, Stockholm: Fritzes, 1996, pp. 53–64, 205–322,
326–350, 363–419.
Falk, R. 'What Future for the UN System of War Prevention?', *American Journal of
International Law*, 97, 3 (2003), 590–598.
Franck, T. M. 'What Happens Now? The United Nations after Iraq', *American
Journal of International La*w, 97, 3 (2003), 607–620.
Glennon, M. J. 'Why the Security Council Failed', *Foreign Affairs*, 82, 3 (2003), 16–34.
Halavais, A. 'Embedded Blowback', News Archives, March 23 2003, available at
http://alex.halavais.net/news/archives/000353.html (accessed 15 October 2003).
Human Rights Watch Press release, 'Iraq: coalition Attack on TV Station May Be
Unlawful', New York, 26 March 2003, Availaible at http://hrw.org/press/2003/03/
iraqtv032603.htm (accessed 15 October 2003).
Human Rights Watch Press release, 'U.S. Using Cluster Munitions In Iraq',
Washington, DC, 1 April 2003, available at http://hrw.org/press/2003/04/
us040103.htm (accessed 15 October 2003).
International Commission on State Sovereignty (ICISS) *The Responsibility to Protect*,
Ottawa: International Development Research Centre, 2001.
ICRC Treaty database, available at http://www.icrc.org/ihl (accessed 15 October
2003).
Jacobsson, M. 'Vart är folkrätten på väg?' *Internationella Studier*, 3, Autumn (2003),
20–31.
Jennings, R. Y. 'The *Caroline* and McLeod Cases' in the *American Journal of Inter-
national Law*, 32 (1938).
Langenkamp, R. D. 'What Happens to the Oil: International Law and the Occupa-
tion of Iraq', University of Tulsa College of Law, 17 January 2003, p. 19, available
at http://www.energy.uh.edu/documents/behind_the_gas_pump/Langenkamp_
FullPaper.pdf (accessed 7 January 2004).
Quinlivan, J. T. 'Force Requirements in Stability Operations', *Parameters, Army
War College's quarterly*, 1995, 59–69, available at http://carlisle-www.army.mil/
usawc/parameters/1995/quinliv.htm (accessed 15 October 2003).
Sperry, P. Operation: Iraqi Freedom, 'U.S. Miscalculations Left Troops Vulnerable', WorldNetDaily Exclusive, 10 July 2003, available at http//:www.worldnet-
daily.com/news/article.asp?ARTICLE_ID = 33505 (accessed 15 October 2003).
Sperry, P. 'No Shock, No Awe: It Never Happened', WorldNetDaily Exclusive, 3 April
2003, available at http//:www.worldnetdaily.com/news/article.asp?ARTICLE_
ID = 31858 (accessed 15 October 2003).
Steiner, H. J. and Alston, P. 'Universal Declaration of Human Rights' and 'Inter-
national Covenant on Civil and Political Rights', *International Human Rights in
Context*, Oxford: Oxford University Press, 2000, pp. 1376–1391.
Taft, W. H. and Buchwald, T. F. 'Preemption, Iraq and International Law', *American
Journal of International Law* 97, 3 (2003), 557–563.
UN/S/RES/1483 (2003), para 16, 18–20, available at http://daccessdds.un.org/doc/
UNDOC/GEN/N03/368/53/PDF/N0336853.pdf?OpenElement (accessed 6 January
2004).
U.S. Congress, Congressional Budget Office, 'Letter to the Honorable Kent Conrad

and John M. Spratt Jr. regarding estimated costs of a potential conflict with Iraq',
September 2002, available at http://www.cbo.gov/showdoc.cfm?index = 3822&
sequence = 0 (accessed 15 October 2003).

U.S. Department of Defense, 'Embedding Release for Iraq 2003', RELEASE,
INDEMNIFICATION, AND HOLD HARMLESS AGREMEENT AND
AGREEMENT NOT TO SUE, available at http:// www.journalism.org/
resources/tools/ethics/wartime/embedding.asp (accessed 15 October 2003).

Wedgwood, R. 'The Fall of Saddam Hussein: Security Council Mandates and Pre-
emptive Self-Defense', *American Journal of International Law*, 97, 3 (2003), 576–585.

Yoo, J. 'International Law and the War in Iraq', *American Journal of International
Law*, 97, 3 (2003), 563–576.

Part II

THEORY AND STRATEGY
DURING THE WAR

8

BRUTE FORCE OR COERCION

Two perspectives on conflict management

Stefan Ring

Introduction

'Everything in war is very simple, but the simplest thing is difficult', Clausewitz writes as he describes the difficulties of prosecuting a war.[1] The course of war we could follow during the offensive of the US-led alliance against Iraq in the late winter of 2003 gave a partially different picture than the one conveyed by this loose quotation. The enormous superiority of the American and British units in firepower, mobility, command, and coordination meant that the Iraqi military resistance essentially dissolved after only about two weeks of combat. The evolution of the war provided an example of the military strength that the United States now has at its disposal. The US can use its military instruments of power in a way that entails small casualties in that the enemy can be fought at long distances and everything takes place at a furious pace. However, the aims of war have not been achieved when military fighting has ceased. A terminal point is not reached until peace is secured.

War thus cannot be judged solely from its dimension of military activity. Clausewitz argues that the political purpose must constitute the basis for conflict analysis. He writes that '. . . war is not a mere act of policy, but a true political instrument, a continuation of the political activity by other means'.[2] From this point of departure follows a clear relationship between the military part of the war and the political aims. What may seem a simple task militarily can prove to be considerably more difficult when the political dimension comes to the fore and peace is to be made.

There is therefore a need to analyse how war should be fought. The analysis must take into consideration not only how the military forces should be deployed, what targets should be attacked, and what territory should be conquered. It is equally important to analyse how the military instruments of power should be used and what factors are governing the chosen line of action. Here the relationship to the adversary becomes central. The situation in which the opponent is to be forced into an unconditional

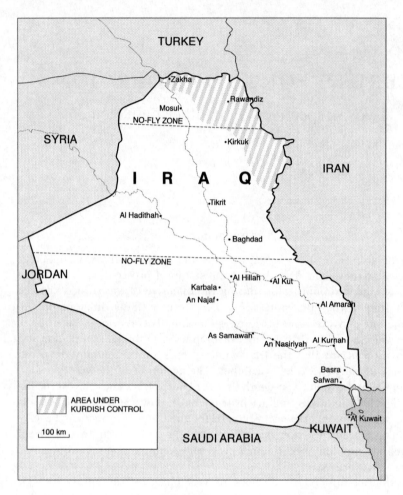

Figure 8.1 Iraq before the war in 2003.

surrender, something that can be called the use of brute force, can be regarded as one of two extremes. The struggle of the Allies against Germany and Japan during the Second World War can serve as an example. The opposite situation, which can be called the use of coercion, would then be represented by a condition where the adversary's political leadership is part of the solution. The Kosovo War, when NATO for political reasons could not pursue a military campaign for the purpose of overthrowing the Serbian regime and occupy Serbia, can be described as such a case. In the first instance, that of brute force, a dialogue with the enemy is completely subordinated to the objective of crushing his military capability. When the aim of the war has been achieved, the resultant defencelessness of the

144

adversary can be used to dictate unilaterally the peace terms. One drawback to such a procedure is that it often generates a need for a protracted occupation in order to create the basic conditions necessary for the vanquished nation to survive. In the second instance, that of coercion, when the political leadership, or rather the government apparatus of the opponent, will remain after the conflict is over, military means are not sufficient. Conflict management in this situation aims primarily not at defeating the adversary militarily, but at bringing about a political will to change. Some form of dialogue, a negotiation, is then necessary. The military efforts, together with a series of other activities, must be directed towards influencing the mechanisms governing political decision-making. The drawback to this procedure is that it requires close and complicated cooperation between many political, diplomatic, and military actors. Usually, this cooperation must extend over national borders and the risk of watered-down compromises is therefore great.

In this chapter, these two perspectives on conflict management, brute force and coercion, are discussed in connection with the war of the US-led coalition against Iraq, taking as a point of departure the theories expounded by André Beaufre and Thomas Schelling.[3]

Schelling – negotiation or military annihilation

In his book *Arms and Influence*, Schelling argues for an approach based on the notion that military victory no longer is a central element in a conflict:

> Military strategy can no longer be thought of, as it could for some countries in some eras, as the science of military victory. It is now equally, if not more, the art of coercion, of intimidation and deterrence. The instruments of war are more punitive than acquisitive. Military strategy, whether we like it or not, has become the diplomacy of violence.[4]

According to Schelling, the greatest difference between diplomacy and military force is not the instruments used, words or bullets, but the relationship between the parties in the conflict. The fundamental idea of diplomacy is negotiation, a dialogue that certainly may contain threats and mutual distrust, but nevertheless is founded on some kind of mutual interest. In contrast, the idea of military capability presupposes the possession of the strength and power to achieve certain aims against the enemy's will, without conferring with him. A state possessing sufficient military strength can theoretically take what it wants and defend what it has. In addition to conquest and defence, military means can be used to cause pain. All wars cause pain. Death and destruction are in the nature of war, but these elements are not the purpose of warfare. Devastation is a result of the military efforts, not an objective in itself. While the traditional way to use military instruments of power implies taking what you want by force, Schelling contends that the ability to make the adversary realize that he can be harmed is one of the most significant options for the use of military force.[5]

The central point in Schelling's reasoning is his suggestion that there is a great difference between:

> taking what you want and making someone give it to you, between fending off an assault and making someone afraid to assault you, between holding what people are trying to take and making them afraid to take it, between losing what someone can forcibly take and giving it up to avoid a risk or damage.[6]

In order to substantiate his argumentation, Schelling employs the concepts of brute force and coercion, but he maintains that the word coercion denotes, on the one hand, forcing somebody to act and, on the other, making somebody refrain from acting through deterrence. He therefore uses the word *compellence* instead of coercion when he is specifically referring to active behaviour sought from the opponent as opposed to the passivity sought in a deterrence relationship.[7]

There are great differences between brute force and compellence. By using brute force, it is possible to achieve the established goals without any consent of the opponent. The use of brute force focuses on the adversary's military capability to defend himself, while his interests are of secondary or no consequence. In most conflict cases, however, it is not only the military capability that is relevant. A nation's will to defend itself is based on more than military strength. Schelling contends that this will can be influenced by causing the opponent damage and pain. Military force as a means of exerting pressure works best when the capability to inflict damage and pain is held in reserve, as a threat. By means of the threat of force, it is possible to influence the opponent's choices.[8] The threat of pain is an attempt to psychologically affect the motives behind his choices, whereas the method of brute force is designed to physically overcome the adversary's strength and thereby gain control over his will.

This reasoning is the foundation for the concept of compellence. While brute force means the use of military force to crush the adversary's defence capability, the theory of compellence is based on the idea of negotiation. Success in negotiations requires good knowledge of the opponent and of what he is aiming at and perceives as most threatening. It is also necessary to make the opponent understand what behaviour on his part will lead to the use of force and what is required to avoid such use.

The starting point for the use of compellence is the presence of an ambition to use as little force as possible and a readiness to use whatever force is necessary. Compellence thus proceeds from the thought of a limited use of power instruments. It requires well-developed communications between the actors involved in order to prevent unwanted escalation. This leads up to a central question in Schelling's reasoning, namely the requirement for an understanding of the rationality on which the adversary's thinking is based. Succeeding in the use of compellence requires that this use is resting on some form of rationality understood and accepted by all actors. The analysis of the situation must be done similarly by the parties. They do not have to favour the same solutions, but both parties must perceive the development of events and the behaviour of the adversary on the basis of similar rational standpoints. In the bargaining situation, which is to be created within the framework of compellence, it is important not to subject the opponent to demands blocking his ability to act in the desired direction or threatening his survival.

From Schelling's view that compellence has the greatest chances of success if military force is held in reserve as a threat, one might draw the conclusion that it is primarily the employment of military force or the amount of force that distinguishes brute force from compellence. However, the distinction cannot be made with reference to the size or quantity of the military force that is used. In fact, the difference resides in the purpose and in the relationship with the adversary. If the German objective in the battle of Verdun had been to remove a military obstacle and if the French soldiers had been looked upon first and foremost as a military resource, this event would have been an example of brute force. If the purpose instead had been to cause the largest possible losses of French fathers, husbands and sons, not for the sake of military effectiveness but calculated to be perceived as intolerable to the French nation, then it would be more appropriate to regard the battle of Verdun as a use of compellence.[9] This example is not central to Schelling's analysis. Still, the reasoning demonstrates very clearly that it is not the amount of force that marks the distinction between brute force and compellence but the purpose of using force. Another evidence for the claim that the size of the military effort is not decisive for the typologization is the Israeli air attack against the Iraqi nuclear reactor at Osirak in 1981. Although only 16 aircraft of the Israeli Air Force participated, the operation is usually regarded as an act of brute force.[10] This can be compared with the Kosovo war when thousands of sorties were carried out. Still, this war is an example of compellence. The purpose of the employment of force and the interaction of the parties involved make up the decisive difference.

In Schelling's conception of compellence, there is a clear ambition to minimize the use of force. The purpose of brute force is to gain control without the adversary's consent by using military force as the primary means. When compellence is used, negotiation supported by military force is the method. This negotiation requires cooperation between diplomats and military men.

Wesley Clark, in his book *Waging Modern War*, provides an account that can serve as an example of the use of compellence. In a conversation with

Secretary of State Madeleine Albright during the Kosovo war in 1999, Clark recognized that initially the build-up of military forces had been used to increase the persuasive power of the diplomatic efforts. After the start of the bombings, the tables were turned. Now the diplomats were instrumental in strengthening the effect of the military weapons employment.[11] This example from the Balkans points to the need for close cooperation between various actors playing different roles depending on the conflict development when compellence is to be used.

While the use of brute force is mainly a question for the military organization, compellence is totally dependent upon the interaction of many actors. Politicians, diplomats, and military leaders must plan and implement operations in close teamwork in order to achieve the synergistic effects central to the use of compellence. There is, however, a natural inclination of the military organization to act as independently as possible in order to reduce the uncertainties on the battlefield.[12] It can sometimes be frustrating for officers to discover that they are not allowed to carry out the military operation in all respects in a manner optimal to achieve military victory and with the smallest possible risk for their units.[13] Politicians are loath to commit themselves and want the largest possible latitude for action. Many politicians and diplomats also do not understand what it is possible to achieve militarily. They may have overconfidence in the capability of the military instruments of power to bring about changes,[14] as well as a reluctance to use such power instruments. There is also an international aspect of the demand for a common view. One of the difficulties of succeeding in compellence is thus made clear.

In attempting to substantiate Schelling's theory, Peter Viggo Jakobsen has put together five different factors that he contends are necessary to achieve success in coercion.[15]

1   The threat must involve so much damage that it is too costly to withstand.
2   The threat must be credible. The threatening party must be perceived as having both capability and will to realize the threat.
3   The threatened party must be given time to yield to the demands that are made.
4   The threatened party must be convinced that concessions will not lead to new demands.
5   The conflict must not be perceived as a zero-sum game where only the threatening party gets benefits. Both sides must feel that they gain more by negotiations and the results these can produce than by using force.

In Jakobsen's interpretation of Schelling, both the stick and the carrot are important elements. The need for a threat, a stick, is fundamental. But for the probability of concessions to increase, the opponent must feel that there is also some advantage, a carrot, in yielding.[16] The conception of threat here should not be taken to mean that the use of force is not a natural component of coercion. Lawrence Freedman observes that even modest objectives may need the backing of 'extremely tough actions'.[17]

The central feature in Schelling's reasoning is the relationship between the parties in a conflict. The conditions for their negotiations and the instruments they use in their interaction are by and large the very framework of his argumentation. At the same time, a conflict can never be conducted in a vacuum. Because of the network of mutual dependencies and interests that is growing stronger in a globalized world, few events do not affect more actors than those who are directly involved. External factors can thus influence the development of a conflict. In order to widen the discussion, it may therefore be necessary to examine another strategy theorist, the French general André Beaufre. Compared to Schelling, he has a broader perspective.

Beaufre – a widened perspective

While Schelling deals with the use of force restricted to the actors immediately affected by a conflict, Beaufre has a wider approach. There are, however, common thoughts evident, for instance in Beaufre's reasoning about direct and indirect strategy. The purpose of the direct strategy is defined as follows: 'In the *direct strategy* "mode" . . . the basic concept being that military force is the principal weapon and that victory or deterrence will be achieved by its use or maintenance.'[18]

The direct strategy can in many respects be compared to brute force, even though Beaufre includes deterrence as one of its objectives. However, the military capability is fully at the centre. The indirect strategy has another purpose:

> Indirect strategy is therefore the art of making the best use of the limited area of freedom of action left us by the deterrent effect of the existence of nuclear weapons and of gaining important and decisive victories in spite of the fact that the military resources which can be employed for the purpose must in general remain strictly limited.[19]

Beaufre's indirect strategy consists of two parts: the exterior and the inner manoeuvre. Together, they make up the totality missing in Schelling's reasoning. Both the conflict's surrounding influential factors, the exterior manoeuvre, and the factors exerting influence in the very conduct of the conflict, the inner manoeuvre, are taken into account.

Beaufre writes: 'the central feature of the "exterior manoeuvre" is to assure for oneself the maximum freedom of action'.[20] This maximum freedom of action is in large measure a question of psychological manoeuvring.

All methods, political, economic, diplomatic and military, should be used. To be successful requires having an adequate military deterrent to dissuade the opponent from resorting to military measures. The combined actions must also obtain '. . . a definite line of policy so conceived that it forms a logical thesis'. Exterior manoeuvring means that 'abstract positions'[21] are to be conquered. This conquest aims at increased political latitude for action so as to make it possible to form or maintain alliances, to get military measures accepted by the international community, and to have the opponent perceive one's position as strong and his own as weak.

The interior manoeuvre consists of 'three variable but interconnected factors: material force, moral force, and time'.[22] Through the relationship between them, flaws in one component can be compensated for by another.

War termination without peace – Iraq 2003

If the two perspectives on conflict management outlined above are accepted, it can be argued that the US chose to use brute force to defeat Iraq and depose Saddam Hussein. This war was terminated officially on 1 May 2003 when President George W. Bush, from the deck of the aircraft carrier *USS Abraham Lincoln*, announced: 'Major combat operations in Iraq have ended. In the battle of Iraq, the United States and our allies have prevailed.'[23] On the ship, there was a large banner reading: 'Mission accomplished.' The message of the slogan was that the military task was now fulfilled, that the war was won after the annihilation of the Iraqi armed forces. Implicit in this language was the view that military units are used solely to attain military victories and that this is enough to win wars. The attitude that military forces should be used exclusively for military warfare has been expressed earlier by President Bush during the war against Afghanistan.[24] A war can hardly be regarded as victorious, however, until peace is concluded. Wesley Clark contends that the Bush administration, especially the Pentagon, underestimated the resistance to an American presence in Iraq and had the idea that 'large numbers of military and police would rally to the Americans, and that the bureaucrats would stay on the job'.[25] Meanwhile, there was a struggle between the Department of State and the Pentagon over responsibility for the reconstruction. The decision allowing the Pentagon to assume this responsibility was not made until January 2003. In the Pentagon, they chose not to make use of the material assembled by the State Department within the project Future Iraq, since persons in leading positions at the defence headquarters felt that the analysis made by the foreign policy leadership was incorrect.[26]

Developments in Iraq after Bush's speech have shown that the task was not fulfilled in early May 2003, not even from a narrow military perspective. The US forces have had to act as 'nation builders' in a way hardly desired by the US Administration.[27] Almost daily during the 15 months after the end of the regular conflict, news about American soldiers having been killed in various types of attack reach us. At the same time, the Iraqi infrastructure does not work. It appears that the threat against the civilian population has shifted from the state terrorism practised by Saddam Hussein's regime to terrorism that may be linked to al-Qaeda and to common criminality, a situation which the Iraqi police and the American troops have great difficulty in handling. The Iraqi armed forces may have been defeated on the battle-field, but the Iraqi resistance seems to live on. American planning and imple-mentation of the military part of the brute force operation demonstrate the enormous military capacity at the disposal of the US today, while the hand-ling of the peace-building part has exposed great shortcomings.

The choice of the brute force option means that the attacking part to a great extent deprives the adversary of responsibility for what happens after the war. Inevitably, a state making another state defenceless by military force must assume responsibility for the disarmed state. In view of the devel-opment we have witnessed so far, it does not seem as if the US appreciated the scope of this problem before the war. On the other hand, the transforma-tion of a nation from dictatorship to democracy takes time; not days, weeks, or even months, but years. It is, therefore, still too early to claim that the US has failed. At the same time, it is difficult to disregard the fact that the suffering inflicted upon the Iraqi people, for instance in the form of increased criminality, including looting in hospitals, could have been limited by better planning of the transition from warfare to occupation.

Is brute force the only alternative?

The Iraq War has been criticized from many different quarters. First, the critics have been against the thought of starting a war at all. There has also been a line of argument, not primarily pacifist but contending that a war could increase the risk of instability in the region. The US, for its part, has justified the military intervention against Saddam Hussein by comparing current international developments to a slippery slope. According to the Bush administration, the attack against the World Trade Center demon-strated an accelerating trend towards an increased risk of terrorist attacks against the West. The Iraqi regime, the US insists, supported this develop-ment and thus posed an immediate threat to Western security. In his 2002 State of the Union address, President Bush branded North Korea, Iran and Iraq as an 'axis of evil'.[28] The speech indicated a fear that these states were developing weapons of mass destruction that could pose a serious global threat and that they possessed technology that could wreak havoc in the West if it fell into the hands of terrorist groups. To meet these threats, the US has enunciated a national security doctrine containing the option to carry out pre-emptive attacks when necessary if a nation is in the process of acquiring weapons of mass destruction.[29]

151

The rationale for placing Iran in the same category as North Korea and Iraq was not only the threat of terrorism. By mentioning Iran in the same context as these states, the Bush administration hoped to support those forces in Iran opposing the religious leaders.[30] This directs attention to another dimension of the analysis that was made by the Administration before the war, a dimension based on what has been called 'the inverted domino theory'. When dominoes are put on end side by side, one falling domino will release a chain reaction knocking down all the others. The belief that international relations can work in the same way as falling dominoes is not new in American politics. At a press conference in April 1954, President Dwight D. Eisenhower put forward the domino theory, which would influence US policy in Indochina.[31] The essence of this thinking was that if Vietnam falls, all of South east Asia will go communist, and then you don't know where it will end. The notion that the domino theory could also be used to spread democratic ideas and not only communist ones germinated among neo-conservative Republicans. Those who most strenuously argued for the inverted domino theory were Deputy Secretary of Defense Paul Wolfowitz and the then-chairman of the Defense Policy Board Richard Perle. That their thoughts have met with sympathy is evident, for instance in a speech delivered by President Bush on 26 February 2003 at the American Enterprise Institute in Washington, where he pointed out that a new regime in Iraq could serve as an inspirational example to other states in the region.[32] Criticism of this suggestion emerged in a report of the US Department of State entitled *Iraq, the Middle East and Change: No Dominoes*.[33] The report was not disseminated publicly but was intended for a small group of high-ranking officials in the US Administration. It criticized the inverted domino theory. Reality could very well produce a completely different development, the State Department asserted: 'Liberal democracy would be difficult to achieve. Electoral democracy, were it to emerge, could well be subject to exploitation by anti-American elements.'[34]

But even within the State Department opinions were divided.[35] With the right methods, the proponents of the inverted domino theory argued, the fight against terrorism would not only ward off the threat of an attack with weapons of mass destruction against the US. A war against Iraq, resulting in democratization of the country, would lead to a positive transformation of the whole region. The Iraqi model would then provide support for the regime critics in Iran and could give them opportunities to topple the Muslim anti-American mullahs. Then Syria would be in line, Saudi Arabia would be forced to modernize its political system and would stop supporting fundamentalist Muslims, and the Palestinians would suddenly find themselves in a situation where they had become completely isolated in the Middle East. The Israeli–Palestinian conflict, perceived by US public opinion as part of the counterterrorist struggle, would then be solved automatically.[36]

If the entire Middle East was to be transformed under US leadership, there was no other option than deposing Saddam Hussein – hardly anyone believed that it was possible to make him resign through negotiations. Brute force seemed to be the only alternative at hand.

Developments in Iraq thus far have not strengthened the US rationale for the chosen line of action. No weapons of mass destruction have been found yet as of this writing in August 2004, and the possibilities of political change in accordance with the inverted domino theory seem remote. Since the difficulties of creating stability and security in Iraq and the region remain, there is reason to ponder the military strategic alternatives the US could have chosen in its attempts to succeed in the conflict with Iraq.

The development of US armed forces

After the fall of the Soviet Union, the armed forces of the United States have experienced great changes in various stages. This process, which is still going on, was started during the Clinton presidency, and even before George W. Bush won the presidential election he expressed a will to make further changes:

> Yet today our military is still organized more for Cold War threats than for challenges of a new century – for industrial age operations, rather than for information age battles. There is almost no relationship between our budget priorities and a strategic vision. The last seven years have been wasted in inertia and idle talk. Now we must shape the future with new concepts, new strategies, new resolve.[37]

When Bush took office, he increased the pressure for change by appointing Donald Rumsfeld Secretary of Defense. During his first months in this post, Rumsfeld advanced two themes.[38] The first implied that he considered the military narrow-minded, old-fashioned, and still equipped, organized and trained to fight 'old' enemies of the type represented by the Soviet Union. The other theme focused on surprise. As a matter of routine, Rumsfeld used to hand out the book *Pearl Harbor: Warning and Decision* written by Roberta Wohlstetter.[39] He also initiated a new transformation of the armed forces in the form of a Quadrennial Defense Review (QDR), presented to the Congress on 2 August 2002.[40] Rumsfeld's QDR is largely a continuation of the Clinton administration's earlier pursuit of a modernized defence, but it also includes an increase in the budgetary funds assigned to increase combat readiness and permit the existence of standing units capable of fighting at short notice.[41]

Rumsfeld also established the Office of Force Transformation to coordinate the transformation work that was to be done.[42] As head of this coordination he selected the retired admiral Arthur K. Cebrowski. Towards

153

the end of his active duty as a military man, Cebrowski was responsible for the thinking behind Network-Centric Warfare (NCW).[43]

Another policy-related concept is what Harlan K. Ullman and James P. Wade call Shock and Awe.[44] In a book with this title, they advocate a method, Rapid Dominance, which amounts to the utilization of military instruments of power to quickly bring about the adversary's collapse:

> The aim of Rapid Dominance is to affect the will, perception, and understanding of the adversary to fit or respond to our strategic policy ends through imposing a regime of Shock and Awe. Clearly, the traditional military aim of destroying, defeating, or neutralizing the adversary's military capability is a fundamental and necessary component of Rapid Dominance. Our intent, however, is to field a range of capabilities to induce sufficient Shock and Awe to render the adversary impotent. This means that physical and psychological effects must be obtained.[45]

The idea of Rapid Dominance relies primarily on a massive employment of air forces and other long-range means. The aim is to cause a system collapse by parallel air strikes within a short time.

Shutting the country down would entail both the physical destruction of appropriate infrastructure and the shutdown and control of the flow of all vital information and associated commerce so rapidly as to achieve a level of national shock akin to the effect that dropping nuclear weapons on Hiroshima and Nagasaki had on the Japanese. Simultaneously, Iraq's armed forces would be paralyzed by the neutralization or destruction of its capabilities. Deception, disinformation and misinformation would be applied extensively.[46]

Large ground forces are to be used only if the opponent does not surrender after the air strikes, and only as a last resort are military forces to be used to occupy the enemy's territory.

Other concepts have been introduced in recent years. The idea of Effects-Based Operations (EBO) is to prepare the ground for more flexible military planning and use of military forces. It focuses on impact rather than the number of targets destroyed or who is executing the employment. The ambition is to obtain cooperation across the entire spectrum between the political, military and economic systems. The aim of EBO is to 'develop capabilities that can rapidly break an adversary's will to fight'.[47]

Rumsfeld's endeavour to modernize the US armed forces in line with these ideas means that the number of soldiers in the US Army must be reduced. When the Chief of Staff of the army, General Eric Shinseki, testifying before a congressional committee, contended that an occupation of Iraq would require several hundred thousand US soldiers during a long time, this interfered with Rumsfeld's plans, and Rumsfeld termed Shinseki's analysis 'far off the mark'.[48] Rumsfeld knows that it is not easy to afford quantity as well as quality – even for Washington. Against the background of what we know now about the development of events in Iraq, surely there can be no doubt that Shinseki had a considerably more realistic understanding of the requirement for US troops in an occupation of Iraq than Rumsfeld was willing to admit.

Yet the outcome of the Iraq war has reinforced the thoughts about the transformation of the US armed forces. Vice-President Dick Cheney announced that the war provided 'proof positive of the success of our efforts to transform our military'.[49] Under Rumsfeld's leadership, US armed forces are headed towards attempting to substitute technology for soldiers. The technological development is to permit another type of warfare than what was planned for during the cold war. Certain modifications can, however, be discerned in the light of the experiences from Iraq.

In recent decades, the US has made great efforts to increase its war-fighting capability. Corresponding measures to improve the capacity of the US armed forces to handle the situation that arises when fighting ends have not been taken.[50] A study by Cebrowski's Office of Force Transformation recommends that two divisions with the primary mission of being able to participate in peace-promoting work be organized.[51] However, this strength, about 30,000 men, is only a tenth of what Shinseki believed was necessary in Iraq. His opinion is supported by a RAND report which suggests that, considering the size of the peace-keeping forces in Bosnia and Kosovo, there should have been 500,000 soldiers in Iraq.[52]

The will to use coercion

Schelling's thoughts about coercion are centred upon the idea of negotiations between the actors in a conflict. It is not the direct employment of military power instruments which brings success. What is sought instead is the indirect effect they have on political decision-making. The pace of the political and diplomatic process, not the speed on the battlefield, determines the outcome of the conflict. The focus of current US policy trends is on quickly overcoming an adversary by military efforts. Room for an outlook emanating from the perspective of coercion appears not to exist. While coercion is grounded on the combination in time and space of politics, diplomacy and military force, the US conceptual development, especially the thoughts of achieving Rapid Dominance, is directed towards separating these various means. In the event of force employment, the forces are to be employed from the start, fully, within the shortest possible time, for the purpose of destroying the defensive capability of the adversary.

Even if the concept Shock and Awe has never been presented officially by any leading representative of the Bush administration, much of the defence

planning and the operations conducted today are based on this concept.[53]
In a congressional hearing, the former deputy chief of staff of the US Air
Force, Lieutenant-General Thomas McInerney, described what a war against
Iraq might be like:

> Now I would like to broadly discuss the combined campaign to
> achieve these objectives using what I will call blitz warfare, to
> simplify the discussion. Blitz warfare is an intensive, 24/7 precision
> air-centric campaign supported by fast-moving ground forces com-
> posed of a mixture of heavy, light, airborne, amphibious, special,
> covert operations, working with opposition forces that will all use
> effect-based operations for their target set and correlate their
> timing forces for a devastating violent impact.[54]

From a purely military point of view, this is an ideal condition. The military
operation can be planned to achieve maximum effect during a short time and
with military control over events. The risk of casualties is minimized and
optimal military solutions can be chosen. At the same time, the military
instrument runs the risk of becoming more static. Either it is employed
fully or it is not used at all. It is doubtful whether reality permits such a
rigid attitude. There will always be conflicts demanding other forms of force
employment. The danger of current thinking is that the central decision-
makers will regard these as disturbing deviations from the ideal. Brute
force will become the preferred approach and coercion will not even figure
as an option. If limited political latitude for action then calls for the use of
coercion, problems will arise. Considering the complexity of cooperation
and the demand for an understanding of the strategic totality inherent in
the practice of coercion, the probability of failure will be high. On the other
hand, choosing brute force over coercion can result in the success of the
military operation at the expense of the strategic goal.

The US analysis seems to be highly focused on the military dimension of
conflicts, with a brute force perspective governing the choice of method.
There is a desire to win wars as quickly as possible by means of great technological superiority. Achieving this technological capability demands that
the number of units, especially manpower-heavy Army units, be reduced.
There has also been a tendency to regard the need for nation-building as
a deviation from the normal. Every conflict management effort in the
1990s has been characterized by improvization in this respect. Reduced man-
power in combination with the absence of a will to handle the occupation,
which in most cases is a consequence of a brute force operation, increases
the risk that peace work will become more difficult. It appears that the
policy-makers want to use brute force without realizing the consequences
of this method.

The exterior manoeuvre and coercion

An important element of Beaufre's indirect strategy is the exterior manoeuvre, designed to provide for maximum freedom of action. The ambition is to obtain the strongest possible moral position: The international community is to perceive my cause as righteous and be suspicious of the adversary's. Furthermore, the moral dimension is to be reinforced by a strong military capability. When coercion is practised, a successful exterior manoeuvre is of the greatest importance. The US military capability built up around Iraq was probably sufficient to pose the threat that is an important component of coercion. US capability and will to use military force had been demonstrated in the three large-scale military operations that had taken place in recent years: the Kuwait War of 1991, the Kosovo War of 1999, and the war against the Taliban regime in Afghanistan in 2001. However, there were no signs that Saddam Hussein was prepared to leave his power position just because he was threatened. One reason for this, perhaps the most obvious, is that Saddam's whole political life revolved around gaining and retaining power. After the Kuwait War, President George H. W. Bush believed that the Iraqi people would overthrow Saddam Hussein: 'Saddam cannot survive . . . people are fed up with him. They see him for the brutal dictator he is.'[55] But Saddam could and did survive as a dictator for 12 more years until US military units took Baghdad in 2003.

Immediately after the Kuwait War, Saddam took advantage of the reluctance of the West to move its ground forces to Baghdad and depose him. Having made a few concessions, including accepting UN resolution 687, he acted with all his force against the insurrection of the Kurds and Shi'ites and suppressed it with great ruthlessness.[56] Saddam's ability to manage political crises was strengthened by the international community's unwillingness to get serious and take sufficient measures. The resolutions adopted by the UN Security Council and the sanctions resulting from these were not enough to diminish Saddam's power base. Instead, he could turn the suffering of the Iraqi people into anger directed against the West. When the Bush Administration finally, after having driven the Taliban regime out of Kabul, began to pay serious attention to Iraq, the disagreement among the permanent members of the UN Security Council was helpful to Saddam Hussein. In this situation, the US would have needed to practise the exterior manoeuvre in order to secure a freedom of action that would have facilitated the management of the conflict.

There were diverging views even in the US on how the Iraq question should be handled. During the summer of 2002, a struggle over the UN's role seemed to be going on within the Bush administration. While one faction, mainly consisting of the neo-conservative group in the Pentagon, wanted to ignore the UN and instead create a 'coalition of the willing' through bilateral agreements, the Department of State under Colin Powell

wanted to act through the UN. The first option presupposed that US political and military strength was sufficient and that there actually was no need
for any foreign assistance. The second option reflected the belief that
broad international support was necessary to succeed in a war against
Iraq. At a dinner in August 2002, Powell, according to Nicholas Lehmann,
managed to convince Bush to take the UN route.[57] Although Bush decided
to try to make use of the UN and even succeeded in getting the Security
Council to agree on resolution 1441, the split among the permanent members
did not end. Washington was not ready to compromise about its basic view
that Iraq was an imminent security threat. Its stand did not make the situation easier, since a majority of the other members of the Security Council
refused to accept the description of reality that Washington presented.

Suddenly, Saddam seemed to be on the same side as world opinion against
the US. As a result of the conflict in the UN, Saddam could play on the
existing anti-Americanism in the Middle East and thereby contribute to
reducing US freedom of action. It has been argued that this distrust, which
often finds expression in disgust, emanates from the Islamic world's image
of itself. Islam is not only one of the world's largest religions, but has also
been a large empire with a very advanced culture.[58] Being subjected to
pressure, threats, and unilateral solutions therefore creates frustration and
resistance. Moreover, the fast-growing anti-war opinion all over the world
induced many governments to strike a cautious or even critical attitude
towards the behaviour of the US. Specifically, this reduced freedom of
action resulted in Turkey's refusal to allow American ground troops to use
Turkish territory as a base for attacking Iraq.

Since the aim of war is to win peace, success in the exterior manoeuvre is
of great importance. If acceptance for the conduct of war is gained, there will
be greater latitude for action when fighting ends. Patience in case of setbacks
will be greater, both among the public at home and among other states.
It will also be more difficult for groups opposing an occupation to obtain
domestic and international support. The difficulties the US encountered in
trying to win approval for its war against Iraq and the huge international
opposition aroused against the war put anti-American groups in the
Muslim countries in a mood conducive to increased recruitment of man-
power and money for terrorism directed against the US and the Iraqi population. The image of strength demonstrated by the US on the battlefield has
turned into an image of weakness in the struggle to restore law and order.

Is it possible to negotiate?

Negotiations require some form of mutual understanding between the different parties and a sense that there is something to gain from an agreement.
There must also be an understanding of the rationality behind the behaviour
of the actors in the conflict. In the case of the US and Iraq, this bargaining

situation probably did not exist after 11 September 2001. The attack against the World Trade Center and the subsequent designation of Iraq as one of the states belonging to the 'axis of evil' made it politically impossible to negotiate. To some extent, the instrument of negotiation had been squandered after the Kuwait War.

The 1990s were characterized by endless negotiations mixed with military actions. In principle, one could say that an attempt was made between the Kuwait and Iraq wars to use coercion through attrition tactics. Operations Southern Watch[59] and Northern Watch[60] barred large parts of the Iraqi air space, and a large number of military actions, primarily against Iraqi anti-aircraft sites, were carried out. Following a conflict between the UN and Iraq, the US and Great Britain in 1998 performed Operation Desert Fox.[61] Thus, the UN's attempt to disarm Iraq with the help of weapons inspections was supported by military efforts without achieving anything that was perceived at the time as a decisive success. One cannot disregard the possibility that weapons production could have resumed once the control of Saddam ceased. Coercion, too, must have a terminal point. It is impossible to negotiate forever. Achieving decisive success requires a situation in which normal relations can be resumed. Such was not the case with Iraq. Coercion, in the manner practised in the 1990s until the Iraq War of 2003, did not work. The core issue was Saddam Hussein. As long as he remained in power, there was no definitive solution of the conflict. The notion of negotiating Saddam away from power was completely unrealistic, no doubt. All his adult life he had struggled for power with all available means, and his conception of reality discouraged him from taking another person's advice.[62] He would probably never have been able to sit at the negotiation table and understand that the game was up.

Hopes that the Iraqi people would have the strength to overthrow Saddam by itself vanished soon after the Kuwait War, when the Kurdish and Shi'ite insurrections were suppressed with all the brutality of which the dictator in Baghdad was capable. From this, it can be concluded that brute force was the only way out and that the use of military instruments of power by the US-led alliance in the spring of 2003 was a logical consequence of the earlier failures.

A combination of brute force and coercion

The choice between coercion and brute force is not obvious. Inherent in coercion is the existence of a comprehensive view and chances of solving a conflict both politically and militarily. However, the requirement for close and constructive cooperation between politicians, diplomats and military people is taxing, not least because the actors involved must often accept compromise solutions. Middle courses can be especially hard to accept for the military organization because they can lead to an increased risk for the soldiers participating in the operation. The use of coercion also demands a skilfully performed exterior manoeuvre so as to increase the political freedom of action and isolate the adversary. In the short run, brute force is a considerably more simple choice, especially if a nation has at its disposal powerful armed forces. By attacking according to the principle of Rapid Dominance, political will can be demonstrated at the same time as the military organization is allowed to employ its resources in an ideal manner. But war is much more than winning victories, especially in a situation where a lasting peace is the goal. The most important objective, then, is not to destroy old systems but to create conditions for the establishment of new ones.

The question is, was it possible to practise brute force against Saddam and coerce the rest of the Iraqi state? Is it possible to depose a dictator while preserving the structure holding a society together? Could the ruling circles in Iraq, not Iraqis in exile but those who occupied such positions that they might be instrumental in preventing the structure of the society from collapsing during a change of regimes, be persuaded to cooperate? Is it at all possible to tolerate some part of the government apparatus or are its representatives so intimately associated with the dictator that their culpability is too great?

In the war against Afghanistan, brute force was used against the Taliban regime, while coercion made the local warlords switch sides. But what was possible in a feudal society like Afghanistan is not as simple in a centralized totalitarian state of the Soviet type. A complicating circumstance in the Iraq case is that Saddam's power structure to a high degree was built on ties of blood. His power base emanated largely from Tikrit and members of the tribe Albu-Nasir. As early as his tenure as vice-president (1969–1979), Saddam gathered his tribal relatives in the Iraqi security service. At the outbreak of the Iraq War in 2003, all central positions in this organization were held by persons from Albu-Nasir.[63] The control of the Iraqi people, not least persons in important positions, was as developed as in most totalitarian states. Saddam had also, during his long time in power, created the image that his regime was irremovable. He seemed to weather all crises, keeping his power, so why not this one, too? The risk of being exposed as collaborator with the enemy was obvious. Attempts from the outside to establish collaboration under such circumstances would probably meet with difficult hurdles. Apart from the control exercised by the security service, the build-up of a government apparatus with blood ties as the idea probably inspired a loyalty among many high-ranking officials directed more towards Saddam Hussein personally than towards the Iraqi nation. Their authority was based on his possession of power, not on the government organization. If the dictator in Baghdad had disappeared, their legitimacy as people with power would probably have come to an end. To have deposed Saddam under such conditions and still have striven to preserve a working government apparatus would have been very difficult.

The alternative that a popular uprising would do the job for the US was nipped in the bud. A complicating circumstance is that the population of a totalitarian state is often dependent on the state to provide for their needs. A popular uprising in Iraq would probably have shattered the state's capacity to render assistance, since many officials in central positions formed part of Saddam's power apparatus. The consequences would probably have been the same as those appearing in connection with the US assumption of power, namely a societal collapse.

Another problem with an uprising in Iraq is that the country is not ethnically homogenous. In other words, there is no uniform national identity.[64] If Saddam had been overthrown by a popular uprising, this could have resulted in the division of Iraq between the Kurdish, Sunni and Shi'ite groups. What might have further aggravated the situation is that the different ethnic groups in many areas are mixed together and have conflicting interests. An uprising against Saddam might very well have turned into a civil war between the ethnic groups. If the Iraqi people had deposed Saddam, its willingness to accept US interference in the government of Iraq would probably have been limited, irrespective of the support received from Washington during the rebellion. An attempt to set up a council, with mostly exile Iraqis as members, would probably have encountered strong resistance. The US might have ended up in a situation where it would have had to separate different fighting groups.

The use of a combination of coercion and brute force against Iraq would initially have required an effort to succeed in an exterior manoeuvre. This political effort could have begun immediately after the Kuwait War. The required foundation would have been a common view among the leading actors in the UN Security Council and an agreement to institute a new regime in Iraq. The no-fly zones imposed over Iraq in 1991 could have been used to reduce Saddam's military capability, but also to show Saddam's incapability. Along with this demonstration, a political alternative to the dictator in Baghdad should have been promoted, both nationally, within Iraq, and internationally. In all likelihood, it would still have been necessary in the end to use brute force to overthrow Saddam because he would probably not have given up power voluntarily. But the use of brute force would have taken place under different political conditions and presumably with more support from the Iraqi people.

Conclusion

History shows that military instruments of power in various situations must be used to create better living conditions for exposed people in a conflict area. Without the international military effort that now has been going on for more than ten years in the Balkans, the suffering that had befallen the population would have been much worse. Sometimes a conflict can be managed by coercion. In other cases, in the struggle against Hitler during the Second World War for example, only brute force is applicable. All conflicts cause suffering, and no single solution can mitigate all the ordeals suffered by the civilian population. It is, however, important to understand and develop the military instruments of power so that they can be used as tools of both coercion and brute force. The choice between these two uses can become involuntary if all actors on the national and international arenas do not cooperate.

When General Maxwell Taylor returned from the Korean War, he was charged with evaluating the conduct of the war. He concluded that the US government had made a mistake when it treated political, diplomatic and military efforts as separate rather than complementary means.[65] Increased and improved coordination of political, diplomatic and military actions would have created the necessary conditions for more successful warfare. Success in coercion requires precisely this coordination. The seeds of failure to prevail in the Iraq conflict without in the end resorting to brute force were sown immediately after the Kuwait War in 1991. An attempt to overthrow Saddam while maintaining the Iraqi government apparatus would have demanded that the international community, as a first step, legitimized a new regime. This would have taken time, but there was time. The 1990s were devoted to various attempts to use coercion against Iraq. The problem has been that the international community distrusted the rationale of US behaviour in the region. This distrust was further accentuated under the current Administration. As a result of the difficulties that the nations of the world have had in cooperating and putting pressure on Saddam, the conflict developed into an application of brute force when the attack against the World Trade Center provided an opening for the Bush administration to act.

Discord among the central actors in the UN Security Council denied the US the legitimacy that even a superpower needs to accomplish a revolution in another country. Instead, Saddam could exploit the distrust of the US in the Arab world to fan opposition against the war and the occupation that eventually toppled his regime. Responsibility for this situation cannot be laid only on the US. During Saddam's time in power, several nations have contributed to the strengthening of his power position. France, Germany, and Russia carry a special responsibility. We will probably not see a more constructive use of military instruments of power in international politics until the permanent members of the UN Security Council act together to solve conflicts and to a less extent act to protect their own interests. Still, there is reason to ponder the question in what situations of conflict management brute force or coercion should be used. Both approaches have a role to play, but their application produces different results and demands different forms of cooperation.

Notes

1 C. von Clausewitz, *On War*, Princeton, NJ: Princeton University Press, 1976, p. 119.
2 Ibid., p. 87.
3 A. Beaufre, *An Introduction to Strategy*, New York: Fredrick A. Praeger, 1965 and T. Schelling, *Arms and Influence*, New Haven, CN: Yale University Press, 1966.
4 Schelling, op. cit., p. 34.
5 Ibid., pp. 1–2.
6 Ibid., p. 2.
7 Ibid., p. 71.
8 Ibid., p. 4.
9 Ibid., p. 5.
10 K. Mueller, 'Denial, Punishment, and the Future of Air Power', *Security Studies*, 7, 3 (Spring 1998) and Washington Report on Middle East Affairs, available at http://www.wrmea.com/Washington-Report_org/www/backissues/-0695/9506081.htm (accessed 31 October 2003).
11 W. Clark, *Waging Modern War*, New York: Public Affairs 2001, pp. 253–254.
12 B. R. Posen, 'Explaining Military Doctrine', in R. J. Art and K. N. Waltz (eds) *The Use of Force*, Boston, MA: Rowman and Littlefield Publishers, 1999, p. 31.
13 This frustration was voiced after the Kosovo conflict by the US Air Force general Mike Short. In an interview in *The Washington Post* 20 June 1999, he said: 'I hope the alliance will learn that before you drop the first bomb, or fire the first shot, we need to lock the political leaders up in a room and have them decide what the rules of engagement will be so they can provide the military with the proper guidance and latitude needed to prosecute the war . . . As an airman, I'd have done this a whole lot differently than I was allowed to do. We could have done this differently. We should have done this differently.'
14 During his time as military adviser in the White House, Colin Powell, after an attempted coup in the Philippines, had to argue for military restraint in opposition to those civilian officials who wanted to use military force immediately. The episode is described in B. Woodward, *The Commanders*, New York: Touchstone, 2002, pp. 146–155.
15 P. V. Jakobsen, *Western Use of Coercive Diplomacy after the Cold War*, London: MacMillan Press, 1998, p. 17.
16 Schelling, op. cit., p. 4.
17 L. Freedman 'Strategic Coercion' in L. Freedman (ed.) *Strategic Coercion*, New York: Oxford University Press, 1998, p. 21.
18 Ibid., p. 43.
19 Ibid., pp. 109–110.
20 Ibid., p. 110.
21 Ibid., p. 112.
22 Ibid., p. 113.
23 Speech by President Bush, 1 May 2003, available at http://www.whitehouse.gov/news/releases/2003/05/iraq/20030501-15.html (accessed 19 September 2003).
24 Woodward, *Bush at War*, New York: Simon & Schuster, 2002, p. 237. 'Look', said the President, 'I oppose using the military for nation building. Once the job is done, our forces are not peacekeepers.'
25 W. Clark, *Winning Modern Wars*, New York: Public Affairs, 2003, p. 89.
26 D. Rieff, 'Blueprint for a Mess', *The New York Times*, 2 November 2003.

27 J. Dobbins, 'Next Step in Iraq and Beyond: Testimony Presented before the Committee on Foreign Relations', United States Senate, 23 September 2003, *RAND-Testimony*, p. 4, available at http://www.rand.org/publications/CT/CT212/ (accessed 4 December 2003).
28 'States like these, and their terrorist allies, constitute an axis of evil, arming to threaten the peace of the world. By seeking weapons of mass destruction, these regimes pose a grave and growing danger. They could provide these arms to terrorists, giving them the means to match their hatred. They could attack our allies or attempt to blackmail the United States. In any of these cases, the price of indifference would be catastrophic.'
29 *The National Security Strategy of the United States*, September 2002, available at http://www.whitehouse.gov/nsc/nss.html (accessed 1 October 2003).
30 D. Frum, *The Right Man*, London: Weidenfeld & Nicolson, 2003, p. 237.
31 'Question: Mr. President, would you mind commenting on the strategic importance of Indochina to the free world? I think there has been, across the country, some lack of understanding on just what it means to us. Answer: . . . Finally, you have broader considerations that might follow what you would call the "falling domino" principle. You have a row of dominoes set up, you knock over the first one, and what will happen to the last one is the certainty that it will go over very quickly. So you could have a beginning of a disintegration that would have the most profound influences.' Available at http://coursesa.matrix.msu.edu/~hst306/documents/domino.html (accessed 12 August 2004)
32 G. Miller, 'Democracy in Iraq Doubtful, State Dept. Report Says Social, Economic Obstacles Work Against Transformation', *Los Angeles Times*, 14 March 2003, available at http://groups.yahoo.com/group/nhnenews/message/4737 (accessed 12 August 2004).
33 Ibid.
34 Ibid.
35 Reiff, op. cit.
36 Frum, op. cit., p. 259. During a visit to the Pentagon in November 2001, Wesley Clark (*Winning Modern Wars*, p. 130) was briefed about plans for a five-year campaign against first Iraq, then Syria, Lebanon, Libya, Iran, Somalia and finally Sudan.
37 Speech by George W. Bush at the Citadel, a military school in Charleston, South Carolina, 23 September 1999, available at http://usinfo.state.gov/topical/pol/terror/01121002.htm (accessed 3 October 2003).
38 Woodward, *Bush at War*, p. 22.
39 The book was published in 1962 and got favourable reviews. The author's conclusion is that the Japanese attack was a surprise because the US intelligence service failed to interpret the warnings. Some in the US have drawn parallels between Pearl Harbor and the attack against the World Trade Center.
40 Available at http://www.defenselink.mil/pubs/qdr2001.pdf (accessed 3 October 2003).
41 M. O'Hanlon, 'Rumsfeld's Defence Vision', *Survival*, 44, 2 (Summer 2002), 108–117.
42 F. W. Kagan, 'War and Aftermath', *Policy Review*, 120 (3 August 2003), 3.
43 A description of NCW can be found in D. S. Alberts, J. J. Gartska, and F. P. Stein, *Network Centric Warfare: Developing and Leveraging Information Superiority*. Washington, DC: Department of Defense, C4ISR Cooperative Research Program, 2000.

44 H. K. Ullman, and J. P. Wade, *Shock and Awe, Achieving Rapid Dominance*, Washington, DC: Center for Advanced Concepts and Technology, National Defense University, 1996.

45 Ibid., p. 10.

46 Ibid., p. 37.

47 D. Saunders-Newton and A. B. Frank, 'Effects-Based Operations: Building the Analytic Tools', *Defense Horizons*, 19 (October 2002), available at http://www.ndu.edu/inss/DefHor/DH19/DH_19.htm (accessed 26 November 2003).

48 B. Bender, 'Top Aides deny Word of Pentagon Rift', *The Boston Globe*, 31 March 2003, available at http://www.globalsecurity.org/news/2003/030331–warplan02.htm (accessed 1 October 2003).

49 Kagan, op. cit., p. 12.

50 Dobbins, op. cit., p. 4.

51 B. Graham, 'Pentagon puts the idea of peacekeeping army into play', *smh.com*, 25 November 2003, available at http://www.smh.com/au/articles/2003/11/24/1069522539567.htm (accessed 1 December 2003).

52 Quinlivan, James T. 'Burden of Victory,' *RAND Review*, 27, 2 (Summer 2003), 28–29.

53 Kagan, op. cit., p. 19.

54 Available at http://www.iraqwatch.org/government/us/hearingspreparedstate-ments/sasc-mcinerney-092302.htm (accessed 26 November 2003).

55 Quoted in C. Coughlin, *Saddam, the Secret Life*, London: Pan Macmillan, 2003, p. 279.

56 Ibid., pp. 280–281.

57 N. Lehmann, 'How It Came to War', *The New Yorker*, 31 March 2003, available at http://www.newyorker.com/fact/content/?030331fa_fact (accessed 10 August 2004).

58 Frum, op. cit., p. 170.

59 Available at http://www.fas.org/man/dod-101/ops/southern_watch.htm (accessed 3 October 2003).

60 Available at http://www.fas.org/man/dod-101/ops/northern_watch.htm (accessed 3 October 2002).

61 Available at http://www.defenselink.mil/specials/desert_fox/ and http://www.fas.org/man/dod-101/ops/desert_fox.htm (accessed 3 October 2003).

62 Coughlin, op. cit., p. 316.

63 A. Baram, 'Saddam's Power Structure: The Tikritis Before, During and After the War' in T. Dodge and S. Simon (eds) *Iraq at the Crossroads: State and Society in the Shadow of Regime Change*, Adelphi Papers, 354 (January 2003), pp. 96–97.

64 J. Hjärpe, 'Var Saddam den siste irakiern?' *Dagens Nyheter*, 17 August 2003.

65 E. R. May and P. D. Zelikow (eds) *The Kennedy Tapes*, Cambridge, MA: Belknap Press, 1997, p. 10.

References

Art, R. J. and Waltz, K. N. (eds) *The Use of Force*. Boston, MA: Rowman and Littlefield Publishers, 1999.

Alberts, D. S., Gartska, J. J. and Stein, F. P. *Network Centric Warfare: Developing and Leveraging Information Superiority*, 2nd edn. Washington, DC: Department of Defense, C4ISR Cooperative Research Program, 2000.

Beaufre, A. *An Introduction to Strategy*. New York: Fredrick A. Praeger, 1965.

Bender, B. 'Top Aides deny Word of Pentagon Rift', *The Boston Globe*, 31 March 2003, Available at http:// www.globalsecurity.org/news/2003/030331–warplan02. htm (accessed 1 October 2003).

Byman, D. L., Waxman, M. C. and Larson, E. *Air Power as a Coercive Instrument*. Washington, DC: RAND, 1999.

Clark, W. *Waging Modern War*. New York: Public Affairs, 2001.

—— *Winning Modern War*. New York: Public Affairs, 2003.

Clausewitz, C. von *On War*. Princeton, NJ: Princeton University Press 1976.

Coughlin, C. *Saddam, the Secret Life*. London: Pan Macmillan, 2003.

Dodge, T. and Simon, S. (eds) *Iraq at the Crossroads: State and Society in the Shadow of Regime Change*, Adelphi Papers, 354. Oxford: Oxford University Press, 2002.

Dobbins, J. 'Next Step in Iraq and Beyond: Testimony Presented before the Committee on Foreign Relations', United States Senate, 23 September 2003, *RAND-Testimony*, p. 4, available at http://www.rand.org/publications/CT/ CT212/ (accessed 4 December 2003).

Freedman, L. (ed.) *Strategic Coercion*. New York: Oxford University Press, 1998.

Frum, D. *The Right Man*, London: Weidenfeld & Nicolson, 2003.

George, A. and Simons, W. W. *The Limits of Coercive Diplomacy*. Boulder, CO: Westview Press, 1994.

Graham, B. 'Pentagon puts the idea of peacekeeping army into play', *smh.com*, 25 November 2003, available at http://www.smh.com/au/articles/2003/11/24/ 1069522539567.htm (accessed 1 December 2003).

Hjärpe, J. 'Var Saddam den siste irakiern?' [Was Saddam the Last Iraqi?] *Dagens Nyheter*, 17 August 2003.

Jakobsen, P. V. *Western Use of Coercive Diplomacy after the Cold War*. London: MacMillan Press, 1998.

Kagan, F. W. 'War and Aftermath', *Policy Review*, 120, 3 August (2003), 3–27.

Lehmann, N. 'How It Came to War', *The New Yorker*, 31 March 2003.

May, E. R. and Zelikow, P. D. (eds) *The Kennedy Tapes*. Cambridge, MA: Belknap Press, 1997.

Miller, G. 'Democracy in Iraq Doubtful, State Dept. Report Says Social, Economic Obstacles Work Against Transformation', *Los Angeles Times*, 14 March 2003, available at http://groups.yahoo.com/group/nhnenews/message/4737 (accessed 12 August 2004).

Mueller, K. 'Denial, Punishment, and the Future of Air Power', *Security Studies*, 7, 3 (1998), 182–228.

O'Hanlon, M. 'Rumsfeld's Defence Vision', *Survival*, 44, 2 (2002), 103–117.

Quinlivan, J. T. 'Burden of Victory', *RAND Review*, 27, 2 (Summer 2003), 28–29.

Rieff, D. 'Blueprint for a Mess', *The New York Times*, 2 November 2003.

Saunders-Newton, D. and Frank, A. B. 'Effects-Based Operations: Building the Analytic Tools', *Defense Horizons*, 19 (October 2002), available at http://www. ndu.edu/inss/DefHor/DH19/DH_19.htm (accessed 26 November 2003).

Schelling, T. *Arms and Influence*. New Haven, CN: Yale University Press, 1966.

Ullman, H. K. and Wade, J. P. *Shock and Awe, Achieving Rapid Dominance*. Washington, DC: Center for Advanced Concepts and Technology, National Defense University, 1996.

Woodward, B. *The Commanders*. New York: Touchstone, 2002.

—— *Bush at War*. New York: Simon & Schuster, 2002.

9

DOCTRINE, EXPERTISE AND ARMS IN COMBINATION

A reflection on the Iraq War

Anders Cedergren

Operational concept

The military victory over Saddam Hussein's armed forces was secured when Baghdad was captured after approximately three weeks of combat. This was a very short campaign in comparison, so it can be interesting to study the principles on which the campaign was based, and to refer back to the theories that were given a practical application. When analysing the campaign in Iraq, we need to remind ourselves that the conflict is not yet over. A different type of war is now (in the summer of 2004) taking place – a low intensity conflict, guerilla warfare. However, the analysis in this chapter focuses on the military victory over Iraq's armed forces in April 2003.

We need to remember that Iraq's warfighting capability was low. It was never rebuilt after the Gulf War in 1991[1] and several factors contributed to this. The *Southern Watch* and *Northern Watch*[2] operations that monitored air space over Iraq after the end of the Gulf War, and operation *Desert Fox*, which during four days of intensive air attacks in 1998 aimed to destroy what was left of Iraq's capacity to produce weapons of mass destruction. The UNSCOM (United Nations Special Commission on Iraq) operation seems to have been highly effective in disarming Iraq of weapons of mass destruction, carriers, and production capacity for NBC weapons. Furthermore, the arms embargo had made it very difficult for Iraq to raise the warfighting capacity of its armed forces after the Gulf War.

Another factor was Iraq's internal inability to prepare itself for a new war. The country created its own *critical vulnerabilities* that were exploited by the coalition.[3] The Iraqi view on strategy was primarily characterized not by the experiences from the war of 1991, but by its geopolitical position and the internal political situation after the Gulf War. Saddam Hussein felt the Kurds in the north were a problem, and had to be kept under control; in the south, a low intensity conflict with the Shi'ites went on for some time, and the border with Iran needed to be guarded and protected. The regime's sensitivity to internal threats also led to several parts of Iraq's armed forces being assigned the task of monitoring each other. The continued allied operation in the no-fly zones meant that the Iraqi air defence concentrated on survival in a low intensity conflict. All these factors meant that the Iraqi armed forces were poorly prepared and lacked much of the necessary capacity to function in a full-scale conflict.

There were signs of limited capacity in the leadership of the Iraqi armed forces, from the top down through the entire chain of command to the lowest divisional units. No aircraft took off, and the land units did not manoeuvre in combat but generally remained stationary in combat positions, with limited anti-aircraft protection. Apart from the visual line of sight, Iraqi capacity was very limited. For the Iraqis, this resulted in positional warfare and aimless, poorly coordinated attacks. These types of attacks would have been effective against internal threats, but totally lacked success against the well-trained, well-equipped and well-protected soldiers in the coalition units. The level of training of the Iraqi units proved to be another critical vulnerability. The coalition units won every battle. Iraqi units lacked the ability to counter-move, and could not exploit the coalition's weaknesses. In other words, Iraq lacked the ability to coordinate its armed forces in jointly operative effects.

Nevertheless, it is still interesting to consider the coalition warfare strategy because it included doctrinal thought based on the manoeuvrist approach. This well-known approach to war seems to have incorporated and utilized new technology in both familiar and new ways of combining arms.

The doctrine that led to the strategy shown in Iraq in 2003 really originated in the *AirLand Battle* concept from 1982.[4] This concept, described in *FM 100-5, Operations 1982*, introduced the operative level and an intellectual approach to warfare. This contrasts with previous American doctrinal thinking where the emphasis had largely been on firepower and winning battles on the tactical level. Even though the doctrine marked the start of the development of a manoeuvre concept, it was far from fully developed. The AirLand Battle concept was focused on Europe and was aimed at preventing a Soviet attack towards the Atlantic. Soviet superiority in terms of conventional forces on the ground necessitated innovation for any chance of success. The distance to the Atlantic coast was only 200–300 km through northern West Germany and the Netherlands. NATO armies and corps had basically a linear deployment with very limited operative depth. The aim was that these would check the first echelons of the Warsaw Pact. The operative depth on the ground was difficult to change, but could be expanded in the air by pushing aside the Soviet air forces and by using air raids to attack the Soviet reinforcement units in the second and third echelons. What was needed, therefore, was intimate collaboration between the land and air forces.

The AirLand Battle concept, developed to protect Europe, was put into practice in the Gulf War of 1991. From the very start, the air forces were attacking targets over the entire Iraqi territory and launched combined attacks with the coalition's cruise missiles, launched mainly from US navy vessels. The targets were Iraq's command structure, the Iraqi air force and anti-air defences, important land targets such as the Republican Guard and targets assumed to be connected with the Iraqi NBC programme. After 38 days of intensive preliminary combat, the decisive action started when the land offensive was launched. The linear deployments from the European continent were retained (most of the American and British units had been redeployed from Europe) and were applied in practice by attacking in a line. Much of the coordination during this offensive land operation[5] concerned keeping the units at the same level in order to protect each other's flanks.[6] In other words, deep attacks were avoided, as shown by the decisions concerning the 24th Infantry Division (24. ID). In this aspect, the operation was more similar to the Schlieffen Plan of 1914 than *Operation Sichelschnitt*[7] of 1940. The Iraqi units could either avoid the allied land offensive by moving in a northerly direction, or confront it by remaining in position and going into combat. The latter consisted mainly of defensive action.[8] The allied land operation, using this concept of a direct approach, resulted in mainly frontal attacks. The success was based on a massive concentration of firepower, both airborne and shipborne, and massed forces on the ground. Movements on the ground were aimed at destroying or suppressing Iraqi units so that Kuwait could finally be liberated.

When this operation was carried out in 1991, the manoeuvrist approach to warfare was fully developed, and several books on the new idea had existed for some years, for example W. S. Lind's *Maneuver Warfare Handbook* from 1985. They all regarded *movement* as a *weapon*. The conceptual development had also resulted in a new *Field Manual 100–5 1986*, for the US army. It emphasized manoeuvre, confusion, penetration and decentralized leadership.[9] The Soviet operative strategy[10] of that time included *Operational Manouever Groups* (OMG), whose origin can be traced to the 1930s and the development of the Soviet operative strategy.[11] The concept was called *deep operations* in military literature, and assumed versatile, independently-acting units that were organized according to the principle of combined arms carrying out their missions with air support. These OMGs were intended to break through enemy defences and cut up the enemy's more sensitive activities at the rear of his operational area. Why was a more distinct maneouvre concept that included *deep battle* not used in the Gulf War of 1991? The reason is probably that it takes time for ideas and knowledge first to be accepted as a doctrine and then to result in new conduct on the battlefield. When a new doctrine has been created, seven to ten years of intensive training are generally needed before it can be fully implemented in practice.[12] What takes time is retraining at the officer level and basic training in new conduct at the unit level,[13] and often new equipment must be supplied.

In order to understand the warfare strategy applied in the Iraq War of 2003, we need to go back seven to ten years and look at the dominant doctrines of that time. The doctrines found concerned manoeuvre warfare. They were developed from the AirLand Battle doctrine using studies of German and (primarily) Russian (Soviet) warfare strategy, and became known as the Manoeuvre Warfare School. The major difference compared with the AirLand Battle model in *Field Manual 100-5 1982* is the balance between the air and land operation, and the clear emphasis on the importance of deep battle for the land operation.[14] The period between 1986 and Desert Storm in 1991 was probably too short for the more sophisticated manoeuvre doctrine and its decree on deep battle to have any great impact. The first part of the American armed forces to adopt the new model was the US Marine Corps. In the Marine Corps' *Warfighting* from 1989, manoeuvre warfare was put forward as the coherent concept that gives a small force the best chance of defeating a larger one:

> Maneuver warfare is a warfighting philosophy that seeks to shatter the enemy's cohesion through a variety of rapid, focused and unexpected actions which create a turbulent and rapidly deteriorating situation with which the enemy cannot cope.[15]

In *Field Manual 100-5 1993*, the US Army also introduced a similar manoeuvre-oriented operational concept. Some of the most distinctive aspects of manoeuvre warfare are as follows:

- Balance between movement and fire. Firepower did not always have a task of *destruction*, but should often be used to allow units to *move* to new positions, from where enemy weaknesses could be exploited.
- The switch from a tactical leadership level to an operative one, i.e. the quest for a joint operation with joint effects.
- Deep operations, i.e. deep attacks or deep battle to unsettle and demoralize the enemy.
- Coordinated attacks on targets over the entire operative depth to create and exploit critical vulnerabilities.
- The systematic use of combined arms.
- Decentralized command, mission tactics.
- Willingness to take risks to rapidly reach strategic and operative objectives.

Although the Reagan administration's increases in the defence budget were over, the intellectual approach to warfare strategy greatly enhanced the US war capacity throughout the 1990s. This was actively promoted by the conceptual philosophy summarized in doctrines about manoeuvre warfare and the resultant improvement in quality. Another factor was the new decisiveness shown at political level in the USA over the conflict with Saddam Hussein in 1991 and in the following years.

US and UK objectives in the Iraq War

The attack on the World Trade Center on 11 September 2001 triggered off the attack on Afghanistan. This attack was directly aimed at the Taliban regime that openly supported al-Qaeda and allowed its territory to be used for bases and training camps. However, the success in Afghanistan did not end the concern the US felt about the threats against itself. The US concluded that the attack on the World Trade Center showed that some countries could ally themselves with terrorist movements and, among other things, provide them with weapons of mass destruction. The Bush administration could not accept this continued threat against the US. The country that concerned Bush the most was Saddam Hussein's Iraq.

In a speech on 21 March 2003, the US Secretary of Defense Donald Rumsfeld described the official US objectives in invading Iraq.[16] The primary objective, according to Rumsfeld, was to topple Saddam Hussein and his regime, and to achieve this, Iraq's armed forces had to be defeated. Another objective was ultimately to destroy Iraq's capacity to produce weapons of mass destruction and thereby reduce the chances of terrorist movements all over the world gaining access to such weapons. A third objective was to access information and evidence regarding terrorist networks and terrorist activity in and outside Iraq. A fourth objective, more controversial, was to create a successful democratic example in the Middle East, a region completely dominated by dictatorships, in many cases with religious overtones. A fifth objective, Rumsfeld stated, was to ensure that the oilfields and the oil industry remained intact under the control of the Iraqi people (and not set on fire as in 1991). The theme of the second chapter of this book is an inquiry into the real US objectives with the war.

The official objectives required that the US defeated Iraq militarily and gained control over its territory. It necessitated establishing *land operative control* as a first step in achieving political and military strategic objectives.[17] Land operative control was set up in Iraq when the Iraqi armed forces had been defeated and Baghdad captured. This created the freedom in which the political level could act. Land operative control is normally a prerequisite for reaching the political objectives. In the longer term, the coalition also needed to achieve land domination so that the territory could be completely controlled. Not until then would conditions exist for the self-government of a democratic Iraq. At the time of writing (August 2004), this has not yet been achieved.

The following section describes three interesting phases in the war that clearly exemplify the doctrinal application. The description also forms the basis of the conclusions presented in the final discussion. The three stages are: (1) the start of the operation, (2) the advances along the Euphrates and the Tigris, and (3) the capturing of Baghdad.

The start of the operation

Many people regarded the attack on Iraq's political leadership on 19 March 2003 as the real start of Operation Iraqi Freedom. After that, hundreds of aircraft and cruise missiles prioritized targets in Baghdad and several other cities such as Kirkuk, Mosul and Tikrit. The land operation began in the south, a couple of hours after the first bombs were dropped, when the 3rd Commando Brigade landed on the Al Faw peninsula and the United States Marine Corps (USMC) advanced towards the harbour in Umm Qasr. The 3rd American Infantry Division (3. ID) started to advance in a northerly direction along the Euphrates river.

At present it cannot be established whether all this military activity was planned to start exactly the way it all turned out. The deadline for when Saddam was to leave Iraq had just expired. The conditions for starting the campaign were only partly fulfilled. On one hand, the units were trained, and were in their starting positions and orders were given. On the other hand, Turkey's rejection of the US request to use Turkish territory to open up a front in the north noticeably worsened the prerequisites of the operation. The 4th Infantry Division (4. ID) allocated to the task had its equipment on board a ship in the Mediterranean Sea and most of its personnel at home in the US. Redeployment to Kuwait, unloading equipment that had been on ships for several months and resetting up 4. ID as a combat unit would probably have taken a considerable amount of time, and, at best, could only be put in place to relieve 3. ID or MEF/USMC[18] when the fighting was over. (The position became to some degree acceptable in the north as the 173rd American Ranger Brigade landed at Harir Airport, thereby allowing the strength to be built up via this air bridge head. This also illustrates a flexibility in adapting the plan to reality.)

The air and land operations therefore started approximately simultaneously, separated by only a few hours. This campaign and that of the Gulf War of 1991 differed considerably. In the Gulf War, a long and thorough preliminary air campaign (38 days) was considered necessary before the land operation could start. The firepower was to have the intended impact first. The operation was based on methodical implementation – first, the Iraqi armed forces were to be reduced to a suitable level, primarily from the air and the sea, and then advances on the ground would follow. This time the coalition decided to introduce an element of surprise by starting the land and air operations at approximately the same time. The campaign plan included a massive preparation phase of two–three days with attacks on around 3,000 targets before the land operation got under way. However, this was cancelled when the opportunity presented itself to topple Saddam Hussein and wipe out the Iraqi strategic command on 19 March.[19] The hope was that this measure, together with a subsequent intensive attack on the Iraqi command system, would overload and demoralize the Iraqi armed forces so that they would not want to fight when there was no longer leadership at the highest level. This speculation by the operative command does not seem unreasonable since the regime was a dictatorship and everything was controlled by the group around the dictator.

The opening move of the operation shows that American warfare strategy had developed during the 1990s. Since the campaign was to be conducted in accordance with US doctrines about manoeuvre warfare, movement and firepower were regarded as two agents that would balance each other. Like firepower, movement was a weapon that would have operative effects. These effects were *surprise, dislocation, demoralization* and *paralysis.*

The events indicate flexibility, decisiveness and an ability to improvise, qualities that had not been particularly pronounced in previous American warfare strategy, which has been more characterized by firepower, methodology, and attrition.

Advances on the ground

On 27 March the land operation had advanced 300–400 km into Iraqi territory. The 3. ID had reached Karbala and the Marine Corps had reached Al Kut. By 24 March the weather had deteriorated and several sandstorms followed each other in quick succession. The tactics had been for versatile and coherent units to maintain a high rate of advance. Opposition along the routes should be localised and passed if possible. The advance should continue towards targets deep in the operative field. The ultimate target of the land operation was the capital of Iraq. Suitable places to cross the Euphrates river were used so that the advance could come from several directions, thereby creating even more chances to select convenient routes, and creating general threats deep inside the opposition's territory. Throughout this phase, the land operation was supported by aircraft, which precision-bombed threatening targets over a great operative depth.

When war broke out, only a small number of units from the regular Iraqi army were deployed in the south to confront an advance along the Euphrates and Tigris rivers towards Baghdad. Most of the units were held in their peacetime garrisons mainly for logistical reasons. No noticeable preparations had been made throughout the operational depth to prevent or hinder the coalition's advance towards Baghdad.[20] This is the reason why Iraq was not more successful at using terrain and rivers to slow the coalition's rapid advance. Iraqi units were deployed in cities, towns and villages, where they had better chances to survive and where they hoped to level the odds. However on a few occasions they tried to attack coalition forces. At Nassiriyah on 23 March, around 100 Iraqi soldiers, supported by tanks and artillery, launched a counterattack, injuring around 100 Americans and killing nine.[21] On 27 March Iraqi units at An Samawah, probably from the 11th Iraqi Infantry Division, attacked the American supply roads west of the town.[22] Parts of the 3. ID confronted the Iraqi attacks in the area. The 101st Airborne Division, with units of a brigade from the 82nd American Airborne Division, were then to protect important nodes on the supply routes.[23] The V American Corps reserves had then been put in action and a new reserve could not be assigned during the ongoing advance. This fact, the poor weather, the Iraqi attacks along the supply roads, and the fact that the 3. ID and 1st Marine Corps Division had been advancing at full speed for over a week and needed to rest and replenish supplies, brought on the need for an operational pause.[24]

The phase exemplifies several interesting aspects of the operation. The rapid attacks on the ground against deeply placed targets are a clear example that the US forces had adopted the concept of deep operations. The targets were reached by maintaining the advance and by only engaging in combat if it was necessary in order to reach the targets, not to defeat the enemy units. Placing the targets for the ground forces deeply also enabled their commanders to manoeuvre at high speed. Coordination at the flanks was not a priority, so the exposure of long flanks was a conscious risk. Depth and tempo place an opponent in a dilemma. The opponent is forced to deal with major threats in unacceptable locations and has difficulty in implementing effective countermeasures in time. If the opponent cannot keep pace, and experiences one crisis after another, deep attacks and rapid movement can even be a way of reducing risk. As Sverre Diesen described it:

> Offensive operations often give the operative commander two choices: to choose a solution that due to the risk factor gives the opportunity for both victory and a catastrophical defeat, or to maximise safety and protect against the catastrophe – but at the same time lose the chance of victory.[25]

The defending party must avoid disruptions in the rear and the collapse of his operation. The choice is often between threatening the attacker's flank/rear, or trying to assemble enough forces to prevent the advance of the attacking party's echelons. The movements of the Iraqi forces indicate that they attempted to do the latter at times. Iraq was dislocated by the attacks in the west along the Euphrates river and in the east along the Tigris river. The Iraqi Adnan division rapidly redeployed under the cover of sandstorms to tighten the defences south of Baghdad, but suffered heavy losses from bombing during the movement.

Already in this phase, the coalition had presented more threats than the Iraqis could cope with. Selected and prioritized targets were precision-bombed from the air over the entire operative area. Deep attacks were carried out on the ground, and these would soon be able to reach Baghdad. The action of special units – to gather information, engage in combat, identify targets for air and artillery attacks, etc. – was successful. At the operative level Iraq had no countermoves. The battlefield only really offered poor alternatives. If the units moved, they were attacked; if they deployed, they were also attacked; and if they confronted the coalition, they would be surrounded or attacked by units that consisted of *combined arms*. A later section, 'The need for combined arms', studies in more detail what this means. The Iraqi forces could not keep up with the tempo of the coalition operations and were therefore unable to establish a coherent defensive operation over a great depth. Units were committed ad hoc into battle, regular units were mixed with the Republican Guard, and this all resulted in dispersed engagements with coalition forces.

Baghdad

In a dictatorship, the country's top leaders and the capital city, with all its symbolic places, are often the strategic centre of gravity. Iraqi units had gathered to protect Baghdad, and decimated units that had previously engaged in combat with the coalition's advancing units, had moved into the city.

When the 3. ID had captured Baghdad's international airport, mechanized units from 3. ID and USMC carried out raids from 5 April. Despite the concentration of Iraqi units in Baghdad, the fighting for the capital was over very quickly. Raids were carried out along motorways and avenues that led in towards the centre of the city. Along these routes, the coalition could use its superior combat and movement capabilities.

When the land operation approached Baghdad, the 3. ID and MEF had been pushing forward for more than two weeks, and were greatly in need of rest and equipment maintenance. The decision to continue into Baghdad in spite of these needs indicates that the commanders in the field had seen great opportunities. The openings that appeared regarding Baghdad, and the ensuing decisions to complete the operation quickly towards the central parts, cannot have been predicted, but with all probability resulted from the course of events. Once again, this indicates that the operative plan was mainly a support for operative and tactical decisions in a dynamic course of events, and that the operational and military strategic *objectives* were more important than the *plan*. The chance to capture the routes into the city, and important locations in the city, was realized by commanders in the field. In reality, it was the commander of 3. ID, Major Gen. Buford

175

Blount, who took the decision and he informed the commander of V Corps, Lt. Gen. William Wallace, who later ratified the decision.[26]

Throughout the war, targets in the Baghdad area were precision-bombed, and the units that retreated into Baghdad were badly decimated by the coalition's air attacks. The coalition's air operation showed that modern air power can also be very effectively used in cities, and causing limited un-intentional damage. Kill boxes (areas in which you expect your opponent's high-value targets to appear) for the coalition's air power were also posi-tioned over parts of Baghdad. Small bombs and bombs with concrete war-heads reduced the damage. The controversial bunker bombs, GBU-27 and GBU-28, with detonation tubes that enabled them to detonate underground, had the same effect and caused little collateral damage.[27] Great accuracy in hitting targets in Baghdad required special units on the ground that could locate, identify and point out targets by using laser technology. For example, Douglas A. Macgreggor states, 'Unmanned sensors do not substitute for informed human judgement'.[28]

The battles in and around Baghdad show partly a new picture of American warfare strategy, including the following:

- The objectives are more important than the plan, even during the risky venture of entering the capital.
- The decisions are taken when the opportunities open up. Commanding Office 3 ID outside Baghdad probably understood that the enemy was soon to be defeated.
- New tactics regarding urban combat. Taking a city by concentrating on important routes into the city and capturing important buildings and functions, instead of attacking block after block thus occupying large areas, is an innovation. However, this requires a weak opponent.
- Coordinating ground-air firepower is possible using modern technology, even in cities.

The need for combined arms

Combined arms has been a tradition in warfare from the ancient times until the present day. The theory of combined arms is also inherited from the Swedish King Gustavus Adolphus, whose brigades contained the three combat services of the time: infantry, cavalry and artillery. German doctrinal development after the First World War gave it the title of *Führung und Gefecht der verbundenen Waffen* (Command and Coordination of Combined Arms).[29] The purpose of combining arms in a unit is to present a versatile threat to the opposition, and for the unit's own benefit to give it the flexibility to cope with various courses of events. If the opposition has the capacity to protect itself from one of the threats, it can be exposed to others. This can be seen when an armoured unit stops when it has driven into a minefield. Stationary, the unit is exposed to direct anti-tank fire and tank-damaging grenades from artillery. However the unit reacts, it is exposed to the opposition's combat capacity. If it remains still, it will be attacked. If it tries to move away, it will incur losses from the mines, and if the vehicles are abandoned, it will also be attacked. All options are poor. The unit is in a dilemma, which will lower combat morale.

To understand the theory of combined arms it must be observed that weapons systems have strengths and weaknesses that are specific for every system. If several weapons systems are integrated, the weaknesses in one system will be compensated by the strengths of others. For example, the tank is most useful in open and mixed terrain where it has great firepower, long range, strong protection and high degree of mobility. It is less effective in steeply sloping forested terrain. Infantry has advantages in this type of terrain in that it can carry its weapons systems and that it can even advance undetected. However, dismounted combat troops have limited weapon impact on hard targets, and are slow and vulnerable in open terrain. Infantry and tanks complement each other when they work together. Protecting land forces from opposition air attacks requires anti-aircraft defence. Anti-aircraft units have their strengths in attacking aircraft, but are vulnerable to the opposition's land units. By operating together with tanks and infantry the weaknesses of the anti-aircraft units are protected and the unit can concentrate solely on its main task – air targets (which protects tanks and infantry). The ways in which the strengths and weaknesses of different weapons systems complement and overlap each other is an important part of the theory of combined arms.[30]

Combined arms also enable units to conduct their own combat to a certain extent. They are versatile, can deal with unexpected courses of events, and have the capacity to operate independently. This type of unit can complete the majority of the most common tasks during a land operation, and do not need to request help from a higher commander every time something unforeseen occurs. (No headquarter needs to decide how the unit is to be organized in order to meet the actions taken by the opponent, nor does the unit need to be reorganized in the field.) The commander of such a unit has great freedom to act in various situations, which is in line with the leadership philosophy of *Mission tactics* or *Auftragstaktik*. The concept of combined arms has lately been associated with manoeuvre warfare.[31] In reality, combined arms is a prerequisite for deep combat or for conducting deep operations.

The coalition's land operation in the Iraq War was based on this theory. As primarily mechanized units, based on the M1A2 Abrams tank or the British Challenger, the units moved in an organized fashion with combined arms deep into opposition territory. They could confront the opposition's best units and win the battles. Iraqi units could never be efficient in battle when American tanks were present. The tanks protected the other weapons systems, whose weakness could otherwise have been exploited by the opposition. The dominance of the tank in a land operation has probably never been greater. As the British Defence Minister expressed it, 'In addition to the quality of our people, the reliability, mobility and protection offered by Challenger 2, Warrior and AS 90 contributed to the coalition's success on land'.[32] Units with combined arms carried out deep attacks at high speed along the Euphrates and Tigris, and the concept also made possible the attacks in Baghdad and Basra.

What is often put forward in the debate of how ground forces are to be organized in the future, is that development is the same as winding down the tank and organizing *light forces* with great operative and strategic mobility. The American tank that was used in the Iraq War, the M1A2, has a maximum speed of 70–80 km/h. It is therefore as fast as other armoured vehicles. It has superior firepower and protects its crew and its own weapon system better than any other combat vehicle. It thereby also protects the other weapons systems in the unit, and the unit as a whole. The command system of M1A2 admitted that an Iraqi vehicle was hit by the first shot at a distance of 4,100 metres. In many cases, Iraqi tanks were destroyed at long distances, more than 3,000 metres. The tanks were so lethal that the Iraqis usually abandoned their tanks in areas where American tanks were operating.[33] Some American tanks lost their combat capacity, but no American tank seems to have been destroyed by Iraqi weapons.[34]

Force transformation is a continuous process. It should not be a matter of creating light or heavy units, but rather a question of creating capacities that are in proportion to the existing needs on the battlefield. Units must be able to survive and function in many different combat situations. It is generally more important with versatile capacity on the battlefield rather than getting there quickly.

There are also some restraints to force transformation. Some take the view that units with special properties can be put together combining different components soon before going into action. Therefore, they argue, it is not necessary to basically organize the units according to the principle of combined arms. Their basic starting point is not the nature of war, most of the time resulting in chaos leading to the fog of war on the battlefield, so well expressed by Clausewitz. The assumption is that the battlefield is overviewable and predictable, and that everything is known about the opposition. Therefore it is assumed that capabilities can be created, as and when necessary, based on accurate information.

Furthermore, capabilities on the battlefield cannot be achieved without basic training and joint training. If units are not trained together, combined arms cannot have the desired effect. The viewpoint may indirectly lead to the *separation of arms.* As is stated in *On the German Art of War: Truppen-führung*, translated by B. Condell and D. T. Zabacki:

> Units that are only superficially held together, not bonded by long training and discipline, easily fail in the moment of grave danger and under the pressure of unexpected events. From the very beginning, therefore, great importance must be attached to creating and maintaining inner strength and to the discipline and training of units.[35]

Another part of the theory of combined arms is the capability to reinforce the basic capacity of a unit thus creating a *combat team* or a *task force*. Further reinforcement consists of *close air support* (CAS). The efforts to achieve synergy effects are promoting the development of agents and methods for CAS. Generally speaking however, the air operation and land operation were not so intimately connected as the first reports tried to claim,[36] even if there are examples of the opposite. In 1st Marine Expeditionary Force (MEF) the CAS seems to have worked well. Forward air controllers from the 3rd Marine Aircraft Wing were present in all manoeuvre battalions in MEF.[37] This made possible continual use of air support to exploit opportunities or to attack targets that could not be attacked in other ways.

One characteristic feature of the coalition action in the Iraq War was the ability to create combat teams. This ability indicates that the input units were well trained in each function, and that the appointed commanders had the expertise and flexibility to make suitable use of the units according to the existing doctrine. According to Murray and Scales, examples of this are found in the 3. ID brigade combat teams, the 1. MEF brigade combat team Tarawa and the 1. Marine Corps division, and in the British 1. Tank Division.[38] These combat teams were built up around a core of mechanized battalions. In addition, the combat teams were equipped with many other systems and so comprised a combination of arms, including tanks, light battle vehicles, artillery, helicopters and the ability to use air combat forces. As the authors expressed it:

> Major General Blount [commander of 3. ID] divided his maneuver battalions – nine armor and mechanized infantry – among the division's brigades to form three brigade combat teams (BCT), either infantry- or armor-heavy. Each was essentially a self-contained close combat unit, which, thanks to the speed and killing power of Bradleys and Abrams tanks, had the ability to command as much ground as an entire division during the Cold War.[39]

Basic capabilities at the operative level

The theory of combined arms and their synergic effects also includes coordinating land, marine and air combat forces, which is the basis of the joint operation. To reach the objectives, the operative command level needs to combine land, marine and air combat forces in different ways, depending on the predominant needs on the battlefield. This creates primary effects, which vary according to the stage of the operation. The primary effects indicated in the impending Swedish Joint Operations Doctrine are *intelligence, command and control, firepower, mobility, protection,* and *durability*.[40]

After air dominance was established in the first hours of the conflict, the air forces were then used to attack targets on the ground. The use of intelligence systems to identify certain target areas, and to select targets and measures, had its origin in the manoeuvre theory about the opposition's center of gravity, decisive points and critical vulnerabilities. A combination of the air operation and the land operation, which had the objective of taking Baghdad, Iraq's strategic centre of gravity, aimed at destroying the unity and morale of the Iraqi armed forces as quickly as possible.

The air operation in 2003 used 1,800 combat planes, as opposed to the 2,700 during the Gulf War. In the Iraq War and the Gulf War, approximately the same number of guided bombs were used, 18,467 and 17,000 respectively. (Chapter 10 in this book focuses on the coalition's air operation.) The big difference is found in the number of unguided bombs. In the Iraq War, only 9,251 were needed, whereas the Gulf War used 210,000. A total of 227,000 bombs were dropped in 1991, compared with only 28,000 bombs in 2003. Fewer bombs were used in 2003 because of the improved intelligence system in the form of JSTARs (Joint Surveillance and Target Attack Radar System) and UAVs (Unmanned Aerial Vehicle), the time period between discovery and action, and increased precision.[41]

It is also interesting to note that most of the bombs were dropped from older bomber planes of the B-52 type.[42] The major technological breakthroughs have been in ammunition. Consequently, bombs could be used containing fewer warheads than previously, thereby causing less collateral damage. Other airborne weapons systems were also used, such as anti-tank missiles, mainly Hellfire and Maverick, and 20 and 30 mm cannons that were used against targets on the ground.

Approximately half of the air force missions targeted the six divisions of the Republican Guard. When the Iraqis tried to redeploy these divisions, they discovered that the JSTARs and UAVs could track them even when sandstorms prevented visual sighting. Most of the knocked out combat vehicles in these divisions seem to have been attacked from the air. Another effect of technological development can be identified here: even under difficult conditions, the opposition units can be discovered, located and identified.

The air operation also largely consisted of providing support to the land operation in the form of *Battle Field Interdiction*. The units on the ground and units in the air complemented each other's strengths and weaknesses so that joint effects could be achieved.

A great deal of the coordination between ground and air, and between the operation's different command centres, was handled via satellite telephony. The importance of the space arena in conducting joint operations cannot be over-stressed. GPS (Global Positioning System) is now part of the units' equipment, sometimes down to group or individual soldier level.

Deep operations demand that units with combined arms advance independently after the breakthrough. They need to be basically organized and jointly trained according to this principle. Their capabilities can be reinforced with a greater number of, and more powerful, systems, thereby forming combat teams. At the operative level, capabilities are created by combining land, marine, and air combat forces to meet different operative needs.

Doctrines and their development

In modern American military terminology, the desirable phenomenon on the battlefield has been given many names, such as *Shock and Awe*, *Rapid Decisive Operations*, *Rapid Dominance* and *Effects-Based Operations*, *Objective Force*, *Overwhelming Force*, *Overmatching Power*. As I pointed out earlier, it takes up to ten years for new doctrines to reach everyone in a country's armed forces and thereby result in sweeping changes to action taken on the battlefield. Common to these modern terms is that they do not concern a new warfare strategy, but are about different phenomena on the battlefield that lie within the application of manoeuvre warfare. According to American tradition, even small changes in conduct on the battlefield are given new names, which often prove to be short-lived. Special military and civil interests often lie behind the terminology.

Two words that regularly recur in the descriptions of these terms are *tempo* and *effect*. They refer to similar things that are found in descriptions of manoeuvre warfare. The following description is taken from the Swedish Joint Operations Doctrine:

> A shift in the balance of power, to create as advantageous a situation as possible, is a fundamental part of the indirect method. This can be followed by disintegration of opposition forces, either directly without combat or via confrontation. The displacement is to be both physical and psychological. Psychologically, the displacement is primarily an effect of logical disorder and a feeling of losing the freedom of action. If opportunities are created before the opposition has recreated its capacity, military victory can follow directly through

181

system shock or through continued combat with advantageous position of strength.[43]

Effects Based Operations (EBO) – Operations that are planned, executed, assessed, and adapted based on a holistic understanding of the operational environment in order to influence or change system behavior or capabilities using the integrated application of selected instruments of power to achieve directed policy aims.[44]

Effects-Based Operations, described by USJFCOM
(US Joint Forces Command)

The EBO concept is similar to the manoeuvrist approach: take action with the aim of achieving something different, preferably at a higher level, i.e. desired effects are expected to occur somewhere other than where the action has been taken.

The current fashionable words used for labelling new phenomenon on the battlefield hide the fact that it is basically about a warfare strategy that is based on manoeuvre theories and which is called manoeuvre warfare. What has happened since the manoeuvrist approach was introduced as a base for the doctrines in the US, first in the USMC *War Fighting* in 1989 and then in the US Army, is that information technology has been introduced to the command system, weapons and ammunition, thereby increasing range and improving precision. For the same reason, the ability to discover, locate and identify targets over the entire operative depth is enhanced. The sensational innovation is the precision in the weapon loads and their noticeably improved effects.

Conclusions

When assessing war, it is often very exciting to concentrate on 'the new'. To understand the operational concept used by the coalition in Iraq, it is necessary to assess the established knowledge *and* the new elements used in the war. It is more complicated to view the war from this broader perspective that assesses the warfare strategy and operations, and not only technology. The documentation that is available after the Iraq War already allows this, even though much is as yet unpublished or is inaccessible due to confidentiality. In this chapter, the warfare strategy used by the coalition has been placed in an evolutionary context. Irrespective of the conclusions drawn from this war for the future, these need to be treated with caution because of the poor quality of the Iraqi opposition. This is not to devalue what is being developed in warfare strategy. War is difficult, uncertain and chaotic. The coalition campaign was carried out under difficult conditions with comprehensive and complicated coordination between land, marine, air and other combat forces operating a long way from their respective home bases.

Another distinctive factor is that the latest technological developments were used. With increased precision and longer ranges, giving greater fire-power and higher tempo, the Iraq War has shown that fewer bombs, fewer take-offs and a smaller number of land combat forces are needed to reach military success. One of the results of this was that there were fewer combat forces than in the Gulf War of 1991, both on the ground and in the air, yet they could generate greater effect. Nevertheless, the most important experience is perhaps that the *total* effect is decisive. Modern warfare must be *joint*, i.e. based on a concept of *joint operations* that aim to achieve *joint effects*. Operational strategy puts together tactical victories to help achieve greater objectives and methods, and so enables tactical victories to help achieve military strategic objectives. A well-planned operation is the key to success, with as few losses as possible, in as short a time as possible. Winning battles is very important for success in a war. However, war is not won at the tactical and technological levels. Above all, warfare capacity cannot be limited to locating targets and precision combat from afar. One of the most important reasons for this is that an opponent is often thoughtful and flexible, with a sophisticated war strategy, and who can use assymmetry to his advantage.[45]

Manoeuvre warfare that combines a mobile objective-oriented land opera-tion with a powerful air operation constitutes a successful concept for the future. Technological developments will affect the methods used and in which combination, because weapons systems are those that most rapidly change through technological development. There will be new ways of combining land, marine and air operations in joint military implementation aiming to achieve synergy effects. In the future, units on the ground must be able to conduct deep attacks decisively and quickly to achieve rapid success. The Iraq War has not shown that the manouevrist approach and manoeuvre warfare have been replaced by any other doctrine. What it has shown is that manouevre warfare was applied with new combinations of arms. However it is possible that new concepts of warfare can be developed from this in the future.

A major innovation in the American war strategy is that, for the first time, a real capacity was shown for a mechanized *deep battle*. The assumption of the concept is that units with combined arms are used on the ground. The air operation, whose main task was *Battlefield Interdiction*, played an impor-tant role. This combination between land and air combat forces can be strengthened by continued technological advancement.

For the first time, the specific capabilities of special forces were integrated in an operation with other combat forces. The advantages are the ability to infiltrate the opposition and thereby acquire intelligence, identify targets for long range precision engagement, and conduct independent combat missions. During the Iraq War, special forces were also given responsibility for an area (western Iraq). The integration of the special operations forces were an important factor in the success of the campaign.

The coalition enjoyed air dominance from day one. The strategic objectives assumed that victory would be achieved on the ground. Consequently, establishing *land operational control* was one of the objectives of the campaign. Not until this had been achieved would the majority of the objectives be reached and the space created for the political leadership to act (which partly was not utilised). As Richard Hart Sinnrech says: 'Whoever has control over the air has control over the war. But in the end, it is on the ground that the war is won.'[46]

The highest quality equipment, personnel and training are vital for dominance on the battlefield. However, other important factors must not be forgotten. One of them is the importance of the doctrines. Technology is worthless without a doctrinal approach. Doctrines and training are powerful factors and can give small task forces superiority over stronger opponents. This was not demonstrated in Iraq, because the Iraqi armed forces were too weak, but history provides other examples, such as Germany in 1939 to 1942, and the wars between Israel and the Arab states.

The coalition's campaign was an example of manoeuvre warfare that displayed known and new combinations of arms. Even with the major technological advances in precision and firepower that were displayed in the Iraq War, intangibles expressed in the form of concept, doctrine, training, morale and leadership are still the most important factors for a country's warfighting capacity.

Notes

1 The allies named the Gulf War in 1991 *Operation Desert Storm*. In this chapter the war is referred to as the Gulf War. The war in 2003 is called the Iraq War, but the coalition named it *Operation Iraqi Freedom*.

2 *Southern Watch* is the name of the operation for the surveillance of no-fly zones in southern Iraq. There were more than 300 targets and Iraq's attempts to build up its air forces were thwarted. A similar operation in northern Iraq was called *Northern Watch*.

3 R. R. Leonhard, *The Art of Maneuver: Maneuver-Warfare Theory and AirLand Battle*, Novato, CA: Presidio Press, 1991, p. 167. Here, Leonard differentiates between the weakness and critical vulnerability of the enemy. Attacking a critical vulnerability will stop the enemy operation.

4 N. M. Rekkedal, 'Grunden till modern manöverkrigföring', in A. Cedergren and P. A. Mattsson (eds) *Uppdragstaktik: En ledningsfilosofi i förändring*, Stockholm: Försvarshögskolan, 2003, pp. 185–190.

5 This phase of *Desert Storm* is called *Desert Sabre*.

6 R. M. Swain, *Lucky War: Third Army in Desert Storm*, Fort Leavenworth, KS: U.S. Army Command and General Staff College Press, 1994, mainly the chapter 'Desert Storm: Battle'.

7 *Operation Gelb* is the German name for the entire campaign in the west of 1940, when the allies were defeated in around three weeks. *Operation Sichelschnitt* is

the name of the part relating to the advance through the Ardennes, the penetration by the Meuse-Ardennes Canal, and the thrust against the English Channel.

8 However, it should be pointed out that large parts of the Iraqi units, which had been given the task of delaying the allies, gave up instead of fighting.

9 R. H. Scales and M. Williamson, *The Iraq War: A Military History*, Cambridge, MA: Belknap Press, 2003, p 47.

10 Operational warfare can be defined as a component of military warfare that concerns theory and application regarding planning, implementing and maintaining large operations and campaigns aimed at reaching operative or strategic objectives in a specific region. See M. N. Vego, *Operational Warfare*, Newport, RI: Naval War College Press, 2000, p. 2.

11 Tuchatjevskij and Triandofillov are regarded as the founders of this concept of deep operations in Soviet warfare strategy. See N. M. Rekkedal, *Modern krigskonst: Militärmakt i förändring*, Stockholm: Försvarshögskolan, 2002, pp. 107–108.

12 The German *Wehrmacht* already had the concept completed in 1921, but it was not until 1927 that the officers could apply it at divisional level (*without* equipment in the form of tanks, artillery and planes). After Hitler's decision on armament in 1935, another five years passed before the *Wehrmacht* could apply it on the battlefield. Another example is the Swedish decision on defence in 1958 and the introduction of independent brigades, and a greater degree of mechanisation. With this came a new doctrine for offensive warfare, which could not be fully applied until the start of the 1970s.

13 D. A. Macgregor, *Transformation Under Fire: Revolutionizing How America Fights*, Westport, CN: Praeger, 2003, p. 24.

14 N. M. Rekkedal, op. cit., pp. 196–201.

15 United States Marine Corps, *Warfighting*, 1989/1997, p. 73.

16 A. H. Cordesman, *The Iraq War: Strategy, Tactics, and Military Lessons*, Westport, CN/London: Praeger, 2003, p. 22.

17 Land operative control is described in the Swedish *Land Operations Doctrine* [*Doktrin för markoperationer*] as follows: 'Land operative control in an area occurs when one side has gained a superior position in an operational area, its units have successfully achieve their tasks with good margins, and where there are connections to areas where domination and the operative base have been established. . . . *Land operative control* can and sometimes must be established far from the combatant's own or allied territory (land domination). When land operative control is achieved, forward operative bases can be established, greatly increasing the strength of the position. The time factor is thereby a consequence. Characteristic of successful land operations are that they establish land operative control over a long period of time.' Swedish Armed Forces, *Remiss ett – Doktrin för Markoperationer*, the chapter entitled Markoperationer.

18 MEF, Marine Expeditionary Force; USMC, United States Marine Corps.

19 Cordesman, op. cit., p. 60.

20 Cordesman, op. cit., pp. 18–19.

21 Cordesman, op. cit., p. 72.

22 Cordesman, op. cit., p. 79.

23 Murray and Scales, op. cit., pp. 62–64.

24 Murray and Scales, op. cit., p. 110.

25 S. Diesen, *Militaer Strategi: En innforing i maktens logikk*, Oslo: Cappelen Akademiska Förlag, 2000, p. 144 (author's translation).

26 Cordesman, op. cit., p. 366.

27 Cordesman, op. cit., pp. 285–286.

28 Macgregor, op. cit., p. 70.
29 J. S. Corum, *The Roots of Blitzkrieg: Hans von Seeckt and German Military Reform*, Lawrence, KS: University Press of Kansas, 1992, p. 202.
30 J. M. House, *Combined Arms Warfare in the Twentieth Century*, Lawrence, KS: University Press of Kansas, 2001, pp. 3–5.
31 Leonhard, op. cit., pp. 41–42 and 91–111.
32 Cordesman, op. cit., p. 352.
33 *Iraq Lessons Learned*, 8 May 2003, available at http://www.strategypage.com/iraqlessonslearned/default. asp (accessed 14 January 2004).
34 Ibid.
35 B. Condell and D. T. Zabecki, *On the German Art of War: Truppenführung*, London: Lynne Rienner, 2001, p. 19.
36 Cordesman, op. cit., p. 285.
37 Murray and Scales, op. cit., p. 67.
38 Murray and Scales, op. cit., pp. 64–67.
39 Murray and Scales, op. cit., p. 97.
40 Försvarsmakten, *Doktrin för Gemensamma Operationer* [Joint Operations doctrine], Stockholm: Försvarsmakten, 2003.
41 *Iraq Lessons Learned*, 19 May 2003, available at http://www.strategypage.com/iraqlessonslearned/ default.asp (accessed 14 January 2004).
42 The B52 has been modernized, including the navigation system, which is necessary for precise targeting.
43 Försvarsmakten, *Militärstrategisk doktrin [Joint Operations Doctrine]*, Stockholm: Försvarsmakten, 2002, p. 83. (Author's translation).
44 The definition is approved and used within JFCOM 2004.
45 Historical examples of attempts to defeat an opponent with combat from afar is the USA's war in Vietnam and NATO's attempts to defeat Yugoslavia with precision bombing from the air.
46 R. H. Sinnrech, 'Relearning Old Battlefield Lessons', *The Washington Post*, 24 April 2003, p. A25.

References

Ankersen, C. and Tethong, L. 'Rapid Decisive Force are Risky Business', *Proceedings*, 129, (10) October 2003, 19.
Cedergren, A. and Mattsson, P. (eds) *Uppdragstaktik. En ledningsfilosofi i förändring*. Stockholm: Försvarshögskolan, 2003.
Condell, B. and Zabecki, D. T. (eds) *On the German Art of War, Truppenführung*. London: Lynne Rienner, 2001.
Cordesman, A. H. *The Iraq War: Strategy, Tactics, and Military Lessons*. Westport, CN/London: Praeger, 2003.
Corum, J. S. *The Roots of Blitzkrieg: Hans von Seeckt and German Military Reform*. Lawrence, KS: University Press of Kansas, 1992.
Diesen, S. *Militaer Strategi: En innforing i maktens logikk*. Oslo: Cappelen Akademisk Förlag a-s, 2000.
Försvarsmakten, *Militärstrategisk doktrin*, Stockholm: Försvarsmakten, 2002.
Försvarsmakten, *Remiss ett – Doktrin för Markoperationer*. Stockholm: Försvarsmakten, 2003.
House, J. M. *Combined Arms Warfare in the Twentieth Century*. Lawrence, KS: University Press of Kansas, 2001.
Hugemark, B. (ed.) *Storm över öknen. 13 uppsatser om Gulfkriget*. Probus, Stockholm, 1991.

'Iraq Lessons Learned', available at http://www.strategypage.com/iraqlesson-slearned/default.asp.

Leonhard, R. R. *The Art of Maneuver, Maneuver-Warfare Theory and AirLand Battle.* Novato, CA: Presidio Press, 1991.

Macgregor, D. A. *Transformation Under Fire: Revolutionizing How America Fights.* Westport, CN/London: Praeger, 2003.

Murray, W. and Scales, R. H. *The Iraq War: A Military History.* Cambridge, MA/London: The Belknap Press, 2003.

Rekkedal, N.-M. *Modern krigskonst: Militärmakt i förändring.* Stockholm: Försvarshögskolan, 2002.

Sinnrech, R. H. 'Relearning Old Battlefield Lessons', *The Washington Post*, 24 April 2003.

Swain, R. M. *Lucky War: Third Army in Desert Storm.* Fort Leavenworth, KS: U.S. Army Command and General Staff College Press, 1994.

Vego, M. N. *Operational Warfare.* Newport, RI: Naval War College Press, 2000.

—— *Operational Warfare*, Draft manuscript, 2003.

10

THE IRAQ AIR WAR IN 2003

Back to the future?

*Magnus Bengtsson, Claes Bergström, Nils-Göran Bernebring,
Roland Jostrup, Richard Lindborg, Lars-Johan Nordlund,
Jan Reuterdahl and Johan Wiktorin*

Introduction

The art of air war is only a hundred years old. The ability to use the third
element – that is, the air and space above the surface of the Earth – is nonetheless today unique among those means of power projection available to
actors that seek to accomplish political and strategic objectives. The Iraq
War in 2003 was no exception to the rule; the Western alliance allocated
considerable air power assets to ensure an early operational success. The
air operations over Iraq did not only shape the battlefield for the Western
ground forces' final advance towards Baghdad, but also seem to have been
undertaken before, during and after the open fighting to support the strategic,
operational and tactical war effort on the ground, at sea and in the air. Why,
then, did the air war prove so successful? What was the actual magnitude of
the allocated airpower assets, at what times during the course of events were
they used, and according to which principles for the planning and conduct of
military operations? The purpose of this chapter is to shed light on these
questions, and to discuss various aspects of contemporary and future use
of airpower. It is worth noting, however, that at the time of writing (in the
summer of 2004) there are relatively few reliable, independent, and open
sources reporting on the war. The conclusions we draw are therefore of a
preliminary nature but may nevertheless provide pointers and give rise to
discussions on the present and future importance of airpower.[1]

The first hundred years of airpower have been characterized by a constant
search for the best target set to attack, the most superior technology, the
most efficient principles for command and control, the most supreme military theory for the application of airpower and so forth. Its development
has been affected by such factors as various actors' political and strategic
objectives, geopolitical situation, contemporary political preferences, their

cultural differences, technological know-how and national economy, as well as the standpoints of leading airpower theoreticians, and their influence on contemporary decision-makers. The first theories for the application of air-power were born out of lessons learned from the First World War (WW I) among the then leading Western countries. These theories had in common the notion of ending wars fast and decisively by creating overwhelming psy-chological effects to the enemy. Their major differences lay in the preferred choice of target sets, and varying views on how to accomplish this objective. Somewhat simplified, the three major lines of development of airpower may be summarized as follows:[2]

- The French–Italian line of development in which the theoreticians initially studied and advocated development of strategic airpower cap-abilities, but that later turned to development of fighting forces for tacti-cal support of ground and maritime forces within the framework of a defensive strategic posture.
- The Russo–German line of development that primarily sought to create superior military firepower in three dimensions. The German develop-ment was based on a concept of short, rapid, and violent offensives, in which ground and air forces operated together. The concept did not exclude the use of strategic airpower, but the main mission for airpower was support of an integrated air–land offensive within the framework of an offensive strategy against Germany's perceived main opponents – its neighbouring countries. The Russian development focused on support of the ground offensive, and the Russian air forces had as their main objective to ensure superior firepower for breakthroughs, and to provide support for the ground forces within a decidedly offensive strategy.
- The Anglo-American line of development focused on strategic airpower. This was born out of these countries' need to protect financial interests in other parts of the world, and to protect sea trades and territories far away from their own coastlines. The airpower theories of these countries were thus shaped to create the necessary preconditions for offensive national strategies, while the leading airpower theorists of these countries simulta-neously were inspired by notions from the early 1900s of the so-called 'knock-out blow' – that is, to hit early and decisively to end wars quickly.

However, the air operations during the Second World War (WW II) showed that none of these lines of development were comprehensive enough, and the post-WWII era was characterized by a continued search. The development was both hampered and dominated by the then evolving, polarized, grand strategic situation with two superpowers that both focused on development of strategic nuclear airpower. The Western war effort in the Korean War in 1950–53, and the Vietnam War in 1965–72 were, however, dominated by tactical airpower.[3] In these wars, concepts for strategic airpower played only minor roles. Also, the allocated strategic bombers were then utilized in primarily tactical roles for which there were no comprehensive theories or doctrines. The United States Air Force (USAF) was forced to try various air war strategies but none of them proved efficient enough to decide the outcome of the wars, despite overwhelming air superiority. The situation at hand, with access to strategic airpower assets and theories, but a primary need for tactical airpower capabilities, came to remain unchanged until 1991 when the Gulf War erupted.

In the beginning of the 1990s, 'new' American airpower theories of 'decapitation' had become predominant. These theories have roots dating back to the airpower development in the US during the inter-war period, or perhaps even further back in time, and show great resemblance with the notions of those days on strategic air war against the financial and industrial infrastructure of the enemy – a type of 'industrial warfare'.[4] The main difference was that in the 1990s technology had caught up with the early theorists' visions. Since the Vietnam War the USAF had invested heavily in weapons and navigational systems for high-precision engagement, stealth aircraft that single-handed or in small units managed to penetrate Iraqi air space unnoticed, and command and control aircraft and satellites that enabled a previously unsurpassed situational awareness and information dominance. The primary objective for the Western war effort was thus possible to redefine from maximum destruction to creating desired effects on the enemy. Modern technologies now allowed direct attacks against the Iraqi leadership and/or to isolate them from the outside world by destroying or disrupting systems for command, control and communications. However, as time went by, this concept proved to be an expensive way of fighting the air war; it presumes access to state-of-the-art technology and a wholehearted national financial commitment.

The development in the Western world from the Gulf War until now has been affected by heavily reduced defence budgets, increasing political requirements for instantly accessible airpower assets, and growing demands to avoid collateral damage when utilizing airpower. The tendency throughout the Western world has therefore been to develop and maintain smaller but more capable fighting forces that accomplish their objectives within the framework of an integrated and coordinated overall operations plan. This trend started in the 1970s when the US Army Training and Doctrine Command (TRADOC) commenced development of 'new' concepts for conventional ground war. Initially, the members of TRADOC thoroughly studied the interwar Russo–German operational concepts and, to them, the importance of close cooperation and coordination between air and ground forces became obvious.

Their new doctrine for ground war that appeared in 1982 – the so-called *FM 100-5 AirLand Battle* – turned out to be a break away from the traditional American views on the use of airpower for 'industrial warfare'. The AirLand

Battle concept was used for the first time in the Gulf War in 1991, but had its first major effect on American views on war fighting during the Iraq War in 2003 – more than two decades after its introduction. Before that, in 1993, the *FM 100-5 AirLand Operations* – that emphasized initiative, speed, deep operations, flexibility, and coordination – had replaced the AirLand battle concept. There is thus reason to believe that contemporary American operational concepts are built on a mix of the Russo–German line of development during the inter-war era, and the visions from the late 1990s on using integrated and technologically sophisticated air, ground and maritime forces in effects-based operations against the enemy's leadership functions and information sphere. The continued analysis in this chapter may, hopefully, show whether this was the case in 2003.[5]

The general course of events

The Iraq air war in 2003 started, and was, effectively, decided in the 1991 Gulf War when the Western coalition almost completely eradicated the Iraqi Air Force.[6] Out of some 750 Iraqi aircraft at least 150 were destroyed or left behind by the retreating Iraqi forces. After two weeks of limited air war more than 120 Iraqi pilots defected with their fighter aircraft to Iran, and of the remaining aircraft most were unserviceable. The year after – on 10 and 26 of August respectively – the Western coalition established no-fly zones over northern and southern Iraq to protect the Kurdish and Shia Muslim minority populations. From that point on, the coalition maintained the no-fly zones through air operations called Northern Watch and Southern Watch and had plenty of time to monitor the Iraqi Air Force's attempts to reconstruct its former strength. From June 2001 to the outbreak of war on 19 March 2003, coalition aircraft flew more than 21,700 missions over Iraq, and destroyed 349 targets that were part of the Iraqi air defence system. The Iraqi Air Force was nevertheless, in theory, a strong opponent at the beginning of the war. It consisted of some 20,000 airmen and over 300 aircraft. It also had at its disposal some 17,000 anti-aircraft troops, more than 850 ground-to-air missiles, and approximately 3,000 units of anti-aircraft-artillery. Against the Iraqi forces, the US-led coalition mounted some 1,800 aircraft of, mainly, American origin and an overwhelming supremacy in terms of technology and know-how. The Iraqi Air Force never got airborne, and the coalition established air superiority almost immediately after the initial strategic air attack on 19 March – the beginning of the war campaign that came to be known as Operation Iraqi Freedom.

The objectives of the coalition's air operation were according to the British Ministry of Defence:

1   to neutralize the Iraqi Air Force and its integrated air defence system,
2   to conduct strategic attacks against leadership targets,

3   to provide armed air support to own ground and maritime forces,
4   to deter and counter possible threats from Iraqi ballistic missiles, and
5   to destroy the Republican Guard.[7]

After the first strategic attacks by F-117 Nighthawk stealth aircraft and cruise missiles against Iraqi leadership facilities in the Baghdad area, the coalition's ground operations commenced in earnest on 20 March, and the main air operations the day after. The coalition's dominance and control of the air was so complete that the main part of the assigned air assets could focus on shaping the battle space – i.e. to create favourable conditions for their own fighting forces' activities – through close air support and reconnaissance missions against Iraqi ground forces. All in all, more than 42,000 missions were flown, including some 20,000 offensive missions, out of which close to 16,000 were close air support missions against Iraqi ground forces, 1,800 attacks on political leadership facilities, 1,400 missions against the Iraqi Air Force and integrated air defence system, and 800 attacks against installations that were suspected to accommodate weapons of mass destruction (WMD) or ground-to-ground missiles. The coalition lost no aircraft in air-to-air battle, and 'only' six AH-64 and AH-1W helicopters and one A-10 air-to-ground aircraft were lost due to ground-to-air fire. There were, however, another 13 aircraft lost, but for other reasons. Yet one may state that the Iraqi Air Force did not take part in this 21 day-long air war. The continued presentation of the events will therefore focus on the activities of the coalition, in particular on how the almost non-existent opposition in the air allowed the 'new' American doctrines for integrated air and ground forces to be tested against the Iraqi ground forces. The continued analysis in this chapter will be made according to the present most common way of describing the main missions for airpower – control of the air; strategic attack; anti-surface force air operations; and supporting air operations.

Control of the air

Control of the air (Counter Air Operations, CAO) may be exercised through both offensive and defensive actions. The first type represents a pro-active and pre-emptive stance on how to create favourable conditions in the battle for control of the skies for the attacker, and is the most commonly advocated method in Anglo-American airpower theories – the opponent's air power assets are to be destroyed or neutralized before they are put to use. Such attacks are known as Offensive Counter Air (OCA) and may, for instance, encompass air-to-ground attacks against the opponent's airbases and command and control facilities. However, in case an OCA campaign should not be completely successful, an ability is also needed to meet and fight the adversary's attacking aircraft before they manage to inflict damage to one's own base areas and airpower assets. In Western hemisphere literature such efforts are often labelled as Defensive Counter Air (DCA) and include air defence fighter aircraft, missile defence, and anti-aircraft artillery (AAA). DCA is often depicted as a necessary, though unwanted, supplement to OCA since DCA is primarily a reactive posture that does not make full use of the entire air power capability spectrum, and thus increases the level of risk-taking in the battle for air control.

A major part of the airpower assets the Western alliance assigned to fight the Iraqi air defence was used in the offensive role. The overall purpose of the coalition's OCA campaign during the Iraq War was to shape the battle space, and to ensure and maintain its dominance in, and control of, the Iraqi airspace. For this purpose, the mainly American and British air activities that took part before the outbreak of war had worked as a catalyst; the Iraqi air defence's activities were monitored, evaluated, and, to a great extent, neutralized before the alliance launched its initial attack. In spite of the Iraqi Air Force's overall inadequacy, the ground-based air defence was still in a position to offer limited resistance. At the outbreak of war, the Iraqis were believed to possess some 210 missile defence and AAA batteries, and approximately 150 radar stations for air surveillance. To establish the best possible state of air superiority, the USAF thus conducted almost 1,500 OCA missions, including massive electronic attacks, and attacks by use of High Speed Anti-Radiation Missiles (HARM) against radars and other electronic emitters.[8] The Iraqis' attempts to defend their airspace were in essence delimited to AAA firing, and a small number of ground-to-air missile launches. Additionally, the latter were probably fired without the support of guidance from ground-based radars, and an educated guess is that these efforts only marginally affected the coalition's freedom of action in the air.

Apart from protecting its own units in the region with ground-based air defence (GBAD) forces, the US also strove to keep Israel out of the war by preventing possible Iraqi missile attacks. The Israeli Arrow 2 anti-ballistic missile (ABM) system was thus reinforced with three American and three German Patriot missiles. However, these were never put to test during the war since no Iraqi missiles were launched against Israel. In January 2003 Jordan requested to be supported by American Patriot units after negotiations had collapsed with Russia about lending the long-range S-300 ABM system. The US took a positive posture to keeping sophisticated GBAD equipment in Jordan – protecting Jordan's capital Amman from Iraqi missile attacks also indirectly defends Israel – and deployed its own personnel to the area. In southern Turkey three Dutch Patriot units were set up to protect inhabited areas and military airbases from Iraqi missile attacks, and in Bahrain two US Patriot batteries protected the Fifth Fleet's headquarters. Kuwait had two Patriot units of its own and was further reinforced by US batteries, some of them of the most modern type – PAC-3.[9]

During the conflict, Iraq launched some 18 to 20 missiles against coalition forces and against Kuwait, out of which 13 were Al Samoud 2 or Ababil-100 short-range tactical ballistic missiles (TBMs), or large unguided ground missiles. Since they were not found to be threatening, three of the Iraqi missiles were not engaged and they landed in the desert or in the water out of the Kuwaiti coast. One Iraqi missile exploded shortly after take-off. The remaining five were probably CSSC-3 Seersucker cruise missiles, a modified version of a Chinese-made missile. At least two of them penetrated the coalition's air defence. Apparently, these were not detected and engaged by the Patriot system radars, probably because of their extremely low altitude in flight. One of these cruise missiles impacted close to a shopping centre in Kuwait City and created minor damage, and another hit a drone target off the Kuwaiti coast.[10]

During the war, three losses were caused by friendly fire. On 23 March an American Patriot PAC-2 unit fired at a British Tornado over northern Kuwait and killed both crew members returning from a mission over Iraq. The next day a Patriot battery locked on to an American F-16 fighter aircraft causing the pilot to fire a HARM electronic countermeasure missile that destroyed the Patriot battery's radar. Luckily, no people on the ground were injured; the Patriot crew were taking cover due to enemy artillery fire and ran the missile system in automatic mode. Finally, on 2 April an American Patriot PAC-3 shot down an American F/A-18 Hornet fighter aircraft, causing the pilot's death.[11] Investigations of these incidents are still going on. Until these findings are made public, no relevant conclusions are possible to draw on the efficiency of the GBAD system and/or on friendly fire.

In general, two own missiles engaged every incoming ballistic missile, which is in line with U.S. Army doctrine. Other, slower, missiles are initially countered by use of one missile. In total, the Patriot system fired some 24 missiles throughout the war. Patriot PAC-3 units fired four missiles and claimed two hits against a total of nine Iraqi ballistic missiles hit. Out of the remaining 20 missiles fired, Patriot GEM claimed six hits and GEM + one.[12] Most of the destroyed Iraqi missiles were Al-Samoud 2 or Ababil-100s that normally are fired at a distance of 100–150 kilometres. Their short-range ballistic missiles have an approximate range of some 150 kilometres. Compared to the Scud missiles that were used in the Gulf War, that had a range of some 650 kilometres, these missiles were slower but were detected at closer range. Though the Patriots proved efficient against these short-range ballistic missiles, no conclusions may be drawn on how the improvement of the Patriot system has affected its effectiveness against Scuds. However, the discouraging overall results of the Patriot systems should render second thoughts since low-flying cruise missiles may become the most common future air threat. When engaging these targets the limitations of ground-based radars become obvious since most GBAD systems require free line of sight. A precondition for success in future

DCA assignments may thus be an extended integration of Patriot and AWACS (Airborne Warning and Control System) systems.[13]

Conclusions on the control of the Iraqi airspace

There was never a true struggle for the air theatre and the right to exploit it in the Iraq War. The Western alliance gained, in principle, complete and exclusive rights to use the Iraqi airspace from the very first day of the war. Therefore, far-reaching conclusions cannot be drawn on the alliance's offensive and defensive concepts as such. However, even without the partial control of the air that a more qualified opponent would have been able to achieve, deficiencies in the tactical abilities of the alliance to conduct OCA and DCA campaigns have become clear. Not least its problems to separate friends from foes have become obvious, regardless of whether one studies the issue from a ground-to-air or an air-to-ground perspective. Without anticipating the results of ongoing investigations, reviews of human and technical aspects will probably be needed with regard to education and training, rules of engagement (ROE), improved equipment for identifying friend and foes, various radar types to separate targets, and methods to avoid interferences between own radar transmissions.

An early positive conclusion that can be drawn is that the Patriot system is an excellent means of countering short-range ballistic missiles and, more naturally, conventional aircraft – in this conflict, regrettably, exemplified by friendly fire. However, a total of seven losses out of 1,800 allotted aircraft has to be regarded as a minor shortfall. A second conclusion is that the Patriot system has to be integrated with other sensors and intelligence sources to ensure that low-flying cruise missiles are detected and destroyed.

Strategic air operations

The overall objective of strategic air operations (Strategic Attack, SA) is to break the enemy's will to resist. This may be accomplished by reducing or shattering the coherence of the opponent's fighting spirit without first having to destroy the adversary's infrastructure, equipment, and/or fielded forces. A decisive precondition for this type of warfare is the ability to identify the enemy's Centre of Gravity (CoG) in terms of time and space.[14] A Centre of Gravity is defined as the person, function, or capability that gives the adversary his strength and will to fight. A CoG may thus be extremely physical, such as a political leader of a country, or exceptionally abstract, such as a religious, political, or moral conviction that unifies the opponent's means of power.

It has not, by mere use of American and British reports, been possible to define what military objectives were considered strategic in nature – that is, what CoG that de facto was considered the most important. It seems natural to conclude, however, that there were at least three strategic objectives: (1) to dethrone Saddam Hussein; (2) to ensure that Iraq did not have access to weapons of mass destruction; and (3) to guarantee the continued flow of Iraqi oil to the world market. One may thus assume that the Iraqi CoG was defined as Saddam Hussein and his family. If that actually was the case, then the strategic target sets would probably have been defined as Saddam and his closest family members, the government, top-ranking military and political leaders, the system of security forces and party organizations that supported and protected Saddam's position as Iraq's leader and communications systems that made it possible for Saddam to control the entire Iraqi territory. Additionally, known and perceived facilities for development and manufacturing of weapons for mass destruction were probably defined as strategic targets.[15]

The first air offensive was an obvious example of the use of strategic attacks. This was an early and direct attempt to accomplish one of the above-mentioned strategic objectives and end the conflict early. American intelligence services believed they had identified a window of opportunity to eliminate Saddam Hussein and several of his closest associates through a direct and precise attack on a building in Baghdad. On 19 March the highest US level of authority ordered the attack, and two American F-117[16] stealth aircraft carried out the weapons delivery. Simultaneously, this initial attempt to conduct a decisive strategic blow was supported by some 40 Tomahawk cruise missiles. The Tomahawks were launched from American warships and submarines in the Persian Gulf and the Red Sea in an offensive air operation against Iraqi facilities for air defence and command and control. The F-117s were also escorted by fighters and support aircraft to make sure any possible opposition in the air was neutralized on their way to Baghdad. The strategic air operation was conducted according to plan, but the results did not turn out as expected.

A second effort to kill Saddam Hussein was undertaken on 7 April when he, allegedly, visited a restaurant. This time a pair of B-1B Lancer strategic bombers were ordered to attack, but the objective was not accomplished. The numerically largest, coordinated strategic attack occurred on 21 March as a beginning of the so-called 'Shock and Awe' campaign. During the offensive attacks were made at 'Iraqi regime leadership, regime command and control, regime security, integrated air defence systems and weapons of mass destruction',[17] i.e. mainly the types of targets defined as strategic. During the air offensive more than 100 cruise missiles were launched, and fixed-wing aircraft conducted almost 2,000 sorties.[18]

Out of a total of some 20,000 targets attacked during the war, some 1,800 targets were categorized as strategic leadership (9 per cent of all targets), and approximately 800 missions (4 per cent) attacked targets suspected to harbour weapons of mass destruction. Some 65 per cent of the attacks were conducted by use of precision-guided bombs. In total, some 950 cruise missiles (most of them being Tomahawks) were used, and 30,000 guided and unguided weapons were fired. This means that on average some 1.5 weapons were fired against each target.[19] More than half of the weapons were fired by the 51 available B-1B, B-52, and B-2 bomber aircraft, a fact worth noticing since these aircraft were only a small fraction of the total amount of allocated airpower assets.[20]

The strategic air operation was built on the principle of manoeuvre theory; by directly and continuously attacking the enemy's CoG – which here probably was defined as Iraq's political leader including his assets for security and command and control – the tempo of the enemy's decision-making processes was slowed down, and his basis for continued opposition removed step by step. The concept also provided favourable conditions for breaking Saddam's will to continue fighting, thereby making it possible to avoid a prolonged conventional war and potentially higher losses on the friendly side.

These strategic air operations would not, however, have been possible in case a number of important preconditions had not been fulfilled. First, when attacking precision is paramount to avoid collateral damage, and the USAF today is fully capable of delivering precision attacks globally through its consistent development and implementation of precision-guided munitions and space-based systems for high-precision navigation (such as the GPS). Second, to maximize the effect of precision-guided weapons high-quality intelligence and communications are needed, and American fighting forces to a large extent build their capability for intelligence gathering and communications on access to space-based satellites for reconnaissance and communications, and on advanced net-based technologies for real-time transfer of data and information. Third, compared to the adversary an asymmetric technological advantage is required. The US is fully capable of creating that advantage through its access to operational UAVs and stealth aircraft. Finally, an integration is needed of systems and organizations to improve coordination and cooperation – one example being between those US intelligence services that report a possible target, the USAF that plans and commands the missions, and the US Navy that possesses the main part of the US's cruise missiles.

Conclusions on strategic air operations

As of this writing in the summer of 2004 the true influence of the strategic air operations on the outcome may only be assumed. Based on the events of the war – incorporating among other occurrences the unexpectedly weak and badly coordinated resistance, and the early fall of Baghdad – it seems fully feasible that the strategic air operation de facto decapitated the Iraqi society; the attacks on the leadership function, including organizations for support and command and control, made it impossible for Iraq's fielded forces to fight in a coherent and efficient manner. This assumption is further supported by the fact that the coalition suffered relatively low losses while simultaneously accomplishing military victories faster than expected even though having considerably fewer forces assigned than in 1991.[21] However, the specific asymmetric relations between the two parties in this war make it difficult to draw definite conclusions for all future wars. The value of being able to conduct strategic air operations has nevertheless been reaffirmed, and strategic attacks are most probably a dimension of air war that will be of increased value in the future.

Air operations against ground and maritime forces (anti-surface force air operations, ASFAO)

During the war it was paramount to take immediate control over Iraq War industry and infrastructure that possibly offered evidence of possession of weapons of mass destruction. It therefore fell upon airpower to support the accomplishment of this objective through precision attacks on selected targets. The two most commonly used precision-guided weapons in this part of the campaign were GBU-12 Paveway (over 7,100 were used) and GBU-31 JDAM (close to 5,100 were launched), all types of flying vehicles including unmanned combat air vehicles (UCAV) had capability to launch this type of weapon. In addition, to achieve the desired effects a large number of cruise missiles were used independently or coordinated with other carrier vehicles.

The overall purpose of the alliance's bombing campaign was clarified through a so-called effects-based operations concept. Herein the focus was on creating events that affected the opponent's ways of acting, rather than on destruction and attrition.[22] The effects-based operational concept included fine-tuning of the targeting process through a leading idea of carefully selecting targets to achieve desired effects rather than inflicting total physical destruction. One example of this was the alliance's choice to attack systems that supported the Iraqi army with electrical power, fuel and communications instead of attacking the entire Iraqi infrastructure, which would have caused unbearable suffering to civilians. Another example was the use of airborne platforms for reconnaissance and intelligence gathering – such as the E-8C Joint Surveillance Target Attack Radar system (JSTARS) – for identification of and attacks on military units in motion, rather than preventing them from regrouping by destruction of bridges and other lines of communications which would have meant too much negative impact on civilian life.[23]

The use of precision-guided munitions was thus a crucial precondition for effects-based operations. In addition, the probability of actually hitting the intended targets by use of laser and/or GPS/INS (inertial navigation system)-guided weapons was high indeed.[24] This meant that the warheads could be made smaller to minimize collateral damage while still achieving the intended effects. During the war, the precision-guided versus unguided weapons ration was two to one.[25] However, the effects-based concept was not only enabled through improvements in air weapons technology. Probably also a combination of developments in reconnaissance and sensor technology – such as improved radars, UAVs, and E-8C JSTARS – improved command and control, and access to a variety of carrier platforms contributed to a high degree of flexibility in planning and conducting the air operations.

Another 'new' air operations concept that was put to use, though on a limited scale, was attacks on so-called Time Sensitive Targets (TST).[26] Examples of such targets were military leaders, moving weapons systems on the ground, weapons of mass destruction, guerrillas and other targets that could not be easily predicted, and against which available lead times between detection and destruction was extremely short. The normal targeting time cycle meant that too much time was wasted before the order was given to attack. Here, TST-targeting demonstrated a need for airborne quick reaction units able to act on extremely short notice, rather than the usual method of 'timetable' attacks against predefined targets.

Conclusions on anti-surface force air operations

The alliance was able to put enormous pressure on the enemy through its ability to transform intelligence into offensive action in mere minutes, combined with its resources that allowed attacks on all types of targets. Its decision-making cycle, the so-called Observation, Orientation, Decision and Action (OODA)-loop,[27] completely outmanoeuvred the Iraqi equivalent. The Iraqi leadership, and their fighting forces, faced increasingly serious difficulties to establish and maintain their cohesion – one result being the wanting air war. However, the alliance's total supremacy in terms of technology, training, and experience in air war make it impossible to draw in-depth conclusions on the future importance and effect of air operations against surface forces.

Supporting air operations (SUPAO)

The latest American study on the future requirements for air transportation was conducted before the terrorist attacks on 11 September 2001. Accordingly, the United States' planners concluded that less resources were required than during the old scenario in which the cold war transformed into a Third World War. At the outbreak of Operation Iraqi Freedom, the USAF's air transportation fleet was heavily engaged in the Balkans, in South Korea, and in support of Homeland Security operations. Despite that, the USAF managed to mobilize sufficient resources by rigorously giving priority to the operation's most critical requirements. Air transportation soon proved to be a crucial capability for the success of the overall operation. During

Iraqi Freedom, USAF's Air Mobility Command (AMC) was noted to produce as much as 1,400 sorties a day.[28] In addition, other transportation aircraft flew a total of 13,616 transport and tanker missions at the request of US Central Command (CENTCOM), and C-5, C-17 and C-130 transport aircraft continuously flew supply, special operations and other transport missions in and to and from the theatre.

The coalition's capability for command and control of the air war was far better than during the Gulf War. As previously mentioned, this was due to the already established no-fly zone that from the start enabled the coalition to monitor and control the activities of the Iraqi air defence.[29] The overall objectives of replacing the regime and eliminating the perceived threat of Iraq using nuclear and chemical warheads did, however, put greater demands than ever before on the alliance's joint operations command and control structure. The great challenge was to satisfy demands for a high tempo of operations while simultaneously increasing the level of coordination between the efforts of various fighting forces – particularly between ground and air forces – to accomplish desired operational effects. In terms of command and control of airpower this meant that tasks and capabilities that traditionally have been the responsibility of the Joint Force Air Component Commander (JFACC) were allocated to the ground force commander to ensure a 'network' of effects were integrated and coordinated in support of the advancing ground forces. However, strategic air operations beyond the predefined Fire Control Support Line (FCSL) were still under the control of the JFACC. Tactical air operations, as well as airspace control management, from real time to 24 hours ahead was commanded and controlled from a Combined Air Operations Centre (CAOC) at Prince Sultan Air Force Base in Saudi Arabia.[30] Additionally, to ensure increased flexibility in the targeting process – thereby enabling attacks on TST targets on the battlefield – and improve the coordination of ground and air efforts, groups of air liaison officers were posted in the staffs of operational and tactical ground forces and the CAOC personnel strength was increased from 672 to 1,966.[31]

Iraqi Freedom also showed an increased need to monitor the theatre on the surface as well as in the air. Before the Gulf War, the decision-making cycle from detection to attack could take days. During that war, the lead times were reduced to hours. In the Iraq War, this cycle was reduced to minutes through the use of reconnaissance platforms and sensors such as JSTARS aircraft, satellites, and various forms of UAV's that delivered near-real time information for quick decision-making. Additionally, these platforms contributed to a superior situational awareness.[32] The fact that the coalition dominated the airspace almost from the beginning also increased its possibilities to forward deploy systems and sensors. They could thus be used practically unhindered over the ground operations area, which as a result increased the efficiency in battlefield monitoring.[33] The coalition's extensive use of space-based intelligence assets also contributed to its superior situational awareness since these sensors could function completely unhindered to deliver real time information around the clock. Compared to the Gulf War, the use of satellite-based monitoring systems is greater than ever before, not least as a result of the lessons learned in the Gulf War, the operations in Afghanistan, and through the development of space technology.[34]

The coalition's level of control of the air and technological superiority also enhanced its possibilities to conduct successful air search and rescue missions. In the CAOC, some 30 people operated a Joint Rescue Center (JRC) in which reports on aircrews in distress were handled. After having received a report, the JRC pinpointed their exact location through the Global Personnel Recovery System (GPRC). This is also used for computer-aided communications between the JRC and the aircrew. Through the GPRC, while awaiting the rescue operation to commence, the aircrew is able to request assistance with medicine, water and other supplies. Rescue operations were conducted by helicopters, mainly HH-60 Pawe Hawks, supported by unique helicopter air-to-air refuelling HC-130P fixed-wing aircraft. These, in turn, were protected by fighter aircraft for suppression of enemy air defences (SEAD) to increase the probability of reaching the crews in distress. During the missions, special operations forces teams most likely accompanied the helicopters. Once the rescue was successfully accomplished, the crews were taken care of and repatriated according to normal routines.[35] The final reports on the efficiency of the search and rescue operation have not yet been made official, but it is reasonable to assume that the loss ratio of aircrew and aircraft per rescue attempt were less in this war than during, for example, the Vietnam War. The positive effects of this type of rescue operations are obvious; compared to previous encounters the number of own prisoners of war becomes less, and morale is enhanced. Official policy statements also suggest that no combat air mission is conducted unless a credible rescue operation is possible to organize within a, relatively speaking, short period of time.[36]

Intelligence has always been of great importance in war and this operation was no exception. The US had deployed vast intelligence resources to the region. Compared to the Gulf War, the assigned intelligence resources were of considerably increased quality. Improved technology in intelligence gathering equipment, complemented by enhanced capabilities for transmission of information, resulted in near-real time availability of intelligence. The US intelligence services were far from flawless, however. Great difficulties emerged as a result of deficiencies in coordination and of intelligence being restricted unnecessarily, but also due to an apparent lack of experienced intelligence personnel that could process and analyse the data gathered. As a consequence Great Britain and Australia, who both to a great extent depended on US intelligence, suffered from these negative consequences.

The coalition had vast access to qualified gathering equipment and platforms such as the JSTARS and various types of UAVs. Since these systems are still wanting in some respects – such as separating small combat vehicles from civilian cars, and to detect bunkers below the surface – more targets than the actual requirement were selected to make sure the enemy was inflicted decisive blows. This proved particularly difficult in urban environments. Subsequently, there were three times as many JSTARS in theatre compared to the Gulf War. These also had increased capability to utilize satellite information, and improved ability to downlink information to units on the ground.[37] The successes of the UAVs became apparent (some ten different types of UAV were in use, which should be compared to one single type during the Gulf War), and the US predicts that the number of operational UAVs will increase from approximately 90 in 2003 to some 350 in 2010. This figure also includes so-called UCAVs.[38]

Compared to previous wars, improvements in intelligence and command and control notably shortened the lead times from detection to attack. However, the tempo and intensity of the war wore down the battle damage assessment (BDA) process.[39] Furthermore, increased precision in terms of weapons delivery also escalates requirements for precision intelligence; in 1991 it may have been enough to define what building to hit, but now and in the foreseeable future targeteers also have to define what window. This is particularly important when attacking targets in urban areas. It is therefore reasonable to conclude that the risk of information overload increases as the speed and magnitude of intelligence gathering overwhelms the information-processing capability.

Before the war, the coalition launched a massive information operation to affect the Iraqi regime's will to fight and to change the attitude of common citizens. There was also a clear strategy of influencing the general opinion, in the home countries of the coalition's contributing countries as well as in other parts of the world. A wide spectrum of methods was in use, primarily through media such as TV, press and the Internet, but also through leaflet bombings of Iraq. The USAF flew some 158 leaflet bombing missions and aircraft such as the A-10, B-52, F-18C, and the F-16CJ dropped more than 31 million leaflets. It proved difficult to measure the effects of the campaign during the war, and it is still hard to draw any definite conclusions with regard to this. However, American analysts have interpreted the passiveness of the Iraqi people, and the large numbers of deserters as a sign of success.[40] The EC-130 Hercules, also known as Compass Call, and the EA-6B Prowler were here used for the first time as a means in psychological warfare for TV and radio transmissions.[41] However, in global information warfare efforts against the enemy are not the sole purpose: it is just as important is to affect general opinion at home, and in the world at large.

Available information on electronic warfare (EW) efforts in Iraq is still scarce. It seems nevertheless as if fewer EW-aircraft were needed to escort strike packages compared to the previous war. This was probably due to the fact that strike aircraft nowadays have better equipment for their own protection, and that they in many cases could launch their weapons out of range of Iraqi GBAD systems. The USAF had in any case deployed vast EW assets to the theatre. In all, these fired some 408 HARM anti-radiation missiles. However, major parts of the Iraqi air defence had been destroyed even before the war, and the systems that were still operational were in many cases obsolete. Still, according to British military press there were a number of incidents involving Iraqi GBAD trying to engage British fighters, though without succeeding. Just before the outbreak of war, the British modified their Tornado F-3 fighter aircraft to carry Alarm anti-radiation missiles, but the system was not considered sufficiently reliable to be used operationally.[42] The massive, primarily American, EW efforts were nevertheless efficient but one has to bear in mind that major parts of the Iraqi air defence were already neutralized before the war. The coalition would have met a completely different threat if Iraq had had access to modern GBAD equipment such as the Russian S-300 or S-400, or modern European type air defence systems.[43]

The logistical effort during the Iraq War was a crucial contribution to the initial military success.[44] Before the war, the coalition had located equipment and supplies to nearby countries (among them Kuwait) and on ships in the area. This is a procedure that is sometimes known as pre-positioned equipment. Once the operation commenced, it was primarily personnel that had to be flown into the theatre. Also, the flow of equipment and supplies was 'streamlined' to the extent that in-theatre depots were only filled up for five to seven days of fighting. This should be compared with the logistics concepts used during the Gulf War, in which depots were expected to support 60 days of fighting.[45] Now the US used a new, technologically advanced, system based on transponders for monitoring the movement and use of supplies – the Radio Frequency Identification (RFID) system. This is a global system that follows the movement of items from the manufacturer to the end user in the battlefield. However, the RFID seems to have faced certain problems due to malfunctioning transponders. The British to an extent used an electronic system for monitoring logistical support – the Total Asset Visibility (TAV) system. This was made operational at first during the latter part of the operation, and then still with a number of deficiencies.[46] Compared to the Gulf War, the British military seems to have altered parts of its logistical organization from one designed to meet the strains of the cold war to an organizational structure better suited to support an expeditionary type of operation.[47]

The coalition conducted somewhere between 7,500 and 8,000 air-to-air refuelling missions including more than 200 tanker aircraft, of which the USAF performed the lions share.[48] Air-to-air refuelling is characterized as a so-called key force multiplier that considerably increases the endurance of airpower assets. This means that, for example, RAF Tornado and Harrier aircraft may stay airborne for up to seven or eight hours. In addition, the RAF and the US Navy found ways of cooperating because their aircraft have similar equipment for air-to-air refuelling: of the total amount of fuel delivered by British tankers some 40 per cent went to US Navy and US Marine Corps aircraft.[49] As the operation continued, tanker aircraft were also positioned far in over Iraqi airspace to stretch the fighters' time in the air even further.[50] To conclude, it is safe to say that air-to-air refuelling capability is, and will continue to be, a crucial key function in this type of complex international operations due to its inherent ability to allow air forces greater freedom of action.

Conclusions on supporting air operations

As a whole, supporting air operations is a diversified, complex and personnel-demanding part of airpower. They are, and will continue to be, a basic precondition for success in the air war. Without the maintenance and overhaul, safe airbases, information gathering and processing, command, control and communications provided through supporting air operations, the technologically advanced airpower assets of today cannot function. Despite this, the functions that are part of any supporting air operation are only marginally considered in the airpower theories that guide modern air operations. As has been the case since the dawn of airpower, these focus mainly on targeting. However, in real life the fact remains that ten or more people support any single air vehicle – armed as well as unarmed – that successfully reaches its target area and accomplishes its mission. The Iraq War has further accentuated this fact, and the number of support personnel and equipment assigned indicates that supporting air operations for the foreseeable future will be the cost-driving Achilles heel of airpower.

Concluding observations – pointers for the future

As in the Gulf War, the conditions in the Iraq War were ideal for airpower efforts. Then, the alliance could utilize its major asymmetric advantage based on technology against an opponent that did not see himself as inferior. Now, the struggle for control of the air was weak, bordering on non-existent, and the main threat against the Western alliance's air superiority was the odd man pad surface-to-air missile. This influenced the preconditions for, and conduct of, the air operations as well as the overall operation in favour of the alliance. Without free access to the third dimension, they would probably not have been able to conduct the operation the way they did. Certainly, the ground offensive would certainly not have been possible to start as early as it did. Herein lies an obvious hazard when trying to analyse the outcome and identify lessons for the future: this was not at a war between equal opponents, this was a one-sided effort at terms decided by the offensive part. The attacker could freely choose targets, methods and means for the offensive, had the initiative throughout the operation, controlled the airspace and had almost complete power over the course of events. There was thus no need to utilize the entire capability spectrum of airpower; the ground war effort could focus unhindered on manoeuvre war based on integrated air/land operations, and on using the alliance's superior technology to destroy the enemy's fielded forces – a reverberation of the interwar Russo–German notions and the early experiments with airpower applications that were done up until the First World War.

In Iraq, the integrated air/land operations proved successful and supported a rapid military victory. However, the course of events thereafter indicated that the war might still be far from over, even though open encounters between fielded forces have come to a close. Depending on the morale and the war fighting capability of the warring parties, the war may transform into a 'new', asymmetric and/or irregular shape. Therefore one cannot claim, based on the lessons identified in the Iraq War in 2003, that airpower is best used in integrated air/land operations against fielded ground forces; other war scenarios, other opponents, varying geographical conditions and new technology may also overthrow these 'new' airpower concepts. Perhaps there is no such thing as a best way of using airpower? The notions on its best use have now come back to the starting point of the first pioneers, and we have learned from history that neither of the early lines of development were successful in all types of efforts and threat environments. Maybe there has to be a multitude of concepts and theories for the contribution of airpower in political interaction and conflict resolution – one concept for every possible scenario? It has also become increasingly clear that, in future conflict resolution, various combinations of the most basic characteristics – speed, reach and altitude – present such advantages in terms of perspective, ubiquity and flexibility that a determined 'actor' hardly can succeed without access to airpower. Are the countries of the Western hemisphere really prepared to accept the considerable strain state-of-the-art airpower technologies put on their national economies to maintain their asymmetric advantage? Rather, the question one should ask is whether they can afford not to, because the destiny of Saddam Hussein's Iraq more clearly than ever before exemplifies the correctness of Field Marshal Bernard Montgomery's laconic statement: 'If we lose the war in the air, we lose the war and lose it quickly.'[51]

Notes

1 Here, the expression 'airpower' is used to depict the collective capabilities of an entity to project power to bear on an opponent in, from and/or through the third element. The term emanates from English science-fiction writer H. G. Wells' book *The War in the Air*, published in 1908.

2 J. Reuterdahl, 'Modern luftmaktsteori: Nytt recept eller uppvärmd skåpmat', in N. M. Rekkedal (ed.) *Luftmakt: En antologi*, Stockholm: Försvarshögskolan, 2003, pp. 265–288.

3 R. Pape, *Bombing to Win: Air Power and Coercion in War*, Ithaca, NY: Cornell University Press, 1996 and M. Clodfelter, *The Limits of Airpower: The American Bombing of North Vietnam*, New York: The Free Press, 1989.

4 J. A. Warden, *The Air Campaign: Planning for Combat*, 2nd edn, New York: toExcel Press, 2000. See also P. S. Meilinger (ed.) *The Paths of Heaven: The Evolution of Air Power Theory*, Maxwell, AL: Air University Press, 1997.

5 N. M. Rekkedal, *Modern Krigskonst: Militärmakt i förändring*, Stockholm: Försvarshögskolan, 2002, pp. 128–136.

6 This chapter is in part inspired by UK Ministry of Defence, *Iraq: First Reflections Report*, London: Ministry of Defence, 2003; A. H. Cordesman, *The Iraq War: Strategy, Tactics, and Military Lessons*, Westport, CN: Praeger, 2003; C. Conetta, 'Catastrophic Interdiction: Air Power and the Collapse of the Iraqi Field Army in the 2003 War', paper presented at the Project on Defence Alternatives, 26 September 2003; and M. P. Noonan, 'The Military Lessons of Operation Iraqi Freedom', Foreign Policy Research Institute's E-notes, 1 May 2003.

7 UK Ministry of Defence, op. cit., pp. 14, 39–40.

8 Cordesman, op. cit., p. 338.

9 There are at present four missile versions in the Patriot programme: Patriot Advanced Capability 2 (PAC-2) – the first missiles to have limited ABM capability; Patriot Guidance Enhanced Missile (GEM) – became operational in the mid 1990s and had improved ABM capability; Patriot Guidance Enhanced Missile Plus (GEM+) – the latest version produced by Raytheon which includes a modified warhead; Patriot Advanced Capability 3 (PAC-3) that uses a technique of direct hit. See D. C. Isby, 'Second Israeli Arrow 2 ATBM Battery Operational', *Jane's Missiles and Rockets*, 1 December 2002, and E. Blanche, 'Patriots Proliferate in the Middle East as Iraq War Looms', *Jane's Missiles and Rockets*, 1 March 2003, and Cordesman, op. cit., p. 338.

10 M. Sirak, 'How does the Patriot System Work?', *Jane's Defence Weekly*, 9 April 2003; D. Lennox, 'Patriot: How did it perform?', *Jane's Defence Weekly*, 7 May 2003; Cordesman, op. cit., pp. 338–339; V. Samson, 'Hold Your Applause: The Patriot Missile Defence System's Wartime Record Reveals a Complicated Mosaic of Innovations and Flaws', *Jane's Defence Weekly*, May 2003 and 'A Daily Breakdown of Patriot Activity', Center for Defence Information, 13 May 2003.

11 C. Hoyle, 'Patriot Potentially Downed Hornet over Iraq', *Jane's Navy International*, 1 May 2003; Sirak, op. cit.; and Cordesman, op. cit., p. 339.

12 'PAC-3 Did Two Out of Nine Engagements', 2003, Missile Defense, Center for Defense Information, available at http://www.cdi.org/missile–defense/technology.cfm (accessed 3 February 2004).

13 'Patriot Needs Help Detecting Cruise Missiles' (2003), Missile Defense, Center for Defense Information.

14 UK Ministry of Defence, *AP3000: British Air Power Doctrine*, 3rd edn, London: Ministry of Defence, 1999; US Air Force, *Basic Doctrine 2-1.2: Strategic Attack*, Maxwell Air Force Base, Alabama: US Air Force Doctrine Center 1998; D. MacIsaac, 'Voices from the Central Blue', in P. Paret (ed.) *Makers of Modern Strategy: From Machiavelli to the Nuclear Age*, Princeton, NJ: Princeton University Press, 1986, pp. 624–647; and P. S. Meilinger, 'Guilio Douhet and the Origins of Air Power', in Meilinger (ed.) *The Paths of Heaven*, pp. 1–34.

15 This chapter is based on announcements in *Air Force News* and Moseley, T. M. *Operation Iraqi Freedom, By The Numbers*, CENTAF, 30 April 2003, http://www.globalsecurity.org/military/library/report/2003/uscentaf_oif_report_ 30apr2003.pdf. USCENTAF is the US Central Air Force. See also http:// www.central.af.mil (accessed 12 October 2003).

16 The F-117 Nighthawk is a stealth bomber/fighter bomber aircraft that is able to penetrate enemy airspace and deliver high-precision munitions with very little risk of being detected by ground-based enemy radars.

17 Moseley, T. M., op. cit.

18 This section is based on announcements in *Air Force News* dated 19, 20, 22, and 31 March, and 8 April, and on Cordesman, op. cit., pp. 280–282.

19 Moseley, T. M., op. cit.

20 Available at http://www.strategypage.com/iraqlessonslearned/iraqwarlessons learned.asp (accessed 3 May 2003).

21 This section is based on President Bush's address to the workers of the Boeing factory in St Louis on 18 April 2003, on Vice President Cheney's speech on 9 April 2003, and on his address to the Heritage Foundation on 1 May 2003. All three speeches can be found on the internet at http://www.whitehouse.gov.

22 I. McNicoll, 'Effects Based Air Operations: Air Command and Control and the Nature of the Emerging Battle Space', *RUSI Journal*, 148, 3 (2003), 38ff.

23 Cordesman, op. cit., pp. 280–282, 256.

24 GPS stands for Global Positioning System, which is a worldwide satellite-based system for high-precision navigation. INS (Inertial Navigation System) is a GPS-supported navigation system that is used in many types of aircraft and cruise missiles.

25 Moseley, T. M., op. cit.

26 Some 150 missions of this type were conducted.

27 According to its 'inventer' – US fighter pilot and military theoretician Colonel John Boyd (1927–97) – the cycle is comprised of Observation, Orientation, Decision and Action.

28 J. A. Tirpak, 'The Squeeze on Air Mobility', *Air Force Magazine*, 86, 7 (2003), 23–29.

29 J. Day, 'Air Power and Combat Operations: The Recent War in Iraq', *RUSI Journal*, 148, 3 (2003), 32–37.

30 M. Knight, 'Air Power Assessment', *Air Forces Monthly*, May 2003, pp. 24–27.

31 Day, op. cit., pp. 32-7, and Cordesman, op. cit., p. 220.

32 Ibid., p. 219.

33 T. Ripley, 'Attacking Iraq', *Air Forces Monthly*, May 2003, 42–46.

34 Cordesman, op. cit., p. 195.

35 R. J. Newman, 'Ambush at Najaf', *Air Force Magazine*, 86, 10 (2003), 61–63.

36 Available at http://www.af.mil/news/opscenter/caoc_special.shtml (accessed 15 October 2003).

37 E. P. Giambastiani, Jr., 'Lessons Learned from Operation Iraqi Freedom', testimony before The House Armed Services Committee, United States House Of Representatives, US Joint Forces Command, October 2003.

38 Cordesman, op. cit., p. 315.

39 Ibid., p. 315.

40 UK Ministry of Defence, op. cit.

41 Moseley, T. M., op. cit.

42 Day, op. cit., pp. 32–37.

43 Cordesman, op. cit., p. 338.

44 UK Ministry of Defence, op. cit., p. 33.

45 US DoD, available at http://www.defenselink.mil/news/May2003/n05192003_
   200305192.html (accessed 15 October 2003).
46 Cordesman, op. cit., p. 205.
47 Day, op. cit., pp. 32–37.
48 Moseley, T. M., op. cit., p. 7.
49 UK Ministry of Defence, op. cit., p. 14.
50 Day, op. cit., p. 32–7.
51 C. M. Westenhoff, *Military Air Power: The Cadre Digest of Air Power Opinions
   and Thoughts*, Maxwell, AL: Air University Press, 1990, p. 17.

References

Air Force News, 'Shock Air Forces Hit Iraq', press release 22 March, 2003.
Blanche, E. 'Patriots Proliferate in the Middle East as Iraq War Looms', *Jane's Missiles and Rockets*, 1 March 2003. http://www4.janes.com/K2DocKey=/content1/janesdata/mags/jmr/jmroos (accessed 1 October 2003).
Center for Defence Information, 'PAC-3 Did Two Out of Nine Engagements', 2003, Missile Defense, available at http://www.cdi.org/missile–defense/technology.cfm (accessed 3 February 2004).
—— 'A Daily Breakdown of Patriot Activity', Washington, DC: Center for Defense Information, 13 May 2003.
—— 'Patriot Needs Help Detecting Cruise Missiles', 2003, Missile Defense.
Clodfelter, M. *The Limits of Airpower: The American Bombing of North Vietnam*, New York: The Free Press, 1989.
Conetta, C. 'Catastrophic Interdiction: Air Power and the Collapse of the Iraqi Field Army in the 2003 War', paper presented at the Project on Defence Alternatives, 26 September 2003.
Cordesman, A. H. *The Iraq War: Strategy, Tactics, and Military Lessons*. Westport, CN: Praeger, 2003.
Day, J. 'Air Power and Combat Operations: The Recent War in Iraq', *RUSI Journal*, 148, 3 (2003) 32–37.
Giambastiani, E. P. Jr. 'Lessons Learned from Operation Iraqi Freedom', testimony before The House Armed Services Committee, United States House Of Representatives, US Joint Forces Command, October 2003.
Hoyle, C. 'Patriot Potentially Downed Hornet over Iraq', *Jane's Navy International*, 1 May 2003. http://www4.janes.com/K2/doc.jsp?K2DocKey=/content1/janesdata/mags/jni/jni006 (accessed 1 October 2003).
Isby, D. C. 'Second Israeli Arrow 2 ATBM Battery Operational', *Jane's Missiles and Rockets*, 1 December 2002. http://www4.janes.com/K2/doc.jsp?K2DocKey=/content1/janesdata/mags/jmr/jmr004 (accessed 1 October 2003).
Knight, M.'Air Power Assessment', *Air Forces Monthly*, May 2003, 24–27.
Lennox, D. 'Patriot: How Did It Perform?', *Jane's Defence Weekly*, 7 May 2003. http://www4.janes.com/K2/doc.jsp?K2DocKey=/content1/janesdata/mags/jdw/jdw04 (accessed 1 October 2003).
MacIsaac, D. 'Voices from the Central Blue', in P. Paret (ed.) *Makers of Modern Strategy: From Machiavelli to the Nuclear Age*. Princeton, NJ: Princeton University Press, 1986, pp. 624–647.
McNicoll, I. 'Effects Based Air Operations: Air Command and Control and the Nature of the Emerging Battle Space', *RUSI Journal*, 148, 3 (2003), 38–44.
Meilinger, P. S. (ed.) *The Paths of Heaven: The Evolution of Air Power Theory*. Maxwell, AL: Air University Press, 1997.

—— 'Guilio Douhet and the Origins of Air Power', in P. S. Meilinger (ed.) *The Paths of Heaven: The Evolution of Air Power Theory*. Maxwell, AL: Air University Press, 1997, pp. 1–34.

Ministry of Defence, United Kingdom *AP3000: British Air Power Doctrine*, 3rd edn, London: The Stationery Office, 1999.

—— *Iraq: First Reflections Report*, London: Ministry of Defence, Director General Corporate Communication, 2003.

Moseley, T. M. *Operation Iraqi Freedom, By The Numbers*, CENTAF, 30 April 2003.

Newman, R. J. 'Ambush at Najaf', *Air Force Magazine*, 86, 10 (2003) 61–63.

Noonan, M. P. 'The Military Lessons of Operation Iraqi Freedom', Foreign Policy Research Institute's E-notes, 1 May 2003. http://www.fpri.org/enotes/20030501. military.noonan.militarylessonsiraqifreedom.html

Pape, R. *Bombing to Win: Air Power and Coercion in War*. Ithaca, NY: Cornell University Press, 1996.

Rekkedal N. M., *Modern Krigskonst: Militärmakt i förändring*, Stockholm: Försvarshögskolan, 2002.

Reuterdahl, J. 'Modern luftmaktsteori: Nytt recept eller uppvärmd skåpmat', in N. M. Rekkedal (ed.) *Luftmakt: En antologi*. Stockholm: Försvarshögskolan, 2003, pp. 265–288.

Ripley, T. 'Attacking Iraq', *Air Forces Monthly*, May (2003) 42–46.

Samson, V. 'Hold Your Applause: The Patriot Missile Defence System's Wartime Record Reveals a Complicated Mosaic of Innovations and Flaws', *Jane's Defence Weekly*, May 2003. http://www.cdi.org/program/document.cfm?DocumentID = 999&frompage = ../index.cfm (accessed 3 October 2003).

Sirak, M. 'How Does the Patriot System Work?', *Jane's Defence Weekly*, 9 April 2003. http://www4.janes.com/K2/doc.jsp?K2DocKey = /content1/janesdata/mags/jdw/jdw04 (accessed 1 October 2003).

Tirpak, J.A. 'The Squeeze on Air Mobility', *Air Force Magazine*, 86, 7 (2003): 23–9.

US Department of Defense US Air Force, *Basic Doctrine 2-1.2: Strategic Attack*. Maxwell Air Force Base, Alabama: US Air Force Doctrine Center, 20 May 1998.

Warden, J. A. *The Air Campaign: Planning for Combat*, 2nd edn. New York: toExcel Press, 2000.

Wells, H. G. *The War in the Air*. London: G. Bell and Sons, 1908.

Westenhoff, C. M. *Military Air Power: The Cadre Digest of Air Power Opinions and Thoughts*. Maxwell, AL: Air University Press, 1990.

11

THE STRUGGLE FOR CREDIBILITY DURING THE IRAQ WAR

Kristina Riegert and Anders Johansson

Introduction

No analysis of modern warfare can be complete without an assessment of the role of the media. The rapid development of communications technologies during the 1990s linking different parts of the world closer together and bypassing the remit of nation states are examples of globalization. The media contribute to globalization through their roles in the changing global infrastructure, as channels of communication, and as messengers about the world that lies beyond our direct experience. The media occupy a unique position in society: they constitute an arena for different communicators, yet they are also actors in the very events being communicated.

This is why it is futile to separate an event from its representation in the media. Questions like 'Did the media cover the Iraq War accurately and objectively?' do not take into account that communication systems are involved when actors relate to each other, that there is a significant difference between an event and its representation in the media, and that actors respond to the ways that media represent a conflict.[1] In other words, the way things 'appear' in the media and the ways various groups try to influence the images emanating from conflicts are just as important, maybe more, than the de facto 'reality'. In modern mediated societies, then, and especially during war, what is at stake is the credibility of the actors who bring us information. While this has always been true, there are a number of indications that the scales on which credibility is weighed are shifting. We argue that many of the stories making headlines in the Iraq War are indicative of a battle for credibility, a battle between governments, between different media outlets and between the media and governments about who is serving the public interest.

In what follows we chart the changes in the global media structure and how these have affected the conditions for foreign news and conflict reporting, and the relationship between the media and warring parties in the Iraq War of 2003. We pay special attention to the Arabic satellite channel

Al-Jazeera, which has not only challenged Anglo-American dominance among satellite news channels, but also revolutionized the media landscape of the Middle East. Al-Jazeera signifies a qualitative broadening of the number of transnational 'micro' public spheres at a time when the credibility of Western news organizations are in question.

The changing conditions for foreign news reporting

This is not the place to discuss the many aspects of the media globalization debate, but two developments have a bearing on foreign news coverage: the commercialization of the news, and the appearance of new information actors. Regarding the latter, the convergence of print and broadcasting with digital media, together with the availability of cheap digital technology, means that virtually anyone can document and distribute spectacular events via the Internet. These new information actors challenge traditional journalism's hegemony when it comes to covering and interpreting the news. Moreover, the ability to capture and distribute images of events as they happen undermines governments' control over the media.

The former trend is a result of national media deregulation along with the decades-old concentration of media companies into the hands of a few multinational conglomerates which control a large percentage of television output. The global television landscape consists of news agencies, global and regional satellite channels, regional conglomerates and exchange unions, medium-sized and small national channels, as well as the Internet. Satellite and cable technology may have greatly increased the number of television channels, fragmenting viewing publics into niche markets, but media concentration means that we access more of the same content.

As far as foreign news coverage is concerned, it is a paradox that the developments associated with globalization (new technologies, deregulation and economic pressures) have made it more, not less, difficult for traditional news organizations to deliver in-depth, quality information about what happens in the world. Most in the news industry have felt its effects in the form of drastically reduced overseas correspondent networks. Typical for many news organizations today is the use of a combination of rewritten news agency material, freelance journalists and 'parachuting' correspondents, who fly off to different hot spots at a moment's notice. Despite the budget cuts and reduced numbers of staff, the amount of time news organizations are expected to be on air has increased with the competition for news in real time. The technologically-driven demands of being on air all the time have increased the already prevalent tendency of television journalism to prioritise performance over analysis, and meticulousness about form over attention to content.[2] It is ironic that while governments, business leaders and special interests have become more media-savvy in their efforts to break through the information 'white noise', the news industry is reducing its ability

to penetrate and analyse these groups. Even European public service organizations, under heavy pressure from deregulation and niche channels, have
been forced into efficiency, commercialization and campaigns to justify the
goals of public service.

Another consequence of commercialization is the blurring of the boundaries between 'hard' and 'soft' news, and between foreign and domestic news.
The hardening competition between channels has had the effect of increasing
the entertainment and human interest factors in news programmes.[3] These
two aspects each deserve their own separate volume, but in the context of
this essay we refer to the packaging of armed conflicts as neat, sanitized,
little narratives with easily identifiable 'tag-lines', where the roots and consequences of conflicts are glossed over. The human interest factor in war
coverage has to do with the increasing tendency of journalists to show 'the
true face of war'. During the 1990s, humanitarian interventions and civil
wars have become the dominant types of conflict. The suffering of civilian
populations is more central in news coverage than before. While emotional
identification with the victims of tragedy may increase audiences' understanding of themselves and others, the aforementioned commercial impera-
tives in news can also exploit the sufferings of others. Jean Seaton warns that,
'. . . representing pain is also always political. Conflict over the interpretation
of pain has always been highly charged, and of real consequence to those in
conflict. Martyrs need a theatre and an audience – otherwise they are merely
victims'.[4]

Justice cannot here be done to these trends in foreign news coverage or
to the debates in their wake; the point is rather that the conditions on
which journalism was based, within the boundaries of the nation-state, are
increasingly coming under pressure through the rapid changes in global
communications.

Journalism's widening credibility gap

In view of the developments in global media structure and foreign news
reporting, it is not surprising that journalists have had difficulty retaining
the trust of the public. Journalists are also well aware of this problem and
to an increasing extent, they engage in self-criticism. According to a survey
undertaken by the Pew Research Center in 1999, a majority of US journalists
see lack of credibility as the most important issue facing the news media
today. The main causes, they say, are the blurring of the boundaries between
commentary and news coverage, and between entertainment and information. Half of the journalists interviewed said that the public's loss of
trust is due to sloppy reporting, factual errors and sensationalism. Especially
television journalists say that the root of the problem has to do with news
executives' pressure to make a profit and other financial concerns.[5] Despite

these pressures, the news media continue to value '. . . getting the facts right, covering both sides and refusing to publish rumors'.[6]

These issues constitute serious problems for journalism in peacetime, but they are compounded in foreign and conflict news coverage, when propaganda and deception are rampant. Few journalists today have personal experience of the military, and the number of specialist correspondents is in decline. In covering an armed conflict, this lack of expertise means that journalists will be less likely to ask key questions of their sources, less likely to analyse the situation as well and more likely to be dependent on the experts who are part of the establishment that journalists should be scrutinizing.[7]

Reporting wars is expensive and places heavy demands on otherwise shrinking news budgets. Instead of maintaining overseas networks, news organizations tend to quickly mobilize a great number of journalists, descending en masse at the scene of a conflict, something hardly likely to overcome the roots of the credibility gap.

Military–media relations during the Iraq War

In modern warfare, parties to a conflict want to control the media image and the information emanating from the battlefield. In order to do this, the protagonists use a combination of restrictions on journalists' freedom of movement, censorship, persuasion, harassment, and physical threats in order to exercise power over the representation of the war. To get public opinion on their side, they play on emotions, interpret events to their own advantage and suppress dissenting views. Warring parties want to deceive the enemy, break morale and the will to fight and split the ties between the people and their leaders. This environment represents a challenge and requires active reflection by journalists so as not to be exploited by the warring parties' interests.

Empirical studies of Western news coverage of the Gulf War of 1991 demonstrated a lack of scrutiny of, and strong dependence on, official US sources. The 'pool system' effectively censored information, restricted access to the battlefield and obstructed the efforts of unilateral (non-pool) journalists. Television images were dominated by the brilliant display of high-tech weapons: audiences followed the war through the green pictures from night vision cameras and satellite imagery of 'successful' hits on 'military' targets. The accuracy of 'surgical strikes' and the sporadic images of civilian casualties contributed to the impression of a bloodless war.[8]

In contrast, the civil wars that have come through our television screens during the 1990s have often been of another nature: here the classic stereotyping of good and evil was difficult, as was the ability of journalists to tell one side from another in situations where the roots of the conflict are not easily understood. Pigeonholing the moral high ground was easier: it was the (often American) forces fighting for human rights and democracy that were the good guys.

One important difference between these conflicts and the Iraq War was that there was much greater pressure on journalists to be critical of the parties to the conflict. This is due to a combination of factors: journalists' awareness of previous mistakes and of their credibility problem, greater competition from niche media, as well as a strong worldwide opinion against the Iraq War. Another difference was the willingness of the Iraqi regime to countenance foreign journalists. The Gulf War in 1991 is thought of as CNN's commercial breakthrough, due to the combination of 24-hour news coverage and its exclusive footage by virtue of being the only news organization allowed in Baghdad. In the period leading up to the Iraq War, CNN had the company of the other major news networks, all of which had invested in new portable digital technology, capable of live transmission, in order to report 24/7 from inside Iraq. As military action drew near, the tolerance of the Iraqi regime for US journalists wore thin. Fox News was expelled before the coalition forces landed, CNN was reportedly ordered to leave on 21 March, and a week later, Reuters came under heavy pressure not to provide CNN with pictures. Despite Iraqi pressure and expulsion, a relatively large number of foreign journalists ended up staying in Baghdad during most of the war. These correspondents were of course assigned 'minders' whose presence was duly noted in the broadcasts, but whose actual control regarding what could be said and seen is open to varying interpretations depending on the correspondent.

The Iraq War was covered by an unprecedented number of news organizations. There were 3,000 journalists following the advancing coalition forces or reporting from neighbouring countries. Eight hundred of these were 'embedded' under the 'protection' of the US-led forces. These numbers are a manifestation, not only of the heightened interest in war, but also of the news media's expansion in terms of channels and broadcast hours. Since the Falklands War, the British and American military have tried to develop a system that gives journalists access to the battlefield without compromising operations security. The new system of embedded journalists can be seen as a logical development of the previous 'pool system'. Each of the different US adaptations of the British 'pool system' from 1983 to the Gulf War was criticized as being too draconian: due to censorship and lack of access to the battlefield. The embedded system promised journalists greater access to the battlefield and less chance of being trapped in crossfire situations.[9]

When the Iraq War was imminent, many news organizations debated the advantages and risks of the 'embedded' system. Would the ability to remain critical be undermined by living together with the Coalition forces?[10] The public discussion of these risks should be understood as a demonstration of journalists' awareness of the ways their environment could affect them. This served to strengthen news organizations' credibility at the run-up to a war, when journalists have to work hard to maintain the impression of independence.

A Cardiff University study on embedded reporting in the British media found that embedded journalists were 'generally able to preserve their objectivity', that the information from embeds was more reliable than the official briefings and, surprisingly, that embeds were more 'balanced' (less obviously pro-war) than studio-based anchor people.[11] The study warns that the distinction between embeds and unilateral (independent) reporters is at times misleading, since embedded reporters could leave their units and report independently, and unilaterals had the possibility of becoming embedded for a period of time. The report concludes that the embed system is not a perfect solution to the key problem of war coverage: indeed, one of the areas in which both broadcasters and the public are in emphatic agreement is that a *multiplicity of sources and perspectives* is essential for objective and balanced war coverage.[12]

While some fears proved unfounded, the Cardiff study points to two areas of ongoing concern in war coverage. First, what is called a 'cultural issue in British broadcasting' – the tradition of restricting graphic images of violence and death – means that although viewers of the Iraq War were brought closer to the front lines, the 'ugly' side of war is still missing. The consequences of this are 'profound', insofar as war itself is made to appear 'more acceptable'. Indeed, the respondents interviewed 'commented on the sanitised, almost "fictional" quality of the embedded reports bringing a "made for TV" version of war into their living rooms.'[13]

The second issue is the extent to which the embed system increases the danger to unilateral reporters in the field. Unilateral and freelance journalists are an important part of war journalism since access to first-hand information reduces the risk of becoming an instrument for propaganda. While media organizations do take great risks, it is often the freelance journalists who do the most dangerous jobs in a conflict. Statements by American officials and the military about unilateral correspondents consisted of warnings that their safety could not be guaranteed: the implication being that if journalists roamed around, it was their own fault if they got killed. This prompted concern about whether there was a conscious strategy by coalition forces to make embedding 'the only option' for future conflicts.

According to the International Press Institute's report, 17 media representatives died during the Iraq War. Like the Cardiff study, the IPI criticizes the discriminatory way that unilateral journalists were dealt with by coalition forces and details the complaints of press freedom violations: harassment, detainment, equipment confiscationd and deportation. Moreover, the US military seemed uncooperative in investigating these incidents: i.e. when US forces fired on and killed two journalists at the Palestine Hotel, they claimed to be answering sniper fire. Witnesses denied the US version and a cameraman from a French news outlet who filmed during this time registered no sniper fire. Since the US military knew that journalists were based at this location, and no alternative explanation was forthcoming, the International Press Institute concluded that not enough care was taken to protect the safety of civilian non-combatants.[14]

How the Jessica Lynch story undermined the credibility of the US authorities and its media

The rescue of 19-year-old Jessica Lynch from Saddam Hospital in Nasiriya illustrates the aforementioned integration of news and entertainment, as well as the battle for credibility between government and media. It also demonstrates a shift in military practice where the role of Public Affairs Officers has become difficult to distinguish from other professionals dealing with Perception Management.

The news of the rescue of private Jessica Lynch in a dramatic operation, carried out under cover of darkness, came at a time of great political importance for US morale. At that stage of the war, the media had begun questioning the military planning. There was a halt in the offensive, supply lines were stretched and US soldiers had been killed in Iraqi ambushes. For the media, Lynch fit perfectly with the open slot for a human interest story with the right dramatic qualities, and it also 'happened' during prime time. Portrayed as a heroine who fought until her ammunition ran out in a battle to the death for the freedom of the Iraqi people, she was also a person American audiences could identify with. She miraculously survived multiple gunshot wounds, stab wounds and other injuries to be rescued in 'a classic joint operation'. The message was clear: American soldiers don't leave fragile blond comrades behind and our troops will prevail.

How did this story come to contain all these ingredients and how well does it stand up to scrutiny? Not long after the story broke, critical voices were raised about its authenticity. Retired US Air Force Colonel Sam Gardiner argues that the Lynch story has all the hallmarks of a 'strategic influence campaign'.[15] It was also unusual that covert Special Operations Task Force 20, a unit designated for only the highest priorities in Iraq such as the capture of Ba'ath party officials, should undertake her rescue. A press briefing was immediately summoned, rousing reporters from their beds, but at the scheduled briefing the following day (2 April), the CENTCOM spokesperson Brooks declined to comment on Private Lynch's injuries. Later that day, several versions of her injuries began appearing in the media, quoting anonymous Pentagon sources. On 3 April, the *Washington Post's* front-page story quoted unnamed officials as saying that Lynch was 'fighting fiercely . . . had sustained gunshot and stab wounds . . . She did not want to be taken alive.'[16]

Conflicting accounts of the circumstances of Lynch's capture and injuries circulated freely in the Anglo-American press during the following month, despite efforts by the *Washington Post* as early as 15 April to correct their original story. Lynch herself, being cared for in a hospital in Germany, was beyond the reach of the press and also reportedly suffered from amnesia. According to Gardiner, classified information was leaked to the press (bypassing official channels) if it fitted with the Administration's 'message', but information which conflicted with this 'message' was deliberately withheld or delayed.

The efforts of some of the American press to redress some of the factual errors did not have much of an impact on the story until the British media started circulating allegations, based on a BBC documentary aired on 18 May, that the rescue of Jessica Lynch was staged. This charge, originating from outside the US, compelled the Pentagon to break its silence and publish details from its own investigation of the events. The *Washington Post* then published an article on 17 June attempting to clear up the details of the Lynch story once and for all.[17]

Jessica Lynch had not been shot or stabbed, but had received multiple fractures when the Humvee she was travelling in crashed after being hit by a rocket-propelled grenade. She had not fired her weapon since it was believed to have jammed. The Iraqi hospital personnel who treated her in fact kept her alive until the rescue.[18] Jessica Lynch has corroborated these facts, insisting that she is no hero, that there was no reason for the rescue operation to be filmed by combat camera and that she had been used by the Pentagon.[19]

Although we agree with Gardiner's strategic news management case, we would point to several other aspects of the Lynch story. In times of war and crisis, factual errors in the initial media reports are common and errors are imperceptibly replaced by the 'correct' facts as time goes on. When information is sketchy, the interdependence of different media outlets increases and initial errors can spiral into a vicious circle. Second, the US military was successful in promoting a story that had clear short-term propaganda effects on American morale, whether or not the operation was staged for that purpose. If the story was consciously manipulated or spun by the US Administration, they took a risk. Media manipulation is an unorthodox practice in the military Public Affairs tradition. Propaganda scholar Phil Taylor says that we are witnessing a development where the US government no longer distinguishes between a press conference and a psychological operations campaign.[20] The assumption in many European media, that it was an intended bluff, demonstrates however that the Pentagon's credibility was undermined by the flaws in the story. The US media's credibility also suffers, since it is only under the pressure of inconsistencies and the catalytic aid of the British media that the US media redoubled their efforts to correct the story. This is an example of the aforementioned developments in media globalization whereby the British media become useful sources when the US media must deal with sensitive domestic issues.

Finally, the Lynch story raises questions about how far a news story can go on its dramaturgic and entertaining merits and where the boundary between the military and the entertainment industry is drawn. At least the latter has, together with the main protagonist, continued to exploit the story resulting in two books, one made-for-TV movie and another in the making.

The Anglo-American media caught between the public and the powerful

Ever since the terror attacks of 9/11, the US media have been under pressure to demonstrate 'patriotism' in news coverage of the government's security policy. Before the attacks on Afghanistan, the US media complied with the government's request not to air Osama bin Laden's speeches in their entirety. The media accepted, grudgingly, the tight restrictions imposed during the attacks on Afghanistan, but some media, notably CNN, also exercised self-censorship due to perceived audience sensitivities.[21] The touchy political climate and the need to rally around the flag was also evident after the initiation of hostilities in Iraq. While a number of events can illustrate this issue, we chose two that gave cause for the European media to question US media organizations' commitment to independence, and to claim to provide an alternative view.

A telling example of how constricted the political space was for the US media during the Iraq War was the case of veteran reporter Peter Arnett. New Zealand-born Arnett had been based in the US for over 25 years and had won a Pulitzer Prize for his Vietnam War coverage. Arnett gave an interview on Iraqi TV after the outbreak of hostilities in which he said that the US military would have to review its war strategy and seemed to have misjudged the Iraqis' will to fight. After attacks by politicians and angry viewers, NBC, MSNBC and National Geographic Explorer fired him.[22] This despite the fact that Arnett's statements reflected what leaks inside the Pentagon had been saying at the time, and Arnett's apology to the American people. The British tabloid the *Daily Mirror* immediately hired him and, in his first article for them, Arnett insisted that he had been penalized for telling the truth.

During the Iraq War, the Director General of the BBC, Greg Dyke, insisted that his organization was able to retain a critical perspective on the war, and that the BBC's 'impartiality' and 'fairness' had enhanced its reputation. Dyke criticized the American media for their 'unquestioning' coverage of the Iraq War. Not all Americans, he said, were satisfied with the patriotic reporting of Rupert Murdoch's Fox News and the radio conglomerate Clear Channel. A 28 per cent increase in hits on the BBC website from the US demonstrated that 'fair and impartial' news was a sound policy in the new multi-channel environment.[23]

Dyke's speech should be seen in light of the overhaul the BBC has undergone during the 1990s under heavy pressure from new media channels, the government and audiences.[24] His defence of the journalistic values of 'fairness and impartiality' was interpreted as a warning against British plans for more deregulation:

> The communications bill currently before parliament will, if it becomes law, allow US media companies to own whole chunks of the electronic media in this country for the first time. . . . In the area of impartiality, as in many other areas, we must ensure we don't become Americanised.[25]

Dyke's warning also reflects an unease over the status of public service broadcasting: can 'impartiality' continue to be an adequate sales pitch in the new competitive global media structure? In the US television landscape, Fox News tries to gain a competitive advantage by appealing to certain political sympathies in news coverage. This line of thinking holds that those viewers who sympathize with the values of the channel in question will feel more at home with its interpretations of news events, which in turn will give stable audience ratings.

New light is shed on Dyke's speech in the aftermath of the Hutton Inquiry about the extent of the pressure the British government put on the BBC. Briefly, the Hutton Inquiry looked into the BBC's allegations that the British government had 'sexed up' its dossier on Iraq's weapons of mass destruction and then 'outed' its senior science advisor, David Kelly, resulting in his suicide. The inquiry proceedings represent an unprecedented and very public battle of credibility between the BBC and the government, after which Dyke himself resigned. Interestingly, although the government was exonerated and the BBC criticized, opinion polls showed a significant majority still supported the BBC and criticized the government. This was attributed to the fact that the remit of the inquiry was too narrow to include the central issue: the government's erroneous claim of weapons of mass destruction in Iraq.[26]

Al-Jazeera: the new kid on the block

If the European media challenged the US media's version of events, then the transnational Arabic satellite channel Al-Jazeera represents an even more forceful alternative. Al-Jazeera reaches an estimated 35 million Arabic speakers around the world and is the first regional broadcaster to successfully challenge Western media perspectives in news coverage of the Middle East. Through looking at the role of Al-Jazeera both before and during the Iraq War, we are looking at a shift in transnational news coverage towards micro public spheres with competing versions of 'reality', a situation that will affect the way future conflicts are played out.

Al-Jazeera first came to the attention of the Western media through its broadcasting of Osama bin Laden's speeches after the 9/11 attacks on the US. It has since become an important referent in Western media coverage as 'providing another perspective' regarding the conflicts in the Middle East. While the US government has seen its coverage of the wars in Afghanistan and Iraq as a provocation, the channel has gained considerable standing in Western news discourse. How has Al-Jazeera gained the respect of its Western colleagues?

A survey of the news articles about Al-Jazeera during the last two years indicates that the channel is characterized as adhering to Western journalistic norms and ideals. [27] The most common epithet given to Al-Jazeera is the 'CNN of the Middle East', despite the fact that neither CNN nor Al-Jazeera like the comparison. The reason for its persistence is that Al-Jazeera was the first Arabic channel to broadcast 24 hours a day getting exclusive footage and interviews. During the war in Afghanistan, Al-Jazeera came to prominence much in the same way as CNN had during the Gulf War: as the only television channel allowed to remain in the country. This meant that, prior to overthrow of the Taliban regime, Western news channels were forced to buy Al-Jazeera's exclusive footage. [28]

It was two years later, during the Iraq War, that Western satellite channels faced serious competition from non-Western transnational broadcasters. Al-Jazeera's success had spawned new Arabic satellite channels such as Al-Arabiya and Abu Dhabi TV, both of which had correspondents inside Iraq during the war. Headlines during the Iraq War describe Al-Jazeera as a counterpoint to the American media image: 'The War from Both Sides' or 'A Tale of Two Wars', where Al-Jazeera is said to represent the 'Arab view' of the war. [29] This characterization is interesting for several reasons. First, these types of headlines assume that there are *only* two homogeneous versions of events: a Western and Arabic one. Second, these headlines are reminiscent of prevailing journalist ideals, which say that if 'both sides' of an issue are covered, then journalists have fulfilled their task of 'balanced reporting'.

That said, there were by all accounts striking differences between the images of the Iraq War on the Arabic satellite channels and their British/ American counterparts. While the BBC, CNN and NBC showed soldiers rescuing POW's, taking Iraqi prisoners, or moving through empty deserts, viewers of Al-Jazeera saw other events. Here, Iraqi soldiers put up heroic resistance against the 'invading forces', a running count of Iraqi civilian casualties was shown at the bottom of the screen, while the bloody 'victims of the Anglo American bombardment are brought to the operation rooms shrieking in pain'. [30] Al-Jazeera's coverage demonstrated how the Iraqi leadership and civilians experienced the war. Scandinavian journalists describe the shock of seeing Al-Jazeera images for the first time: suddenly the war was the 'blood, tears, fear and anxiety of the civilians'.[31] While the focus on gruesome pictures of dead and wounded was seen in Washington as ideological slant, Western journalists tend to attribute them to cultural differences. Director of BBC News Richard Sambrooke described Al-Jazeera as '. . . a perfectly straightforward Arab television news channel which is still learning . . . They have different values and a different tolerance for gruesome pictures and so on. They have to pay heed to their – principally Arab – audience'.[32]

This view is common among Northern European and US television journalists, who see it as part of their 'journalism culture' to avoid graphic images of death and suffering, in contrast to other cultures, which do not have such norms. Regardless of the bloodiness of the images themselves, Al-Jazeera certainly also broadcast these images to reflect the prevailing anti-war stance in the Arab world.

This did not prevent a number of Western media outlets from using Al-Jazeera as a way to corroborate information from the US-led coalition about what was happening inside Iraq. According to Norwegian television correspondent Sigrun Slapgard, Al-Jazeera had some 20 reporters inside Iraq and one correspondent embedded with the coalition forces.[33] During the first phase of the war, when officials at CENTCOM were saying that the population inside the city of Basra had risen up against Saddam Hussein, Al-Jazeera's correspondent in Basra observed nothing out of the ordinary. Coalition forces told the press they would not force a military confrontation in Basra, but journalists could see Al-Jazeera's pictures of civilians being bombed. In the days preceding this, CENTCOM kept insisting that it had secured the vital port of Umm Qasr, but in reality, the city fell four days later. It is difficult to see how these discrepancies strengthened the credibility of Coalition press relations' efforts.

In view of the way Al-Jazeera is described it is not surprising that foreign correspondents use Al-Jazeera as a source for their news coverage. The working methods ascribed the channel are the same as for any Western media outlet. They 'scoop' the competition with exclusive information and footage, they are on the scene and they broadcast 'newsworthy' information in real time. But the question is whether these characteristics coincide with 'good' journalism and if not, could the media discourse on Al-Jazeera have more to do with Western journalists' attempts to defend their credibility vis-à-vis audiences on the one hand and governments on the other?

Al-Jazeera caught between the public and the powerful

A typical Western news article will describe how different Arab governments have censored or put pressure on Al-Jazeera: it is banned in Saudi Arabia, its offices have been closed in Kuwait and Jordan, it has infuriated the

221

governments of Egypt, Morocco, Algeria, Yemen and Syria. So irritating was Al-Jazeera's coverage of the advancing coalition forces that the Iraqi leadership demanded that the channel 'correct' its coverage. The Iraqi regime gave in when Al-Jazeera threatened to leave the country if its reporters could not work freely.

Perhaps one of the reasons Al-Jazeera wears these conflicts like a badge is in order to counter charges that its financial dependency on the Emir of Qatar, Sheikh Hamad bin Khalifa Al-Thani, may have strings attached. Initiated by the BBC Arabic Service together with Saudi-owned Orbit Radio and Television, Sheikh Hamad stepped in with a five-year loan when the partnership soured. In short, Al-Jazeera is a Pan-Arabic channel where outspokenness and critique is allowed when it comes to other countries than the one in which it is based.[34]

The governments angered by Al-Jazeera have not only been Arab ones. The channel has interviewed not only high-ranking al-Qaeda and Hamas members, but also British Prime Minister Tony Blair and senior officials from the Bush administration, such as Defence Secretary Donald Rumsfeld. It was during the war in Afghanistan that the US government became sharply critical of Al-Jazeera's 'aggressive' interview style, saying that it prefers to get its message across 'in other ways'. The interviews with officials from conflicting camps serve to strengthen Al-Jazeera's claim of 'balance' and showing 'the opposite opinion'.

One of the most controversial features of Al-Jazeera's coverage of the Iraq War was when the channel broadcast footage of coalition soldiers taken prisoner by the Iraqis. London and Washington accused Al-Jazeera of violating the Geneva Convention: however, experts for the Index on Censorship maintain that under Article 13, prisoners must be 'protected from insults and public curiosity', and it is questionable whether this extends to publishing photos or filming prisoners.[35] Al-Jazeera said their job was to transparently report what happened on the ground: coalition soldiers were just as much victims as Iraqi women and children. They questioned the double standard inherent in the US/UK accusations: Anglo-American television news stations regularly air footage of enemy prisoners or dead soldiers, and they are not accused of violating the Geneva Convention.[36]

Al-Jazeera paid a high price for its coverage of the Iraq War when its Baghdad correspondent was killed, and another colleague wounded, in the US bombing of the offices of Al-Jazeera and Abu Dhabi TV. Al-Jazeera, whose Kabul office was hit during the US-led invasion of Afghanistan, claimed it had informed the coalition of the exact coordinates for its Baghdad office. The reaction of US officials seemed to add insult to injury: first insisting on their original version of events, then delivering regrets with the caveat that war zones are dangerous places, and finally by dragging on too long with an investigation into the causes of the mistake. Al-Jazeera concludes that the US deliberately bombed their office.[37] There were other indications of the pressure brought to bear on Al-Jazeera for its decision to 'show the human cost of the war'. It was, for example, the only news organization whose press accreditation was taken away by Wall Street during the Iraq War. US hackers took down Al-Jazeera's English website, which remained unavailable for much of the war, although its Arab-language website was only down for almost a week.[38]

To summarize, Al-Jazeera defends its Iraq coverage with reference to Western journalistic ideals: their journalists were both embedded and uni-lateral (balance), they are independent from government, and they provide transparent, timely and newsworthy (relevant to Arabic audiences) accounts of events.[39] Most news articles about Al-Jazeera balance government accusations of bias with Al-Jazeera's defence of these ideals, together with evidence that Al-Jazeera provided unique insight into the Afghanistan/Iraq Wars, despite enduring shelling, sabotage, verbal attacks and indeed death. Like other non-Arabic speakers, our judgements are dependent on second-hand sources, but in light of the conflicting claims between Al-Jazeera and Anglo-American officials, Al-Jazeera comes out of the Iraq War with greater credibility than its detractors.

Credibility in a multi-channel environment

In light of the increase in information actors in this globalizing world, the Al-Jazeera phenomenon highlights how democratic journalistic ideals are reflected back to us in an unexpected way. We are reminded that journalistic methods and ideals are no guarantee of 'truth', but can vary according to the environment and media landscape. Journalists, decision-makers and audiences are confronted with a fundamental contradiction in journalism: between independence and patriotism, and between impartiality and loyalty to audiences in this new culturally relativistic broadcasting landscape with its multiplicity of 'micro'-public spheres.

We noted that while Western journalists continue to adhere to notions of accuracy, balance and timeliness, journalistic ideals are changing: not only towards entertainment values but also toward a journalism of attachment. The micro-public spheres of Al-Jazeera and Fox News claim to give us balance while showing us not simply competing views of the world, but different realities. The danger here is the development, not of a common world stage, but of separate conservative or religious micro-public spheres whose realities never meet.

That governments use propaganda, persuasion and censorship in war-time is not new. The changing digital environment makes it more difficult for governments to control the images emanating from the battle zone and the long-awaited renaissance in the Arabic media landscape has upped these stakes. In this media-saturated, commercially driven environment, there is a need to rethink the clash between the media's ability to comfort audiences in times of crises and its duty to inform them about what is being done in their name. This is a pressing issue for journalism, especially now.

We have shown that the attempts to silence and censor the media are losing strategies for democratic governments. That warring parties and the bureaucracies who support them are spending more time and effort spinning the news media is something that cannot have escaped anyone during the 1990s. The Iraq War shows that the pitfalls are numerous. Al-Jazeera was not only mandatory viewing for millions of Arabic speakers, but gained the respect of its Western colleagues when it was able to counter the claims of the coalition forces. The BBC, which has traditionally relied on its status as a dependable source, consolidated its position as independent and impartial, even for journalists and audiences outside of Britain. The question is how long this type of organization will last in the face of deregulation and whether the price for taking on the government may have been too high.

Even if audiences prefer news perspectives consonant with their cultural and social values, there are signs that certain audiences are utilizing the possibilities of the new global media environment. Despite the inherent flaws in the system regarding the ability to deliver high quality war journalism, the changing media environment does increase the possibilities for audiences to balance different perspectives against each other. At least for those who have the knowledge, the time and the money to compare.

Notes

1 R. Brown, 'Spinning the War: Political Communications, Information Operations and Public Diplomacy in the War on Terrorism', in D. Thussu and D. Freedman (eds) *War and the Media: Reporting Conflict 24/7*, Thousand Oaks, CA: Sage, 2003.
2 K. Riegert, *The Image War: NATO's Battle for Kosovo in the British Media*, Örebro: Örebro University, 2003, Chapter 5.
3 D. Thussu, 'Live TV and Bloodless Deaths: Infotainment and 24/7 News', in Thussu and D. Freedman op. cit., 117–133.
4 J. Seaton, 'Understanding not Empathy', in Thussu and Freedman op. cit.
5 Pew Center for the People and the Press, 'Striking the Balance, Audience Interests, Business Pressures and Journalists' Values', 30 March 1999. Section I. p. 1. Available at people-presp.org/reports/display.php3?ReportID=67 (accessed 20 November 2003).
6 Ibid., section I.
7 Thussu, op. cit., p. 126.
8 W. L. Bennett and D. Paletz (eds) *Taken By Storm, The Media, Public Opinion, and U.S. Foreign Policy in the Gulf War*, Chicago, IL: University of Chicago Press, 1994 and P. M. Taylor, *The War and the Media: Propaganda and Persuasion in the Gulf War*, Manchester: Manchester University Press, 1992.
9 Joint Chiefs of Staff, *Doctrine for Public Affairs in Joint Operations*, Joint Publication 3-61, 1997, pp. III-2–III-5. The new US Department of Defense policy for embedded reporters can be found at www.militarycity.com/iraq/1631270.html (accessed 5 December 2003).

10 H. Kurtz, 'Embedded in Controversy', *Washington Post*, 27 March 2003.
11 J. Lewis *et al*. 'The Role of Embedded Reporting During the 2003 Iraq War: Summary Report', Cardiff School of Journalism, Media and Cultural Studies. Commissioned by the BBC, 2003, p. 2.
12 Ibid. p. 3.
13 Ibid. p. 3.
14 G. Leaper, A. Löwstedt and H. Madhoun, 'Caught in the Crossfire: The Iraq War and the Media, A Diary of Claims and Counterclaims', International Press Institute (IPI), 2003, Conclusions. Available at www.freemedia.at/ index1.html (accessed 25 March 2004); C. Byrne, 'US Soldiers Were Main Danger to Journalists, Says Simpson', *Guardian Unlimited*, 27 June 2003. Available at media.guardian.co.uk/broadcast/story/0,7493,986599,00.html (accessed 20 November 2003).
15 S. Gardiner, 'Truth from These Podia; Summary of Study of Strategic Influence, Perception Management, Strategic Information Warfare and Strategic Psychological Operation in Gulf II', 2003. pp. 25–26. Available at www.usnewp.com/ usnews/politics/whispers/documents/truth.pdf (accessed 4 December 2003).
16 D. Chinni, 'Jessica Lynch: Media Myth-Making in the Iraq War', *Journalism.org*, 2003, pp. 1–3. Available at www.journalism.org/resources/research/reports/war/ postwar/lynch.asp (accessed 3 December 2003).
17 D. Priest, W. Booth and S. Schmidt, 'A Broken Body, a Broken Story, Pieced Together', *Washington Post*, 17 June 2003, p. A01. Available at www.washington post.com/ac2/wp-dyn?pagename = article&node = &contentId = A2760–2003Jun 16&notFound = true (accessed 4 December 2003).
18 Detailed interviews with Iraqi hospital personnel were the basis of the allegations that the rescue was staged. D. Sawyer, 'Jessica Lynch Condemns Pentagon', *BBC News*, 7 November 2003. Available at newp.bbc.co.uk/2/hi/americas/3251731. stm (accessed 4 December 2003).
19 R. Bragg and J. Lynch, *I Am a Soldier, Too: The Jessica Lynch Story*, New York: Alfred A. Knopf, 2003.
20 P. Taylor, 'Desert Storm Blowback: Psychological Operations in Operation Iraqi Freedom 2003', in L. Nicander and M. Ranstarp (eds) *Terrorism in the Information Age: New Frontiers?* Stockholm: Swedish National Defence College, 2004, pp. 108–128.
21 K. Riegert, 'Know Your Enemy, Know Your Allies: Lessons Not Learned from the Kosovo Conflict', *The Journal of Information Warfare*, 1, 3 (2002), 79–93. See also H. Kurtz, 'CNN Chief Orders "Balance" in War News. Reporters Are Told To Remind Viewers Why U.S. Is Bombing', *The Washington Post*, 31 October 2001, C.01.
22 *National Geographic News*, 'National Geographic Fires Peter Arnett', 31 March 2003. Available at newp.nationalgeographic.com/news/2003/03/0331_030331_ arnettfired.html (accessed 3 December 2003). See also C. Cozens, 'Arnett Fired by NBC after Iraqi TV Outburst', *Guardian Unlimited*, 31 March 2003, available at www.media.guardian.co.uk/broadcast/story/0,7493,926551,00.html (accessed 21 March 2004).
23 D. Timms, 'Dyke Attacks "Unquestioning" US Media', *Guardian Unlimited*, 24 April 2003, available at media.guardian.co.uk/broadcast/story/0,7493, 942640,00.html. See also J. Deans, 'Americans Turn to BBC for War News', *Guardian Unlimited*, 17 April 2003, available at media.guardian.co.uk/broad- cast/story/0,7493,938595,00.html (accessed 7 November 2003).
24 B. McNair, *News and Journalism in the UK*, 4th edn, London: Routledge, 2003.

25 Dyke cited in Timms, op.cit. For an assessment of the relaxation of owner-
ship rules, see L. Cohen and S. Postlethwaite, 'Al-Jazeera: In an Intense Spotlight', *Business Week Online*, 27 March 2003. http://search.epnet.com/direct.
asp?an9393283&db = bsh.

26 R. Norton-Taylor, 'The Hutton Inquiry and its Impact', *Guardian Unlimited*,
6 February 2004, pp. 5–7. Available at www.guardian.co.uk/hutton/story/
0,13822,1142377,00.html.

27 The articles were collected from different electronic data bases using the search
terms Al-Jazeera/Al-Jazira.

28 R. Zednik, 'Inside Al-Jazeera', *Columbia Journalism Review*, 5 April 2002, available at www.alternet.org/story.html?StoryID = 12793 (accessed 15 November
2003).

29 J. Poniewozik *et al.* 'The War on TV from Both Sides', *Time Canada*, 161, 14
(2003), 60–61.

30 This is Robert Fisk's description of Al-Jazeera's image of the war in S. Rampton
and J. Stauber, *Weapons of Mass Deception: The Uses of Propaganda in Bush's
War on Iraq*. London: Robinson, 2003, pp. 200–201.

31 S. Slapgard, *Krig og Løgn: Drama i ti akter* [*War and Lies: A Drama in 10 Acts*],
Trondheim: Gyldendal, 2003.

32 C. Byrne, 'War Reporting "Changed Forever" says BBC', *Guardian Unlimited*,
31 March 2003, available at media.guardian.co.uk/print/0,3858,4637353-
105236,00.html (accessed 27 March 2004).

33 Slapgard, op. cit.

34 M. El-Nawawy and A. Iskander, *Al-Jazeera: How the Free Arab News Network
Scooped the World and Changed the Middle East*, Cambridge, MA: Westview,
2002, p. 49. See also Z. Sardar's criticism of El-Nawawy and Iskanders' book,
Z. Sardar, 'A Voice of Reason', *New Statesman*, 9 September 2002, 131, 4604.

35 Index on Censorship, 'Live from indexonline!', 4 April 2003, available at
www.indexonline.org/news/20030328_iraq.shtml (accessed 26 March 2004).

36 *Correspondent Special*, 'Al-Jazeera – Exclusive', BBC 2, 1 June 2003, available at newp.bbc.uk/nol/shared/spl/hi/programmes/correspondent/transcripts/
3047501.stm.

37 *Reporters without Borders*, 'War in Iraq', www.rsf.org/article.php3?id_article =
6024, 26 November 2003; *Correspondent BBC News*, 'Al-Jazeera Defends War
Reports', 24 May 2003, newp.bbc.co.uk/1/hi/programmes/correspondent/
3047501.stm.

38 Slapgard, op. cit. p. 157.

39 C. Byrne, 'Al-Jazeera Wins Anti-Censorship Award', *Guardian Unlimited*, available at media.guardian.co.uk/iraqandthemedia/story/0,12823,922497,00.html
(accessed 20 November 2003).

References

Bennett, W. L. and Paletz, D. (eds) *Taken By Storm, The Media, Public Opinion, and
U.S. Foreign Policy in the Gulf War*. Chicago, IL: University of Chicago Press,
1994.

Bragg, R. and Lynch, J. *I Am a Soldier, Too: The Jessica Lynch Story*. New York:
Alfred A. Knopf, 2003.

Brown, R. 'Spinning the War: Political Communications, Information Operations
and Public Diplomacy in the War on Terrorism', in D. Thussu and D. Freedman
(eds) *War and the Media: Reporting Conflict 24/7*. Thousand Oaks: Sage, 2003,
pp. 87–101.

Byrne, C. 'Al-Jazeera Wins Anti-Censorship Award', *Guardian Unlimited*, 27 March 2003. Available at www.media.guardian.co.uk/iraqandthemedia/story/ 0,12823,922497,00.html (accessed 15 November 2003).

Byrne, C. 'War Reporting "Changed Forever" says BBC', *Guardian Unlimited*, 31 March 2003. Available at www.media.guardian.co.uk/broadcast/story/ 0,7493,926367,00,html (accessed 5 November 2003).

Byrne, C. 'US Soldiers Were Main Danger to Journalists, Says Simpson', *Guardian Unlimited*, 27 June 2003. Available at www.media.guardian.co.uk/iraqandthe media/story/0,12823,986601,00.html (accessed 20 November 2003).

Chinni, D. 'Jessica Lynch: Media Myth-Making in the Iraq War', *Journalism.org*, 2003. Available at www.journalism.org/resources/research/reports/war/postwar/ lynch.asp (accessed 20 March 2004).

Cohen, L. and Postlethwaite, 'Al-Jazeera: In an Intense Spotlight', *Business Weekly Online*, 27 MArch 2003. http://search.epnet.com/direct.asp?an9393283&db = bsh.

Correspondent Special, BBC 2. 'Al-Jazeera– Exclusive', aired 1 June 2003. Available at www.news.bbc.uk/nol/shared/spl/hi/programmes/correspondent/transcripts/ 3047501.stm (accessed 15 November 2003).

Correspondent, BBC News, 'Al-Jazeera Defends War Reports', 24 May 2003. Available at www.news.bbc.co.uk/1/hi/programmes/correspondent/3047501.stm (accessed 8 November 2003).

Cozens, C., 'Arnett Fired by NBC after Iraqi TV Outburst', *Guardian Unlimited*, 31 March 2003, available at www.media.guardian.co.yuk/broadcast/story/ 10,7493,926551,00.html (accessed 21 March 2004).

Deans, J. 'Americans Turn to BBC for War News', *Guardian Unlimited*, 17 April 2003. Available at www.media.guardian.co.uk/iarkandthemedia/story/ 0,12823,938596,00.html (accessed 7 November 2003).

El-Nawawy, M. and Iskander, A. *Al-Jazeera: How the Free Arab News Network Scooped the World and Changed the Middle East*. Cambridge, MA: Westview, 2002.

Gardiner, S. 'Truth from These Podia; Summary of Study of Strategic Influence, Perception Management, Strategic Information Warfare and Strategic Psycho-logical Operation in Gulf II', 2003. Available at www.usnews.com/usnews/ politics/whispers/documents/truth.pdf.

Index on Censorship, 'Live from indexonline!', 4 April 2003. Available at www. indexonline.org/news/20030328_iraq.shtml (accessed 26 March 2004).

Joint Chiefs of Staff, *Doctrine for Public Affairs in Joint Operations*, Joint Publica-tion 3–61, 1997, Washington, DC: Joint Chiefs of Staff.

Kurtz, H. 'Embedded in Controversy', *Washington Post*, 27 March 2003.

Kurtz, H. 'CNN Chief Orders "Balance" in War News. Reporters Are Told To Remind Viewers Why U.S. Is Bombing', *The Washington Post*, 31 October 2001.

Leaper, G., Löwstedt, A. and Madhoun, H. 'Caught in the Crossfire: The Iraq War and the Media, A Diary of Claims and Counterclaims', International Press Institute (IPI), 2003. Conclusions. Available at www.freemedia.at/index1.html (accessed 25 March 2004).

Lewis, J. *et al. The Role of Embedded Reporting During the 2003 Iraq War: Summary Report*, Cardiff: Cardiff School of Journalism, Media and Cultural Studies, Commissioned by the BBC 2003. Unpublished report.

McNair, B. *News and Journalism in the UK*, 4th edn. London: Routledge, 2003.

National Geographic News, 'National Geographic Fires Peter Arnett', 31 March 2003. Available at www.ews.nationalgeographic.com/news/2003/03/0331_030331_ arnettfired.html Accessed 3 December 2003).

Norton-Taylor, R. 'The Hutton Inquiry and its Impact', *Guardian Unlimited*, 6 February 2004. Available at www.guardian.co.uk/hutton/story/0,13822, 1142377,00,html (accessed 12 July 2004).

Petley, J. 'Foxy Business', *Index on Censorship*, 32, 3 (2003).

Pew Center for the People and the Press, 'Striking the Balance, Audience Interests, Business Pressures and Journalists' Values', 30 March 1999. Section I–V. Available at people-press.org/reports/display.php3?ReportID=67 (accessed 20 November 2003).

Poniewozik, J. *et al.* 'The War on TV from Both Sides', *Time Canada*, 161, 14 (7 April 2003) 60–61.

Priest, D., Booth, W. and Schmidt, S. 'A Broken Body, a Broken Story, Pieced Together', *Washington Post*, 17 June 2003, A01. Available at www.washington post.com/ac2/wp-dyn?pagename=article&node=&contentId=A2760–2003Jun16 &notFound=true (accessed 4 December 2003).

Rampton, S. and Stauber, J. *Weapons of Mass Deception: The Uses of Propaganda in Bush's War on Iraq*. London: Robinson, 2003.

Reporters without borders, 'War in Iraq', 2003, available at www.rsf.org/article. php3?id_article=6024 (accessed 26 November 2003).

Riegert, K. 'Know Your Enemy, Know Your Allies: Lessons Not Learned from the Kosovo Conflict', *The Journal of Information Warfare*, 1, 3 (2002) 79–93.

Riegert, K. *The Image War: NATO's Battle for Kosovo in the British Media*. Örebro: Örebro universitet, 2003.

Sardar Z. 'A Voice of Reason', *New Statesman*, 131, 4604, 9 September 2002. Book review.

Sawyer, D. 'Jessica Lynch Condemns Pentagon', *BBC News*, 7 November 2003, available at www.news.bbc.co.uk/2/hi/americas/3251731.stm.

Seaton, J. 'Understanding not Empathy' in D. Thussu and D. Freedman (eds) *War and the Media: Reporting Conflict 24/7*. Thousand Oaks, CA: Sage, 2003, 45–55.

Slapgard, S. *Krig og Løgn: Drama i ti akter*. Trondheim: Gyldendal, 2003.

Taylor, P. M. *The War and the Media: Propaganda and Persuasion in the Gulf War*. Manchester: Manchester University Press, 1992.

Thussu, D. 'Live TV and Bloodless Deaths: Infotainment and 24/7 News', in D. Thussu and D. Freedman (eds) *War and the Media: Reporting Conflict 24/7*. Thousand Oaks, CA: Sage, 2003.

Timms, D. 'Dyke Attacks "Unquestioning" US Media', *Guardian Unlimited*, 24 April 2003, available at www.media.guardian.co.uk/broadcast/story/0,7493, 942640,00.html.

Zednik, R. 'Inside Al-Jazeera', *Columbia Journalism Review*, 5 April 2003, available at www.alternet.org/story.html?StoryID=12793 (accessed 15 November 2003).

12

CONCLUSIONS

Jan Hallenberg and Håkan Karlsson

Introduction

In its yearly assessment of the global strategic situation published in May 2004, the International Institute for Strategic Studies (IISS) writes:

> If the US is seen to fail in Iraq, America's foreign policy will have to be rethought. The long-term instability of Iraq would act as a potent symbol, highlighting the limited power of the US to intervene successfully against rogue states . . . But if US plans succeed, Iraq, as a westward-leaning beacon of democracy and free markets, is likely to inspire a measure of political and economic reform that could both ameliorate the region's endemic problems and improve the chances of a better accommodation between the Arab world and the West.[1]

As the last chapter of this anthology on the Iraq War is being completed, four months have passed after the publication of the IISS book, but the fundamental uncertainty about the final outcome of the war, so well captured in the quote, still remains as acute as it was when the book was published. Success for the US war effort is far from assured. The Iraq War of 2003 was not just a modern case of planning for and waging a large war, it was also a central element of the grand strategy of the only superpower that the world has known since the collapse of the Soviet Union more than a decade ago. As such, the war in Iraq and the diplomacy before and after the conventional war-fighting phase, plus the insurgency in the country after the fall of Saddam Hussein's regime, all have profound implications for the future of global politics as well as for the future of warfare. In addition, the Iraq War is connected to the so-called War on Terrorism that the Bush administration has waged since 2001. The fundamental issues in this respect are whether or not it was legitimate to say, as the Administration has done, that the war in Iraq is a part of the war on terrorism, and whether, as a result of the toppling of the Saddam regime, the risk of terror attacks against the US homeland, or against US interests abroad, has increased or decreased.

In this chapter, we pull together the threads of our analyses of the Iraq War and also attempt, if not to clarify, then at least to shed some light on the unclear situation in Iraq precipitated by the war. The decision by the Bush administration to invade Iraq has led to consequences fundamentally different from those that the Administration seems to have envisioned during the many months that it planned for the coming war. At this time (the late summer of 2004) we believe that the judgement on the Iraq War as to whether the Administration so far has reached its goals, elaborated by Hallenberg in Chapter 2 of this volume, must be a negative one. In particular, the process by which the US and its allies intended to build a new Iraq, with a broadly representative government that respects the country's ethnic and religious minorities and does not threaten its neighbours, is currently on the road towards failure. If this basic goal is not reached, then the objective of creating a push toward democratization of the Middle East region is bound to fail as well. These tentative conclusions may be disproved by developments in Iraq in the future, but at the present moment they seem warranted. Anyway, a provisional assessment is the best we can do in the complex circumstances at hand. In this context, the overriding question that we seek to address is whether some part of the answer for why the invasion of Iraq turned out so badly for the US can be provided by the analyses undertaken in the chapters of this book.

The basic structure of the chapter is provided by the three main analytical questions posed in the introduction to this book. These questions are: (1) When did the war in Iraq take place? (2) Why did the war in Iraq occur? (3) How was the war in Iraq fought? Drawing largely on the preceding chapters, we endeavour in this chapter to advance possible answers to the central puzzles. In a concluding section we suggest remaining puzzles and ask questions that may form the basis for new research into the Iraq War and into modern war more generally.

When did the war in Iraq take place?

It is a recurring trait in studies of the two wars that the US has initiated against Iraq since 1990 that in a sense there was never any complete cessation of military hostilities in the inter-war period. President George H. W. Bush has acknowledged that he expected that, as a result of Saddam Hussein's defeat in the Gulf War, Saddam would be overthrown in fairly short order.[2] When the expected regime collapse did not occur, the first Bush administration proceeded to undertake several steps to weaken and eventually to undermine the Saddam regime. The first of these was the at least tacit encouragement given to the Kurds in the north of Iraq and the Shi'ites in the south to rise against Saddam in the wake of his defeat in the Gulf War.

When these uprisings failed, the US eventually, in a second step against the Saddam regime, undertook to support the development and maintenance of a zone in northern Iraq where the Kurds could develop a political sphere of their own, consisting of probably between four and five million people. Third, as further detailed in Chapter 10 of this book, the US, at first together with both France and the UK, and after 1998 only together with the UK, established, and for more than a decade maintained, no-fly zones over large areas of Iraq where Saddam's air force was prohibited from flying, and where attempts by Iraqi air defence forces to even lock in on allied planes were met by military responses. Particularly in the six to nine months before the start of the Iraq War, the two allies increased the air attacks against Iraqi targets without acknowledging that a new war was being planned. A situation in which there had been intermittent air attacks on various targets in Iraq was thus gradually changed into a state in which these attacks grew substantially in number and intensity. It seems to us that it would be hard to find any clearer illustration of the difficulty of determining when there is war and when there is no war than the case of the US and Iraq between August 1990 and March 2003.

We have come to the somewhat awkward conclusion that it is easier and perhaps also more useful to pose the question 'when did the Iraq War begin?' than to provide a definitive answer. The same applies to the question 'when did the war end?' Indeed, what has happened in Iraq after the country fell to the US-led coalition provides yet another illustration of the grey zone that may exist between regular war and no war. As a characterization of the situation in Iraq in the spring and summer of 2004, the word 'peace' seems hard to use. The war ended in May 2003 in the sense that the coalition forces had by then finished their major combat operations. However, the main fighting was superseded by mass riots, assassinations and increasingly organized guerrilla attacks. In a sense, then, some kind of war is still going on against the occupation forces. Anders Cedergren in Chapter 9 argues that the conflict is not yet over. In his view, a different type of war is now taking place, a so-called low-intensity conflict.

In Chapter 8, Stefan Ring deals with the post-war troubles resulting from the use of military force against Iraq and traces some of their origins back to faulty American war planning. He analyses the choice the Bush administration had in terms of ways in which it could utilize military force after it had decided, probably late in 2001, that the regime of Saddam Hussein would have to go. Ring's analytical point of departure is the classical distinction between coercion and brute force. He argues that the successful use of coercion necessitates a seamless integration of several power instruments, prominently including military force. In coercion, the acting state is prepared to accept something less than the total surrender of the adversary that it is attempting to influence, but it is also clearly ready to use military force to reach its minimum goals. Brute force, in contrast, means the use of military

231

power to crush the adversary's defence capability. One crucial difference between coercion and brute force in Ring's analysis is that in the case of coercion, the logic of the procedure leads to an outcome in which the acting state does not need to accept responsibility for occupying the territory and administering the society of its opponent, whereas in the case of brute force, the logic of the procedure leads to just such immense responsibility. Ring's analysis makes clear that the Bush administration's choice of brute force to reach its goals in Iraq led to consequences including the necessity to assume responsibility for occupying and administering Iraq after the thorough destruction of the Iraqi armed forces and the ensuing toppling of Saddam. It is also obvious in Ring's analysis that the planners in the Bush administration, acting in line with current conceptual developments within the American defence establishment, had concentrated on quickly and unequivocally reaching certain goals such as toppling the Saddam regime and ending the threatening weapons programmes that the Administration believed that the Iraqi regime pursued and, accordingly, on acquiring the military means by which they wanted to reach these goals. At the same time, it seems equally obvious that the planners in the Bush administration devoted considerably less time to planning for the consequences that would necessarily follow from the use of brute force, consequences that involved complete responsibility for the occupation and administration of a state of roughly 25 million people.

The lack of foresight on the part of the Bush administration with respect to this enormous undertaking continues to baffle many observers. One strength of Ring's analysis is, however, that it helps explain why Washington was preoccupied with the very use of brute force to the detriment of planning for the inevitable consequences.

Why did the war in Iraq happen?

In a sense, the fundamental puzzle in the whole complex of issues that makes up the planning for and fighting of the war in Iraq and then the post-war operations is why did the Bush administration decide to invade the country? As alluded to in Chapter 1, in the study of international relations one analytical distinction is often made when trying to explain an event or a pro- cess, that of levels of analysis. Starting from the bottom, one can distinguish between four levels of analysis: the individual, the state, the region and the international system. It seems fair to say that most explanations of the Bush administration's Iraq decision, including the ones provided by Jan Hallenberg in Chapter 2 of this book, focus on the first two levels. Many attempts at explanation concentrate on the individual traits of George W. Bush, the US President. His tendency to see matters in black and white, often linked to his religiously-based beliefs in which there are few nuances, only a right

way and a wrong way, are prominent here. On what may perhaps be classified as the state level, the existence of a strong current of beliefs within the
Republican party called neo-conservatism provides a second explanation.
The influence of decision-makers who subscribed to these views, it is often
stated, was crucial in making the decision to attack Iraq inevitable.

It is not our intention here to repeat all the various state-level explanations
for the US invasion of Iraq offered in Chapter 2. In our concluding analysis
of this matter we would, instead, like to consider the explanatory power of
the fourth level of analysis, the system level. As strategists, we would argue
that in an international system where there is only one power that possesses
overwhelming military might and where no actual or even potential actor
will match that superpower in terms of military strength in the near future,
there are few, if any, restraints on the sole superpower's use of its military
capability. It is thus, following this reasoning, to be expected that such a
superior power will feel free to utilize military means in situations where
it views its security as threatened. As our colleagues Ove Bring and Per
Broström have so ably explained in Chapter 7 of this volume, what systemic
restraint there might be on the superpower's choice of whether or not to use
military force in the current international system comes in the form of international law and the authority of the UN Security Council under this legal
regime. The events leading up to Iraq War of 2003 are to us evidence that
this restraint is not sufficient to prevent the American superpower from
using military force in situations where its leadership is convinced of the
necessity to do so. The fact that the military expedition in Iraq has proved
to be much more difficult and costly in many respects than the Bush administration believed initially does not, in our view, invalidate the fundamental
point that the US is not really restrained in its use of force in current international relations.

During the summer of 2004 it was often discussed what it would mean for
future US grand strategy if President George W. Bush lost power to the
Democratic challenger Senator John F. Kerry. As a matter of fact, the US
presidential election, whatever its outcome, would do nothing to influence
the strategic situation at the system level that we have discussed here. It
should be remembered, however, that explanations on the system level are
different from those on the individual and state levels. In the case of the
latter two levels of analysis, the explanations provided are typically intended
to provide the basis for clarifying specific decisions. When it comes to explanations on the system level, we are talking about identifying general tendencies. Such a tendency follows from the system characteristics outlined above.
In a system where a military superpower reigns supreme, that power has a
larger propensity to use military force than would be the case if there were
one or more powers that could counterbalance the superpower. We do not
believe that the proposition derived from system-level analysis that a largely

unrestrained superpower tends to wield its power provides a satisfactory explanation for the single decision on the part of the Bush administration to invade Iraq. We do believe, however, that the mechanism delineated here is really at work in the current international system.

As an analytical observation, we conclude that a continuation of the highly asymmetrical power distribution in the world that we have noted here is not conducive to global strategic stability. Presumably, the chances for more stable international relations, with a lower probability of super-power-initiated wars, would be increased by the appearance of an entity with sufficient military might to counterbalance the US. According to the logic of realist balance-of-power theory, balancing against the US is inevit-able. Structural realists therefore suggest that the present international system dominated by America's preponderant power is in itself unstable.[3] Whether counterbalancing is altogether desirable can be debated, of course. Bo Huldt (in Chapter 3) is obviously sceptical on this point. If a true counter-balancer does appear in the future, let us hope that such an actor will be another democracy or group of democracies.

There is, as presented in Chapter 1, a second notion, also belonging to the system level of analysis, which should be brought into the discussion here, that of the security dilemma. According to this conception, if a state cannot know whether other states that are believed to amass threatening weapons are doing that in order to defend themselves or in order to be able to use the weapons for offensive purposes, the state in question is apt to act on the basis of the believed capabilities of the other states, rather than on what it believes to be their likely intentions. The basis for this reasoning is the assumption that in the current system of international relations, there is no authority higher than the state itself when it comes to defending national security interests.

We would like to highlight, once again, that for the leadership in the US what happened on 11 September 2001 was to all intents and purposes a military attack that showed that not even the superpower was invulnerable against this type of attack. If we follow the strategic reasoning in this section, a state that in this brutal way has been deprived of its cherished notion of at least continental invulnerability is bound to perceive the international environment in different ways than it did before the attack. It is here that the question of Iraq's alleged possession of weapons of mass destruction (WMD) necessarily enters the reasoning. After the conclusion of the conven-tional phase of the Iraq War, the stated purpose of the Bush administration finally to disarm Saddam's Iraq of all WMD and WMD-related programmes has been widely derided because very few indications of such weapons or such programmes have been found. Still, from the perspective of the security dilemma, it seems clear to us that potential threats that could be regarded as acceptable when a state viewed itself as invulnerable became less acceptable, if not unacceptable, when this invulnerability was shattered.

234

The result of our attempt to explain the decision of the Bush admini-stration to invade Iraq by applying the notion of the security dilemma is less than conclusive. First, it is doubtful whether the Administration fully appreciated the extent of its dilemma. After all, it seemed woefully ill-prepared for the negative consequences of the invasion. Second, even if it is accepted that the leading members of the Bush administration did indeed believe that the Saddam regime possessed WMD, then why was the option of a military solution to this kind of problem applied to only one of the states known or believed to possess WMD or carrying out WMD-related programmes? In other words, why did Washington not use the same means to eliminate the threat from North Korea and Iran, to mention but the two most obvious examples? To be sure, opting for a military solution in these cases would have been much more dangerous than in the case of Iraq, which was a relatively weak adversary. North Korea and Iran thus repre-sented even worse security dilemmas for Washington. At the same time, however, the threat was more imminent. This reservation notwithstanding, we still believe that the notion of the security dilemma carries some explana-tory weight when it comes to answering the question why the Bush admini-stration undertook to invade Iraq. We would like to repeat our belief that complex events and processes in international relations cannot be explained by simplified monocausal explanations that are so often employed in the popular debate.

While the question why the US invaded Iraq is here considered the main question within the larger puzzle of why did the Iraq War occur, the ques-tions about Saddam Hussein's enigmatic behaviour posed by Jan Angstrom in the introductory chapter are interesting and relevant. Obviously, any attempt to answer them must be based on conjecture. It is difficult to make sense of Iraq's contradictory policy before the war. Roger Karlsson in his chapter shows that the Iraqi regime sought to avoid war. As the threat of invasion loomed larger, the regime insisted vehemently that Iraq no longer had any WMD and even allowed UN weapons inspectors to return to the country. However, Saddam's record inspired no confidence. His previous repeated refusal to cooperate with the UN on weapons inspections had created the impression that Iraq was hiding something. Even after the inspec-tors returned, ambiguity persisted. So why did Saddam not come clean? Perhaps he wanted to leave some uncertainty. One possible key to the puzzle is Saddam's obsession with power, alluded to in Stefan Ring's and Roger Karlsson's chapters. By 2003, the dictator's situation was precarious. On the one hand, he realized that he would have to make concessions. On the other hand, he was anxious to maintain his domestic power and his influ-ence in the Arab world. By leaving outsiders in some doubt as to what weaponry he actually had, he may have tried to regain prestige both at home and abroad.

How was the war in Iraq fought?

In an article published in *Foreign Affairs* in the summer of 2003, Max Boot attempted to draw some early lessons from how the US forces fought the Iraq War:

> Spurred by dramatic advances in information technology, the U.S. military has adopted a new way of warfare that eschews the bloody slugging matches of old. It seeks a quick victory with minimal casualties on both sides. Its hallmarks are speed, maneuver, flexibility and surprise. It is heavily reliant upon precision firepower, special forces and psychological operations. And it strives to integrate naval, air, and land power into a seamless whole. This approach was put powerfully on display in the recent invasion of Iraq, and its implications for the future of American war fighting are profound.[4]

More than a year later, this early assessment still seems on the mark in some respects, but remarkably outdated in others. The analyses provided of the ground operations and of the air war in Chapters 9 and 10, respectively, in this volume agree to a large extent with several of the points made by Max Boot. Anders Cedergren, in his analysis of the ground operations in Chapter 9, highlights several aspects of US war-making that correspond to those identified by Boot. One of these is the flexibility with which the US ground forces carried out their tasks, not least evident in the rapid operations by which they first established positions on the outskirts of the Iraqi capital Baghdad and then proceeded, within a couple of days, to conquer the resistance and occupy the city. One explanation for this rapid advance, which laid the basis for the quick victory in Iraq, was the successful ability for mechanized deep battle shown by the US forces. Cedergren writes:

> A major innovation in the American war strategy is that, for the first time, a real capacity was shown for a mechanised *deep battle*. The assumption of the concept is that units with combined arms are used in the ground arena. The air operation, whose main task was *Battle Field Interdiction*, played an important role. This combination between land and air combat forces can be strengthened by continued technological advancement.[5]

One phase of the war in Iraq that turned out to be vastly less destructive than expected by many commentators was 'the Battle of Baghdad'. According to many observers, there would be huge casualties, not least on the civilian side. These largely failed to materialize. Cedergren makes clear that one explanation for this was the versatility and flexibility of the US forces and that another likely cause was the ineptness of both the Iraqi war strategy and of the practical application of this strategy on the ground. Additional explanations for the lack of any real 'Battle of Baghdad' is provided by Roger Karlsson in Chapter 5. First, in his assessment Iraq's military strength in the 2003 war was only about 20 per cent of what it was during the Gulf War. In two key sentences, Roger Karlsson, in our view, clarifies another fundamental reason why the Iraqi military forces were so feeble during the War:

> By creating a network of mutually supervising military organiza-
> tions, the Ba'ath Party successfully subverted the collective identity
> of the military ... The regime thereby deliberately sacrificed the
> military effectiveness of the units so that they would constitute no
> threat whatsoever to Saddam's continued rule.[6]

Despite its efforts to control the armed forces, the Iraqi regime evidently viewed the military with suspicion. Units from the regular army were not deployed in Baghdad. Instead, the defence of the capital was entrusted to the Republican Guard and the Fedayeen.

A regime possessing a military force depleted by a dozen years of sanctions, and geared more towards maintaining the regime in power than towards achieving conventional military efficiency, cannot be expected to put up much of a fight against an adversary having the most modern and technologically advanced forces that have ever existed in the history of mankind. In addition, there is much evidence that in the state created by Saddam the military was profoundly affected by the aggressive tactics on the part of the Baathist regime to jail and subsequently to kill by firing squad all officers suspected of any kind of disloyalty whatsoever. After decades of intermittent purges, the officer corps in Iraq was anything but a strong professional force ready to give unvarnished assessments to the Leader of what was occurring on the battlefield, or able to undertake forceful and independent military manoeuvres to try to prevent military developments threatening to lead to disaster. To state this is also to put the military achievements of particularly the US attacking forces in some perspective. The feats that the latter performed on the battlefield were no doubt impressive in many respects. Still, there was a world of difference between the opposition that these forces faced as compared to that faced by the forces performing *Blitzkrieg* in 1940, the German forces that overtook France in 44 days.

When it comes to the air aspects of the war in Iraq, Jan Reuterdahl *et al.* state in Chapter 10 of this volume that the use of coalition planes in the war took place under nearly ideal conditions. The adversary did not have air forces to speak of. Indeed, no sorties by Iraqi planes were ever undertaken during the war. There was a measure of air defence but even this was less efficient than had been feared by coalition planners. The fact that the adversary was so weak in these respects may, however, mean that the lessons for future conflict are less direct than may at first be thought. The air forces of some potential opponents of the US are capable of reasonably effective resistance. This is not to suggest that fierce air battles are likely to be fought in the future. The US Air Force will surely remain much stronger than that of any conceivable opponent and will therefore have little difficulty in achieving air superiority in war. Moreover, future wars may also be fought in areas where interference by opposing air forces will be almost non-existent and where there are few suitable targets for air attacks, as was largely true in Afghanistan in the autumn of 2001.

The Iraq War and the future of international relations and international law

The conflict in Iraq in 2003, the developments that led up to it and the processes that it has triggered, both inside and outside the country, have already had important ramifications both for the relations between the most important states and other players in international relations and for the role of international law in the handling of international conflicts. The purpose of this final section is to comment upon these wider ramifications on the basis of the analyses appearing in this book. In addition, we highlight some additional questions that we feel need further study by international relationists or strategists.

The Iraq War can be seen as evidence of a serious weakening of the role of law in world politics. A situation where the world's most powerful state is breaking the basic rules of international law with impunity inevitably calls into question the strength of the existing legal regime. Bring and Broström, in their analysis of the legality of the Iraq War, state unequivocally that the invasion of Iraq did not fit into the bounds of international law. The US-led coalition, they conclude, waged war in the absence of legality under *jus ad bellum*. This does not mean that international law no longer matters as a legitimizing factor. While the US went to war against Iraq without UN Security Council sanction, it returned to the UN soon after the war to achieve legitimacy. In US-sponsored Resolution 1483, the UN Security Council recognized the authority under the Geneva Convention of the US and Great Britain as 'occupying powers' in Iraq.[7] The resolution was supported by France, Russia, and Germany, the principal opponents of the war. Russia, for its part, insisted that the resolution did not retroactively endorse the use of military force against Iraq.[8] As for the US, it maintained that it had operated under legal right provided by UN Security Council Resolutions 678, 687 and 1441, and therefore did not need any new legitimacy from the UN with respect to the war.[9] Nevertheless, passage of Resolution 1483 was a significant achievement for the US because it did legitimize the occupation of Iraq as a fait accompli and involved the UN in Iraq's post-war reconstruction.[10] The resolution could be read as a legalization of the outcome of an illegal invasion. Hence, a potentially debilitating consequence for international law is the legal precedent that was set by the resolution, a risky precedent that could be invoked by the US and other militarily strong states in future international conflicts.

One of the most important effects of the Iraq War has been on transatlantic relations. As discussed by Bo Huldt in Chapter 3 of this volume, the Iraq conflict has had profound implications for the transatlantic relationship. The historical context into which Bo Huldt places these events enriches our understanding of what happened, and makes us realize more of the conditions for what may happen in the future. The chances for any real cooperation between the two main protagonists in the political quarrel over the Iraqi conflict, the US and France, seem small as of this writing in the late summer of 2004. The parties have been able to agree that NATO should play a role in training Iraqi soldiers, but they have quarrelled about the details of this agreement, finally coming to terms in September 2004. It appears very unlikely, at least if president Bush is re-elected in November 2004, that there will be any more important undertaking on the part of the European critics of the Iraq War to contribute to the reconstruction of that unfortunate country in any substantial way. If the Democratic candidate, Senator John F. Kerry, wins, the chances are admittedly somewhat better for an opening on this point. This does not mean, however, that such an equation is as easy to solve as it has appeared to be in some of Senator Kerry's speeches.

Charlotte Wagnsson, in her chapter on Russia, shows that the Russian leadership was not willing to sacrifice what she has identified as its two main principles of foreign policy, that of maintaining the world order and combating international terrorism. For President Putin and his associates, the Bush administration's decision to invade Iraq threatened both of these principles, which made it hard, if not impossible, for Moscow to support the US undertaking. Wagnsson also believes that the Russian leadership correctly calculated that the consequences of the principled opposition by Moscow to US plans would not be as harmful to bilateral relations between the two countries as France's more aggressive denunciations of Washington have been for the bilateral relationship between Washington and Paris. The Russians are likely, one can surmise, to support the US generally in the 'War on Terrorism'. That support, however, will clearly not be unquestioning. The case of Iran, which has aspects of both the fight against terror, with the alleged activities by al-Qaeda operatives inside that country, and of the proliferation of nuclear arms, is another issue where there might very well be a difference between the US and Russia on how to proceed.

In the case of Iran, many of the political questions raised by the Iraq War come back into sharp focus, in our view. One such question is whether or not to believe intelligence reports that Iran is indeed pursuing a build-up of nuclear weapons? A second question is, if Tehran is indeed engaged in such activity, what should the international community, or its leading members, do about it? A third question is, if the US and/or Israel somewhere down the road decide that it is imperative to stop the development of a nuclear force in one of the strongest nations of the Middle East, what would be the reaction of the European allies and of Russia to a military strike, by airplanes and/or cruise missiles, undertaken by either Washington or Jerusalem? A fourth, even more hypothetical question is how the European Allies, Russia and the international community at large would react if the US, with or without the cooperation of Great Britain, decided to invade Iran and topple the government, giving as its reasons for invasion both that country's impending nuclear capability and its support of terrorism?

We believe that the last question will not become acute because it is exceedingly unlikely that Washington will ever seriously contemplate such an invasion. This is so because the costs to the US of the invasion of Iraq have proven to be immensely larger and more burdensome for the superpower and for its leadership than the latter ever imagined. There have been more casualties than expected, particularly after the end of the conventional war phase. There are many more US troops deployed in Iraq in August 2004 – about 140,000 – than the Administration believed would be needed to stabilize the country. There is such disorder in the reconstruction of both Iraqi society and polity that the ability of the US and its allies to construct a political system in Iraq that is stable, broadly representative and non-threatening to the country's neighbours can be seriously questioned. Hundreds of Iraqi civilians have died since the end of major fighting 15 months ago with no let-up in sight. Insurgents are, in the summer of 2004, gradually consolidating their hold of several cities in the so-called 'Sunni triangle' in the country.[11] In addition, the risks to civilians from various countries supporting the US and Great Britain who are working in Iraq have led several countries as well as individual companies to withdraw their forces or to stop working in Iraq.[12]

In Chapter 1, Jan Angstrom asks to what extent the current resistance to the US and to the newly installed provisional government in Baghdad is organized and hierarchical. We cannot pretend to be able to answer this question conclusively at this stage. However, we feel that it is possible to state that the resistance to the US is indeed organized. There are at least two active organizations that are both ready and able to attack US forces and Iraqi forces allied to the US. One of them is the so-called Mahdi Army, a militia controlled by the young Shi'ite cleric Moqtada al-Sadr and based in the holy city of Najaf and in the part of Baghdad now called Sadr City. This force seems to be better organized and probably more hierarchical than the second, more elusive force primarily based in cities such as Fallujah. If the Mahdi Army is Shi'ite, it seems equally clear that the second force consist of Sunnis, who oppose any representative Iraqi government established by free, general elections because in such elections Sunnis are bound to lose the control that they have traditionally had of modern Iraqi society. It is difficult to ascertain whether or not there is any organized third force fighting against the US and its Iraqi allies. We have in mind groups allied with international terrorists, perhaps even to the al-Qaeda network itself. The fact that there have been several suicide attacks against US forces points in the direction that there is indeed some third force distinct from the others. The reason for this is that regular Muslims are believed not to be able to contemplate suicide attacks for religious reasons. Al-Qaeda and its allies have, however, shown no hesitation whatsoever in carrying out such attacks.

None of these developments, seen in isolation or even together, prove that the mainly US undertaking of building a broadly representative Iraq that is stable, treats its minorities justly, and poses no threat to its neighbours, is bound to fail. It does certainly mean, however, that any administration in Washington will make very conservative calculations when it contemplates military interventions, particularly in the Middle East, in the future. The enormously impressive US military capability, so well analysed in three chapters in this book, will no doubt increase further. At the same time, however, developments on the ground in Iraq are showing every day how insufficient even this incomparable military capability is when it comes to rebuilding and reconstructing a complex country in a volatile region after the government of that country has been toppled by mainly US military might. It has, once again, proven difficult to install democracy in a foreign land by the use of military force.

A final issue that has to be addressed, however briefly, in this concluding chapter is the connection between the war in Iraq and the war on terrorism. The Bush administration has consistently claimed two things in this respect. First, it has claimed that the invasion of Iraq was part of the war on terrorism. Second, it has claimed that, as a result of the toppling of Saddam, the US has made gains in the war on terrorism, including reducing the risk of future terrorist attacks against the US homeland. We have no ambition to conclusively prove or disprove either of these claims. We must, however, take note of the fact that knowledgeable observers have seriously questioned both of them.

Jeffrey Record, in a recent article, has formulated the fundamental issue very well:

> Threat discrimination is essential to sound strategy, which is about making intelligent choices within the constraints of limited resources. Failure to discriminate between greater and lesser threats, and between immediate and distant threats, invites disastrous mis- calculation and even strategic exhaustion. It encourages entry into unnecessary wars of choice against lesser, distant threats at the expense of wars of necessity against manifestly deadly threats. This

is what happened to the [US] in the 1960s when it mistook a logical insurgent war in a small Southeast Asian country for a challenge to the architecture of its security interests worldwide.

This is also what happened to the [US] in 2003, when it mistook a vicious but deterred and contained rogue state for an extension of an undeterrable global terrorist threat and proceeded to invade and occupy Iraq. Osama bin Laden somehow morphed into Saddam Hussein and the [US] went after Iraq in the name of the war on terrorism.[13]

In a final conundrum for the US, the war on terrorism and the war in Iraq interact to influence an audience that is crucial to the future of the war on terrorism and important also for the future of Iraq: Arab public opinion. Kristina Riegert with Anders Johansson analyses how the media coverage of the conflict in Iraq in 2003 differed from what peoples in Arab nations had experienced before. In 2003, Al-Jazeera provided them with an alternative view of the events in Iraq. This was in stark contrast to the Gulf War in 1991 when CNN reigned supreme in terms of multinational TV coverage of the war.

It is very difficult to determine what causes broad changes in public opinion, but what we can state with authority is that the peoples of most Arab countries have become more adverse to the US. Zogby International, a US polling firm, has twice, in April 2002 and in June 2004, measured broad Arab opinion in six countries.[14] Responding to the question whether the US was viewed favourably or unfavourably, opinion in four of the six countries polled turned even more negative in 2004 than it was in 2002. In Morocco, the percentage responding that they had an unfavourable view of the US increased from 61 per cent in 2002 to 88 per cent in 2004. In Saudi Arabia, corresponding figures were 87 per cent and 94 per cent, in Jordan 61 per cent and 78 per cent and in Egypt 76 per cent and 98 per cent! Only in Lebanon and in the United Arab Emirates was opinion fairly stable or turned only marginally more negative.

If there is truth to the old saying that 'guerrillas need a sea to swim in, and if the sea is emptied, they will have trouble to continue swimming', and if the adage can be transferred from guerrillas to the al-Qaeda network, then the US is in trouble considering the expansion of the potential recruitment base for this network. As noted above, in four of the most populous Arab nations, opinion of the US has turned from negative views held by a large majority, to near-unanimous negativity. The poll also indicates that part of the reason why opinion has turned more negative is US policies and conduct in Iraq. When this is coupled to the fact that a large majority of the people in the Arab world continue to detest US policies on the Middle East conflict, and that they are also sharply critical of Washington's behaviour in the war on terrorism, it becomes obvious that it will be very hard indeed for the US to change these attitudes, without a sea change in US policies on the Middle East. It is our contention that highly negative figures in public opinion of the US generally, such as those reported here in four large Arab nations, are positively linked to the chances for al-Qaeda and similar organizations to recruit new suicide bombers that will continue to attack US forces and interests in Iraq and in other Arab countries as well. This is another sense in which the outcome of the Iraq War is problematic for the US, at least as this outcome can be tentatively assessed in the late summer of 2004. It is very difficult indeed to estimate the likely consequences of the public opinion figures reported here with respect to the willingness of individuals to be ready to fight the US and its interests in one way or another. What can be said with some confidence, however, is that to the extent that such movements in public opinion do have an effect on the matters mentioned, that effect is bound to serve to increase the recruitment to organizations ready to use violence against US forces and interests.

Notes

1 *Strategic Survey 2003/4: An Evaluation and Forecast of World Affairs.* Oxford: Oxford University Press for the International Institute of Strategic Studies, 2004, p. 162.
2 G. H. W. Bush and B. Scowcroft, *A World Transformed*, New York: Alfred A. Knopf, 1998, p. 488 as quoted in J. Record, *Dark Victory: America's Second War Against Iraq.* Annapolis, MD: The Naval Institute Press, 2004, p. 5.
3 K. N. Waltz, 'Structural Realism after the Cold War', in G. J. Ikenberry (ed.) *America Unrivaled: The Future of the Balance of Power*, New York: Cornell University Press, 2002, pp. 29–67.
4 M. Boot, 'The New American Way of War', *Foreign Affairs*, 82, 4 (2003) 41–58, the quote is from p. 42.
5 A. Cedergren, 'Concept, Expertise and Arms in Combination – A Reflection on the Iraq War,' this volume.
6 R. Karlsson, 'Iraq's Political Strategy before and during the War', this volume.
7 UN/S/RES/1483 (2003), preambular paragraph 13.
8 'Moscow to Support U.S.-backed UN Resolution on Iraq', *Radio Free Europe/ Radio Liberty Newsline*, 22 May 2003. Available at http://www.rferl.org/newsline/ 2003/05/220503.asp (accessed 28 August 2004).
9 Remarks by Colin S. Powell, Secretary of State, and Kim R. Holmes, Assistant Secretary of State for International Organization Affairs, 22 and 23 May 2003. Available at http://www.state.gov/secretary/rm/2003/20909.htm and http:// fpc.state.gov/20930.htm (accessed 28 August 2004).
10 On the UN involvement, see W. J. Durch, 'Picking Up the Pieces: The UN's Evolving Postconflict Roles', *The Washington Quarterly*, 26, 4 (2003) 195–210 and M. Berdal, 'The UN after Iraq', *Survival*, 46, 3 (2004) 83–101.
11 See A. Huseen and N. Pelham, '"Rebels" Writ Runs Large Across the Trouble-some Sunni Triangle', *Financial Times*, p. 7, 30 July 2004 and F. J. Bing West, 'Iraqification, Part II', *The Wall Street Journal*, p A10, 2 August 2004.
12 Christopher Marquis, 'Bush Faces New Obstacles in Keeping Allies' Support', *The New York Times*, available at http//www.nytimes.com, 31 July 2004.
13 J. Record, 'Threat Confusion and Its Penalties', *Survival*, 46, 2 (2004) 1–7.

14 *Impressions of America 2004: How Arabs View America. How Arabs Learn About America*, A Six-Nation Survey Commissioned by The Arab American Institute, Conducted by Zogby International, available at http://www.aaiusa.org/PDF/ Impressions_of_America04.pdf (accessed 21 August 2004).

References

Berdal, M. 'The UN after Iraq', *Survival*, 46, 3 (2004) 83–101.

Boot, M. 'The New American Way of War', *Foreign Affairs*, 82, 4 (2003) 41–58.

Durch, W. J. 'Picking Up the Pieces: The UN's Evolving Postconflict Roles', *The Washington Quarterly*, 26, 4 (2003) 195–210.

Huseen, A. and Pelham, N. ' "Rebels" Writ Runs Large Across the Troublesome Sunni Triangle', *Financial Times*, p. 7, 30 July 2004.

Marquis C. 'Bush Faces New Obstacles in Keeping Allies' Support', *The New York Times*, available at http//www.nytimes.com, 31 July 2004.

Record, J. *Dark Victory: America's Second War Against Iraq*. Annapolis, MD: The Naval Institute Press, 2004.

Record, J. 'Threat Confusion and Its Penalties', *Survival*, 46, 2 (2004) 51–72.

Strategic Survey 2003/4: An Evaluation and Forecast of World Affairs. Oxford: Oxford University Press for the International Institute of Strategic Studies, 2004.

Waltz, K. N, 'Structural Realism after the Cold War', in G. J. Ikenberry (ed.) *America Unrivaled: The Future of the Balance of Power*. New York: Cornell University Press, 2002, pp. 29–67.

West, F. J. Bing 'Iraqification, Part II', *The Wall Street Journal*, p. A10, 2 August 2004.

INDEX

Abd-el-Azez, Emir of Nejd 105
Abdülhamid, Sultan 100
Abdullah I, King of Jordan 106
Abdullah II, King of Jordan 85
Abdullah, Saudi Crown Prince 84
Abkhazia 66
ABM Treaty 41, 70
Abu Dhabi TV 220
Adnan division 174
af Wirsén, Einar 112–13
Afghanistan 2, 8, 42, 133, 150, 157, 160;
  Al-Jazeera coverage 220; and
  al-Qaeda 25, 43, 171; and
  international law 123; and NATO 52;
  and war on terrorism 24, 25, 27, 43,
  65, 171
aftermath of the war 10, 52–3, 131–5,
  150–1, 229–30, 240
air defences 83, 169, 177, 192–3, 203,
  237–8
air power: air power debate 10–11;
  anti-surface operations 198–9; attack
  on Iraqi leadership 172, 196;
  bombing in December 1998 121; and
  collateral damage 127–8; combined
  arms 10–11, 169, 176–81; control of
  the air 192–5, 200; development of
  188–91; objectives 191–2; pre-war
  period 1, 231; strategic air operations
  195–8; supporting air operations
  199–204; targets 196–7
air search and rescue 201
air-to-air refuelling 203–4
Airborne Division 174
airborne platforms 198
Airborne Warning and Control System
  (AWACS) 195

aircraft 196, 197, 201, 202, 203; losses
  192, 194, 201; number of 180
AirLand Battle 168–70, 172–3, 190–1
Al Kut 173
Al-Arabiya 220
al-Dulaymi, Abd-al-Razzaq 86
Al-Duri, Muhammed 84, 86, 90
al-Fatat 101
Al-Jazeera 91, 92, 93, 210–11, 219–23
al-Karmali, Père Anastase 113
al-Khazraji, Nizar 82
'Al-Mu'taasim' Missile Plant 89
al-Qaeda 9, 30, 45, 222; and
  Afghanistan 25, 43, 171; links with
  Iraq 6, 27–8, 68, 91, 124, 151, 242;
  and weapons of mass destruction
  (WMD) 26–7, 90
al-Sadr, Moqtada 240
al-Thawra 86
Albright, Madeleine 148
Albu-Nasir 160
Aleppo 100
Algeria 222
All Dailies 88, 94
Allenby, General Edmund 104
America see USA
'American way of war' 12
Amman 106
Amsterdam treaty 40
An Samawah 174
Anatolia 100
Annan, Kofi 83, 84
Aquinas, St Thomas 119, 126
Arab League 84, 87
Arab-Israeli conflict 98
Arabs 56, 78, 83, 106, 108
Arafat, Yassir 31

245

combined arms 10–11, 169, 176–81,
183, 205
commercialization of the news 211–12
Compass Call 202
compellence 146–9, 163n
Condell, B. 178–9
conduct of the war 10–12, 236–8;
capture of Baghdad 175–6; ground
advances 173–5; Iraq 11; start 172–3,
180, *see also* air power; combined
arms; conflict management
Conference on Security and
Co-operation in Europe 39
conflict management 143–62; Baufre,
André 149–50, 157; brute force 146,
147–8, 150–3, 156, 159–61; coercion
148–9, 155, 157–8, 159–61, 162,
231–2; compellence 146–9; and
negotiation 158–9; Schelling, Thomas
145–9; US armed forces 153–5
Constantinople 99–100, 103, 107, 111
control of the air 192–5, 200
cost 131; human cost 53
Counter Air Operations (CAO) 192
credibility 79, 94; Iraq 88–91; and USA
90–1
Creveld, Martin van 6
Croatia 99
Ctesiphon 109
Cyprus 103
Czech Republic 41

Daalder, Ivo 42
Daily Mirror 218
Damascus 100, 105
Dardanelles 103
dating the war 2, 3–6, 230–2
Davos World Economic Forum (2004)
52, 56
decision process 8, 21–33, 44–7, 91–4,
157–8
decision-making cycle 199, 200
deep operations 169, 170
Defensive Counter Air (DCA) 193, 195
democratizationof Iraq 30–1, 152, 171,
229; of Middle East 27, 28, 30, 31,
130, 152–3
Denmark 50
Diesen: Sverre 174
diplomacy 145
Diplomaticheskii Vestnik 62

Diyarbakir 106
doctrines 181–2, 184
Dodecanese 101
Dominican Republic 133
'domino theory' 152, 164n
Dyke, Greg 218–19

EA-6B Prowler 202
Eadie, Major 110
'Eastern' European states 50
EC-130 Hercules 202
Effects-Based Operations 154, 181–2
Egypt 103, 105, 222
Eisenhower, Dwight D. 152
Ekéos, Rolf 89
electronic warfare (EW) 202–3
embedded journalists 94, 129
end of the war 52–3, 132, 150–1, 231
Erasmus, Desiderius 135
Erzerum 103
Europe: attitudes to the war 50–2; as
'counterweight' 56; 'Eastern states'
50; partition 50–2; and terrorism
50–1; and warfare 48
European Security and Defence Policy
(ESDP) 71
European Security Strategy 56
European Union 39, 40–1; division over
Iraq 51–2, 54; and Russia 65, 71

F-117 stealth aircraft 196
Faw peninsula 108, 172
Faysal, King 104–5, 106, 112
Fedayeen 237
Fedayyin militia 11
Feith, Douglas 29
Field Manual 100–5 169, 170, 190, 191
fighting in cities 92–3
First World War 100, 101–11, 189
force, legal use of 47–8
force transformation 178
Foreign Affairs 236
4th Infantry Division (4. ID) 172
Fox News 214, 218, 223
France 72, 99, 111, 112, 231, 238; First
World War 103, 104, 105; opposition
to use of force 47–8, 50, 51, 87, 89;
and UN Security Council 8, 45, 46,
49; and USA 239
Freedman, Lawrence 4
Future Iraq 150